YOUTH IN JEOPARDY

Keeping Kids Out of Trouble

For concerned parents and professionals who
want practical approaches based on the author's
20+ years of working with at-risk teenagers

DEREK V. SCHUSTER, ED.D

BOOKS

Contents

Introduction

DISCOVERING NEW FRONTIERS OF OUR CITY

Consider this book to be like a journey that may shock you at times. But I promise at the end of the journey, you will feel emboldened in your relationship with teenagers. Are you ready to try on new behaviors?

I probably could have gone through my entire life without meandering through the ghettos of New York City. But something made me choose to expose myself to violent altercations in the most downtrodden and anger-intensive living environments. What made me choose the often dangerous path over the insulated cushy surroundings of a Wall Street or corporate office?

I am a Caucasian male who grew up on the comfortable Upper East Side of Manhattan. That opulent neighborhood has for ages extended with almost total precision to 96th Street, where East Harlem begins. Most Upper East Siders have been able to lead the good life without feeling the need to cross that line of demarcation. I was different—although I don't remember an exact moment when I began to care about the people north of 96th Street.

As a toddler, I developed polio and couldn't walk without my legs being shrouded in braces. I was fortunately cured of the disease at age 5 through the intervention of an Australian nun known as Sister Kenney. But this experience helped me identify with and care about the underdogs of our society—those who, in some way, had to do without. Since I attended St. Bernard's, an elementary school located a block from East Harlem, I noticed early on the dramatic change in conditions north of 96th Street—trash everywhere, blasting radios, poorly maintained buildings. And then, when my older brother Ronald started doing volunteer work in East Harlem, I became more aware of the obstacles facing the residents of that community.

Launching My Career

When I graduated from Colby College in Maine and pondered how I would delve into a career, I was unsurprisingly drawn to the helping professions. My first job in New York was with a city agency called Addiction Services. I had a role in establishing drug abuse prevention programs within the New York City public schools. My colleagues and I found ourselves up against educational and substance abuse bureaucracies, which created enormous obstacles to our achieving successful outcomes. Nevertheless, despite the frustrations of working for a city agency, several of my colleagues and I went on to new social service endeavors in less complicated environments.

I became increasingly interested in the prevention of urgent social problems before they reach a serious stage. Once youngsters become involved with the criminal justice system, they tend to cut or drop out of school and lack employment-related and pro-social skills. There are some similarities in how one might prevent drug abuse and how one might intervene before children are abused or neglected. There is accumulating evidence that early prevention activities contribute more to crime reduction than reactive approaches.

Wouldn't it be more effective and far less costly, I wondered, if programs could be directed at an earlier stage of the problem when the suffering had not reached epic proportions? Could we, for each of these types of abuse, looking back, develop a number of early indicators of greater levels of abuse to come? (Some of these indicators might include emotional and/or financial stress, a lack of positive parental role models, or a lack of understanding of issues related to child development and parental discipline.)

So, in the 1980s, I started an organization called "Family Dynamics." (I have marveled at how the title has gone on since to become a part of the English language vernacular.) Family Dynamics' mission was to prevent the maltreatment of children in Central Brooklyn (the communities of Bedford-Stuyvesant, Bushwick, Brownsville, etc.). I felt good that our organization was serving communities with huge problems but far too few programs.

My "Family Dynamics" Experience

I ran Family Dynamics for eight years. Then, having become the father of five children, I felt the need to make some money. That circumstance led me to join the Family Dynamics Board and enter the equally combative world of commercial real estate. I have become very proud of the accomplishments of those who followed me as Executive Director of Family Dynamics. The mark of success of a child abuse prevention program is its ability to reduce the risk of parents' maltreatment of children while still keeping them at home or at least moving the children to an institution near their parents. Fortunately, there was an amazing group of my successors who ran Family Dynamics. Several of them were able to reduce the risk of child maltreatment (substance abuse, domestic abuse, economic stress, etc.) to unprecedented levels—consistently at a level of 90% plus—without creating insurmountable physical distance between parent and child.

As proud as I was of the statistics, I felt an urge around the year 2000 to get back into providing direct service to at-risk youngsters. I was not interested in managing a large program where most of my time would be spent on administrative duties. I wanted instead to stress quality over quantity, to have a personal caseload, and to experience first-hand what seemed to work and not work when it comes to the prevention of the arrests and re-arrests of teenagers.

Finding a New Home

The issue of what organization I would seek out to pursue my violence prevention goals now emerged. SCAN New York, which had been managed successfully for over 20 years by Lew Zuchman, immediately came to mind. I had met Lew much earlier when he interviewed to be my successor as executive director of Family Dynamics. Lew landed at SCAN, where he embarked on a 40-year-plus career as a true innovator and producer. I was ecstatic when Lew agreed that SCAN and the Violence Prevention Program I was contemplating were a good fit for each other. I went to work for SCAN in the fall of 2000.

The organization's mission is to provide a safety net for at-risk children from 0 to 18 years of age in its target communities. Today, SCAN-Harbor—as the organization came to be known—is the largest provider of youth services in East Harlem and the South Bronx, reaching more than 8,000 children and 700 families each year. The population served is overwhelmingly Black or Latino and low-income.

I prefer to operate programs with 100% private funding. In fact, our Violence Prevention Program has conducted its work for twenty-plus years without the benefit of even one public dollar. I have observed that the concerns of public sources of funding and the conditions found in their Requests for Proposals make successful outcomes more difficult to achieve. The reason why governmental agencies sometimes issue counter-productive criteria for funding is usually their perception of what is "cost-effective from a documentable standpoint." One example of how this rationale runs amuck might be the case of parent training. Though many studies have demonstrated the potential effectiveness of various types of parent training, it is often disallowed in Requests for Public Funding Proposals.

But How Will the Client Families React to Me?

Before reaching out to the mostly poor, overwhelmingly Black or Latino families, I wondered how somebody from a different background would be received. Would they think that I was capable of understanding their particular life situations? Would any such doubts on their part make it difficult for them to listen to me—or even to see me as a bonafide family clinician? As a cautionary step, if I sensed such doubts, I would try to assign another case worker whose background matched clients more closely. But, as our program moved along, I usually found that the families were more concerned about the level of sincerity and skills I brought to their situation than my personal background.

What Violence and Delinquency Prevention is About

SCAN New York's Violence Prevention Program opened its doors in the year 2000. When references are made in this book to "our program," that program is SCAN's (now SCAN-Harbor's). Our at-risk teenage clients are overwhelmingly Black or Latino and come from poor families, and are usually referred to us by the New York City Probation Department, lawyers, or social service agencies. They are ordinarily in the program for a period ranging from four to twelve months. But the primary reason for youngsters graduating from our program has little to do with calendar watching. They are required to complete several benchmark activities, including the following:

- Individual Counseling
- Family Counseling
- Skills Development (based on our 300-page curriculum)
- Peer Group Counseling
- Self-Defense (focusing on 12 specific defensive skills making carrying weapons unnecessary)
- A Prison Visit
- A Challenge Trip [parent(s) usually invited to enhance their relationships with their children]
- An Apology Letter

Measuring Success Over the Past 20 Plus Years

The primary goal of SCAN-Harbor's Violence Prevention Program is to reduce re-arrests.

Pre-Tests of our teenage clients cover the period before entering the program. Post-Test covers the period from entrance into the program to six months after leaving it. Our evaluation system tracks the degree to which the following goals are accomplished:

Re-arrests	Decreased by 72%
Physical Confrontations with Family Members	Decreased by 69%
Violent Threats made to Others	Decreased by 71%
Significant Confrontations with Non-Familial Adult Authority Figures	Decreased by 63%
Physical Confrontations with Peers (fellow students, campers, rival gang members, neighborhood youth)	Decreased by 74%
Violent Acts and Threats Made in Dating Situations	Decreased by 71%
Anger-Driven Destruction of Property	Decreased by 72%
Weapons Possession Detected	Decreased by 82%
Participation in Gangs	Decreased by 83%

Youth in Jeopardy is designed for parents and professionals who are struggling to find ways to keep 'at-risk children' from getting into trouble. It is my hope that readers of this book will find their interactions with youngsters more fulfilling since they will be approaching them from a position of strength. Parents and professionals will begin to see themselves as less a part of the problem and more part of the solution.

Many books have been written about parenting, but almost none have been targeted at parents of children who are at a severe level of risk of getting into trouble. I would argue that ALL children—without proper parenting—can get into trouble. So my book provides the methodology that can prevent that from happening. Furthermore, those who write parenting books usually do so from their academic perches—rather than based on experiences in the streets and in the homes of at-risk families.

Why My Book is Different

My book offers an alternative to others dealing with juvenile misbehavior. Instead of presenting dry academic studies, *Youth in Jeopardy* draws upon my twenty plus years of experience in delinquency prevention work in the Bronx and East Harlem. Filled with emotion-laden anecdotes, it delivers what parents, therapists, and teachers nationwide desperately seek: fresh, practical approaches to violence prevention for rebellious tweens and teenagers.

Readers may wonder what the need for *Youth in Jeopardy* might be at this particular time. The book is designed to address the frustration of Americans who are confronted with daily headlines and blasts of yet another deadly act of violence and who don't understand the causes and potential remedies surrounding these tragedies. They may be asked, "Who would do that and why? Are parents and professionals powerless to prevent this onslaught on our population?"

Youth in Jeopardy seeks to provide techniques that have been found to be successful in keeping youngsters out of trouble. Many exercises from SCAN-Harbor's Violence Prevention Curriculum are included so that parents and professionals will be able to use them with youngsters without "reinventing the wheel."

Practical Techniques, Humorous Anecdotes

Highlighted in *Youth in Jeopardy* are a description of the factors contributing to teenagers being at risk of delinquent behavior—and approaches to reducing the risk. Humorous and sometimes bizarre anecdotes are included. One memorable example concerns "Truant Thomas," who hid his shoes so that I wouldn't be able to walk him to school.

As the founder of a child welfare organization in addition to the Violence Prevention Program at SCAN-Harbor, I consider myself uniquely qualified to author this work. Even as an administrator, I've always maintained a personal caseload. My prevention and early intervention efforts—and those of others in the program—have reduced the arrests and re-arrests of many hundreds of youngsters. I'm also a former teacher and the father of six children, aged eighteen to adulthood.

My background as a parent, an educator, and a caseworker has provided me with a level of experience and insight that will almost surely have a positive impact on readers of this book. Particularly important is the measured success of our program in reducing arrests and re-arrests as well as achieving other goals over a 20-plus-year period.

What follows in the ensuing chapters is a discussion of the origins of juvenile misbehavior, but the pain caused by it, and the many specific techniques used successfully with hundreds of at-risk teenagers over the past twenty-plus years. Will you just keep wondering what can be done to keep kids out of trouble, or will you dive into my book and find out what you, as a parent or professional, can do about the threat posed by juvenile misbehavior?

Chapter 1

The Problems Underlying Youth Crime and Violence

You may have an idea about the extent of juvenile misbehavior but perhaps not realize just how great a problem it is. Sadly, in 2018, the number of 10 to 17-year-olds arrested by law enforcement agencies in the United States was 2.1 million (National Center of Juvenile Justice, July 2020 Report). Of that figure, property crimes (burglary, motor vehicle theft, arson, etc.) accounted for 131,500 arrests, assault for 125,030, larceny and theft for 92,630, and drug abuse violations for 90,670. Males accounted for 70% of the arrests, and Caucasians for 62%. In order to put these statistics in a cross-national perspective, youth homicide rates are typically 3 to 40 times higher than in other highly developed countries (David-Ferdon, C. and Simon, T.R., "Preventing Youth Violence," Atlanta, National Center for Injury Prevention).

In this chapter, I hope that you will come to more fully understand the reasons for the uptick in juvenile delinquency. Of course, teenagers are not only the perpetrators of violent acts but also the victims. Research estimates indicate that 28% of teenagers were physically assaulted at least once in the prior year. A recent study found that more than 200,000 adolescents were treated for physical assault injuries in each of the past five years.

Violence can be considered to be aggression with the intent to cause bodily harm. Activities that can be viewed as violent include kicking, hitting, stabbing, or shooting. Curbing violent behavior is often accomplished by assisting the youngster in expressing anger in an appropriate manner, which can produce positive results rather than getting him or her into trouble.

Aggressive Personalities and Violence

The future perpetrator of violent behavior often grows up in a home where parents resolve disagreements physically. The early exposure to this form of conflict resolution lays the foundation for the development of an aggressive personality. Aggressive people often see others as being hostile toward them without any factual basis for jumping to such a conclusion.

One example would be if someone feels they are looked at "the wrong way." An interpretation is often made that this is an act of hostility. Another example would be when someone accidentally bumps into another in the street or on the subway, perhaps creating a perception of intentional oppositional behavior. The troubling result is that the perpetrators of so-called "intentional acts" are "asking for" a hostile response. This is often how the cycle of violence starts.

One of the problems is that youngsters with aggressive personalities have too seldom been exposed to non-violent alternatives to perceived hostile behavior. Aggressive behavior in the short term may create a sense of relief for some persons. Down the road, however, new problems are created. Once aggressive behavior becomes the norm, it is difficult to control or reduce it. Impulsivity now rules.

Unmet Need for Early Intervention

If there's anything in life that I wanted to make my little niche of expertise, it is the early intervention into social problems.

When I looked around the social landscape, it occurred to me how many types of abuse there were—drug and alcohol abuse, bullying, child abuse, domestic violence, etc. Then I started to focus on the programs that dealt with these tragic problems, and I realized how many resources were allocated to after-the-fact approaches. There are, in fact, plenty of prisons and various types of costly residential treatment centers. But surely, the foremost proponents of these brick-and-mortar tactics are chasing horses that have already left the barn.

Wouldn't it be more effective and far less costly, I wondered, if programs could be directed at an earlier stage of the problem when the suffering had not reached epic proportions? Could we, for each of these types of abuse, looking back, develop a number of early indicators of greater levels of abuse to come? (Some of these indicators might include emotional and/or financial stress, a lack of positive parental role models, or a lack of understanding of issues related to child development and parental discipline.)

The Internal Struggles All Adolescents Face

Teenagers, of course, are undergoing a transitional passage into adulthood. As such, there are normal and abnormal personality traits that mark adolescence. There are a number of internal struggles virtually all teenagers face. They try to reduce the amount of control adults have over them. They attempt to test the limits they are constrained to. They decide whether to focus on the present or the future. They seek intimate relationships while fearing extremely intimate ones. They also may want sexual activity but not necessarily be emotionally ready for it.

Levels of Aggression Ranked by Degree Of Severity

Many teenagers will proceed from the above normal struggles to abnormal aggressive and/or illegal behavior. The following are various levels of negative behavior as outlined by Daniel Daley in "Working with Aggressive Youth":

Level I - Making Threatening Statements or Gestures and/or Non-compliance

A youth frequently responds with verbal and non-verbal threats along with aggression.

The following are examples of non-compliance:

- Association building
- Excluding or ignoring others
- Teasing
- Criticism—the youngster is criticizing other individuals' behavior or attributes through verbal or non-verbal negative actions
- Sarcastic responses—the youngster is mocking the behavior/attributes of others
- Whining and weeping
- Refusing the directives or orders of a parent, teacher, or other individuals

Threats:

- Depicting physical aggressiveness
- Occupying others' personal space
- Ultimatums
- Rumor spreading or malicious gossip
- Yelling and cursing
- Compressing a fist
- Staring and glaring
- Recurring verbal or non-verbal annoying actions
- The use of demeaning statements

Level II — Causing Damage to Property

A youngster regularly engages in damaging property.

Examples:

- Arson
- Fire-setting
- Stealing

- Vandalism
- Kicking or punching immobile objects
- Throwing objects

Level III — Killing or Harming Animals

A youngster frequently is cruel to animals or tortures or kills them.

Examples:

- Hitting or kicking an animal
- Poisoning an animal
- Stabbing or shooting an animal
- Torturing an animal
- Setting an animal on fire

Level IV — Physically Harming Others or Self

A youngster consistently responds with behavior that physically hurts others or self, but does not produce long-lasting or permanent physical or psychological damage.

Examples:

- Poking a finger in someone's chest
- Pushing or shoving
- Pushing, throwing, or kicking objects at others
- Wrestling
- Punching
- Fighting
- Attempting to hurt self (carving on own skin)

Level V – Using Violence toward People, with the Potential for Causing Serious Injury or Death

A youngster responds with behavior that physically hurts others or self and produces long-lasting or permanent physical or psychological damage.

Examples:

- Stalking
- Bomb threats
- Terrorism
- Aggravated assault
- Rape
- Suicide
- Murder

Adolescents may advance to one or another of the above levels of aggression in different ways. Some will proceed from one level to a higher level in a sequential manner. Other teenagers may abruptly move to a high level of aggression with few warning signs.

Awareness of the above five levels can be a useful guideline for parents and other caregivers. Understanding what level a youngster is on will help in developing the most appropriate treatment options. Also, as the treatment process proceeds, it will be helpful to see if the teenager has moved back to a lower level. This insight will help caregivers determine if the treatment plan is working or if it needs to be adjusted.

Personality Traits Leading to Criminal Behavior

Crime-prone teenagers will usually have some combination of the following personality traits:

1. Having an Overly Aggressive Personality

We have just listed some of the levels of aggression as well as the behaviors associated with them. Particular youngsters will respond to various "triggers" that spark their aggression. Some of the triggers include the following:

- When one's personal space is invaded
- Competition over boyfriends or girlfriends
- In retaliation for negative gossip
- A response to bullying/cyber-bullying

- An out-of-control argument
- Being looked at in a certain way
- In retaliation for stolen property

2. Disregard Of Other Persons' Property

Some of the attitudes that would lead teenagers to steal are:

- Feelings of entitlement to "my fair share of what my parents have"
- Feelings of entitlement to what their peers or persons they see in the media have
- Feelings that "I need more stuff to be an equal part of the group"
- Feelings of boredom that can lead to a desire to "get away with it"

3. Rejection of the Need to Be Accountable to Authority Figures

It is important for youngsters who reject the need to be accountable to adults to understand what experiences made them feel that way, which authority figures at home or at school "pushed their buttons" and what they said or did for that to happen?

Some parents have a passive, hands-off style of parenting. They do not set limits for their children's behavior. Kids sometimes do not view such parents as authority figures over them. In those situations, the children feel that if they self-parent, their life will turn out just fine.

Youngsters who are skeptical about the legitimacy of authority figures—especially inner-city minorities—may also feel that they have been harassed by the police. Of course, how they react to these authority figures can have legal consequences. It is important for teenagers to be aware of what they need to do to avoid overreacting to police "harassment" and to avoid getting into worse trouble.

4. Inclination of Abusive Behavior Toward Others

Some individuals develop over time a need to be emotionally and/or physically abusive toward family members, peers, boyfriends/girlfriends, etc. Abusive youngsters may be consciously or subconsciously trying to satisfy the following sorts of needs:

- The need to control how others spend their time and with whom
- The need to criticize others' ideas and behaviors as a means of placing themselves in a superior position
- The need to call the shots about when and how to have sex or regarding other emotional aspects of a relationship
- The need to provide others with true or untrue information about subjects their partner would prefer to be confidential
- The need to make all decisions affecting the relationship

5. Vulnerability To Negative Peer Pressure

Some teenagers will place satisfying the demands of others—regardless of how damaging they could be—ahead of considering what is best for themselves. Examples of succumbing to negative peer pressure might include the following:

- Making decisions to please others and to be popular
- Making decisions that help the youngster perpetrate an image of "coolness"
- Placing loyalty to others as more important than what is best for themselves
- Being manipulated by gang members who tell kids they are their true family rather than their biological relatives
- Being lured into illegal activities to make some "easy money"

6. Getting A "Rush" From Illegal Activities

Some youngsters are helpless to overcome their need for emotional excitement—regardless of whether they have considered what the consequences of illegal behavior might be. Examples might include the following:

- Fighting rival gang members
- Stealing cars
- Selling drugs
- Discharging a firearm
- Being chased by the police

Above, personality traits leading to criminal behavior have been outlined. In Chapter Two, a broader description of what today's teenagers are like will be presented.

Chapter 2

Who are Today's Teenagers, and What Do They Want?

At the risk of stereotyping, this chapter will describe some of the trends occurring in those who are experiencing adolescence during the 2020s.

There are certain basic needs that teenagers have had in any era. Let's start with those:

1. Biological Factors Cause Teenagers to Be Impulsive

Teenagers' brains are not fully developed. One area of the brain which undergoes transitions during adolescence is the frontal cortex. For this reason, it is not usually until their mid-twenties that people develop impulse control, emotional stability, and planning skills. During that period, the brain continues to be molded by environmental factors. Certainly, the stressful and dangerous information which can be found on the internet is one of those factors.

A key part of the brain structure, the amygdala, is especially susceptible to hormonal changes that affect emotional behavior. This process can contribute to adolescent explosive outbursts. Teenagers are particularly vulnerable to Post-Traumatic Stress Disorder (PTSD). Stress added to an already overactive stress-response system can have seriously challenging effects on a teenager's brain. Consequences may include aggressive behavior, hypersexuality, and substance abuse.

This process can further deteriorate into a state of depression. This condition is facilitated by a gradual dysregulation of the Hypothalamic – Pituitary – Adrenal axis (HPA) caused in adolescence by an abnormal release of cortisol from the brain. And the often-present teenage anxiety can deteriorate into a full-scale anxiety disorder. The still-maturing teenage brain may not be able to counteract this process.

2. Teenagers Want to Act Older Than Their Age and Be Treated That Way

Tweens want to lead the life of a teenager. When they actually turn 13, they are already focusing on the freedoms granted to those who have achieved Sweet Sixteen status. And once they become 16, they are already focusing on graduating from adolescence and being on their own.

Sadly, teenagers are so intent on moving on to the next level that they do not fully appreciate the benefits which accrue to 13, 16, and 19-year-olds. Of course, youngsters also tend to dwell more on the privileges associated with those ages and not on the responsibilities that are expected of them. Parents would be well advised to tie the parceling out of privileges to the youngster's performance with regard to educational and family-related expectations.

3. Teenagers Need Clear Boundaries in Terms of What is Acceptable Behavior

At first, it is the parents who establish boundaries for their children—often for reasons of health, safety, and emotional factors:

> "You will be in bed by 8:00."
> "You can only have ice cream twice a week."
> "You will not go into a certain part of town because it's a high crime area."

It is important, however, that adolescents feel that there are not too many rules or that the rules lack reasonable flexibility. If they perceive otherwise, they will feel that their parents' primary motive is to control them. This feeling can result in rebellion and even depression. For that reason, parents should set limits that have a sound rationale and are easily understood by their children.

Eventually, youngsters will hopefully be capable of setting boundaries for themselves. By way of example, Darlene met Tony at school. She realized after a while he was saying things that made her feel uncomfortable. He might ask her what she wore to bed—a nightgown or pajamas. Tony proceeded to inquire about her sexual experience and "What kinds of things turn you on?"

Eventually, Darlene decided that she had to protect herself from Tony's steady stream of questions, which made her feel so uncomfortable. So she set some boundaries for Tony. If Darlene were to remain friends with him, Tony would have to refrain from asking sex-related and other overly personal questions. This story indicates the need teenagers have to set boundaries—though they may not actually follow through with doing so until sensing an urgent situation.

4. Teenagers Need Positive Feedback Conducive to Higher Self-Esteem

People are more likely to make sensible decisions and exhibit positive behavior when they feel good about themselves. They need to approach life with a sense of confidence that their existence matters and that they can have, to some degree, their desired impact on those around them.

What contributes to self-esteem in youngsters? Among the facets are one's level of achievement in school; one's participation and acceptance by their family; one's level of achievement in non-classroom activities, and one's popularity with their peers.

Perhaps a factor most contributing to self-esteem is positive feedback from friends and family. Examples of positive feedback might take the following forms:

"John, I really appreciate your washing your dishes and taking out the garbage yesterday."

"Sally, it was really nice to see how you welcomed the new student so warmly."

"Rick, I noticed how you were able to come home and do your homework without being reminded."

5. Teenagers Need Opportunities to Laugh

Laughter is considered to be a form of medicine—especially when life isn't going so well. It provides youngsters with a break from feelings of aggression and stress. A sense of humor on the part of caregivers can insulate kids—at least for a while—from negative feelings or thoughts.

6. Teenagers Need to Feel They are Being Listened To

One way or another, all human beings need attention. Children soon become experts at attracting negative attention through various types of misbehavior. But life would be easier for everyone if youngsters felt free to express their opinion to someone who cares what they have to say. Of course, teenagers need to learn how to express their feelings in a manner that attracts willing listeners. It is also imperative that those in the role of listener must demonstrate warmth, interest, and a sense of caring on their end.

7. Teenagers Need to Feel They "Fit In"

Our 15-year-old client Wanda enjoys her pack of four to six friends. They like to gossip, comb the neighborhood, and play games together. Wanda's circle contains a number of girls who are seldom afraid to express their opinion. As you might imagine, not all of their sentiments are wholesome. Wanda, being a positive thinker, finds herself frequently disagreeing with her buddies.

Herein lies Wanda's dilemma. She would like to jump in with her own opinion, but she believes that she would often be a minority of one. She desperately wants to remain a part of the group and doesn't want to provide a reason for the others to push her out. Like so many other adolescents, Wanda usually keeps her mouth shut in order to "fit in."

8. Teenagers Need to Feel Comfortable in Their Bodies

Adolescence is a time when the human body undergoes drastic changes and—not always in a predictable manner. There can be an interval of a couple of years between the time when classmates of the same gender go through puberty. Also, the growth of different parts of the body may vary from one kid to another. As an example, one of our young clients, whom we shall call Jake, had a gangly body whose feet had grown much faster than the rest of him.

So individuals may at times feel clumsy, fat, skinny, or hairy. And, of course, their peers are only too happy to tease them about such irregularities.

Some of the most serious cases of anxiety about body shape are labeled "anorexia nervosa." Youngsters (usually girls) will do almost anything to control their weight. They will starve themselves for extended periods of time. Anorexia can often be maintained for only so long—and may lead to bulimia or "binge eating." Youngsters will allow themselves to eat large amounts of food, but after doing so, will induce forced vomiting to rid themselves of the "evil substance."

Parents of children who feel uncomfortable in their bodies must first acknowledge their feelings of discomfort and then offer encouragement, support, and possibly medical and/or mental health support.

Then there are those needs teenagers have which seem particularly a product of the 2020s or at least more acutely felt these days. These needs include the following:

9. Teenagers in the 2020s Often Focus Only on Short-Term Goals

Youngsters today can have feelings of invincibility and can act impulsively. They can live for the moment without considering how their behavior relates to the sort of life they want for themselves down the road. This trend can be understood if we break down how youngsters use their free time. It is somewhat shocking to see how much time is spent on inhaling entertainment (often screen time) as compared to participating in activities with long-term benefits—reading, exercising, developing marketable skills in such areas as music, dance, drawing, technology, etc.

10. Today's Teenagers Have a Propensity for Risk-Taking

One of the defining features of the adolescent persona is a desire to be granted more freedoms—to go where and do what they want, come home later, etc. In a growing number of communities—most certainly in the inner city—the granting of excessive freedom to youngsters creates a risk factor.

Teenagers often believe they are invulnerable and, therefore, immune to the dangers adults face. At other times, they are aware of their vulnerability, but they tend, often erroneously, to believe that the benefits of a decision outweigh the risks involved. Decisions are often made based on such perceptions.

Also contributing to risky decisions is low self-esteem. Youngsters with positive self-images feel valued. Those whose character and behavior are constantly criticized feel low self-esteem. If they don't feel their life counts for much, they are inclined to take increasingly larger risks.

11. Today's Teenagers Tend to Be Prone to Distorted Thinking

All-or-Nothing Thinking, also known as black-and-white thinking, involves evaluating a situation using an extreme analysis rather than a more balanced explanation. Words often spouted include "always" or "never" rather than "sometimes" or "usually." All-or-nothing thinking puts pressure on youngsters to be perfectionists who are seldom content with anything short of perfection.
Catastrophic Thinking is, of course, a line of thought that involves a disaster with horrific results—destroyed homes, bank-

rupt businesses, etc. Those who frame ordinary situations as catastrophes imagine that their worst fears will come true. They resign themselves to frequent periods of extreme worrying and stress.

Intolerance of Uncertainty. Teenagers in the 2020s are often worriers. They worry, especially when a situation is unclear or if there are multiple ways a situation can turn out. For youngsters, a lack of certainty may cause them to dwell on the worst scenario imaginable.

Examples might be:

My mother asks me to come home immediately after school. ("I'm in trouble.")

Test results are taking a long time after a visit to the doctor. ("I must be really sick.")

My grandparents aren't responding to my emails. ("They don't care about me anymore.")

Unfortunately, teenagers have to live with uncertainty. They have to be willing to be patient while additional information will allow their hopes or fears to be confirmed.

12. Teenagers' Lives Are Often Molded by Their Usage of Electronic Devices

Our caseworkers have found on many occasions that their teenage clients are on their phones, social media, and Netflix for between five and ten hours a day. The effects of this obsession with electronic screens, which will be examined in Chapter XV, are numerous.

As there are only so many hours in the day, clearly, other would-be priorities, such as homework and family time, are often neglected.

With youngsters' personal relationships often restricted to remote communication, there is often not much depth to the relationships. They are frequently superficial but assumed by youngsters to be "meaningful."

Remote relationships eliminate the need to develop empathy for others and effective social skills.

Remote relationships are not conducive to caring about others or even regard for human life.

For some teenagers, even killing others has become an enjoyable act—an opportunity to transmit the slaughters occurring in video games to real life.

13. Teenagers Can Be Fearful of First-Time In-Person Meet-Ups

Social media usage poses a number of challenges and problems for adolescents. One of them is that it does not require youngsters to develop social skills to the extent that in-person relationships do. Superficial conversations and relationships are the norm. Sensitivity to subtle verbal and non-verbal cues is often not part of the routine.

So whether teenagers are meeting up with a dating prospect or a potential buddy, they can feel somewhat intimidated. If they say the wrong thing or act awkwardly, they may feel that future relationships can be instantly blown out of the water. So a youngster who is anticipating such a situation may come across as nervous—leading to a self-fulfilling prophecy. If a parent senses this sort of insecurity, they might be advised to reassure their children that if they relax, they will do just fine.

I hope that this chapter has been an illuminating journey inside the mind of today's teenagers. Do you recognize any or all of these characteristics in the teenagers you know?

A Positive Parental Pearl
"Rick, I noticed that you were able to come home and do your homework without being reminded."

Chapter 3

The Many Risk Factors Teenagers Face

In this chapter, you will be introduced to Kevin, who will discuss his experience living in a homeless shelter. You will also know how Roger dealt with a filthy living environment and how Jessie coped with her drug-addicted mother. Juan will describe how his father's incarceration affected him, and Martin will discuss the impact of his grandmother's death.

Why are today's teenagers more likely to be at risk than those of previous generations? It sometimes seems that each generation, compared to the previous one, has more challenges when it comes to raising children. In today's social-media, instant-gratification-driven world, parents certainly have much to compete with and often need help. In turn, there is the challenge of maintaining standards expected of children's behavior so that they grow into responsible and independently-functioning adults.

Quite possibly, parents may have picked up this book because they are struggling to find that very important balance between them and their children. However, take heart and remember that the most dangerous scenario is when adolescents are allowed to function with little or no supervision or accountability for their actions.

As for those who work with teenagers, such as caseworkers, the implications are clear, especially when being presented with teenagers who have not had that most-necessary supervision from early on. Whether you're a parent or caseworker, it's important to understand the risk of negative behavior, which often feeds on itself. How many times have we heard an adult threaten to penalize bad behavior without any follow-through? More often than we would like, to be sure, because the more youngsters take risks without experiencing negative consequences, the more they will believe that they don't have to avoid behaving badly. Partially, for this reason, there are youngsters who find themselves in legal trouble on a regular basis.

Of course, parents of teenagers and service providers from the helping professions would like to prevent at-risk youngsters from getting into trouble in the first place. The key to this is to recognize which risk factors are most likely to lead an individual down the wrong path. Here are some of those risk factors to consider:

MENTAL HEALTH FACTORS

☐ **Behaviors Indicating Depression and/or Contemplation of Suicide**

- Continual anxiety and sadness
- Fatigue and reduction of energy
- Expression of feelings of worthlessness or of a wish to die
- Alterations in sleeping patterns
- Difficulty in making decisions or even concentrating
- Alterations in weight or appetite
- Irritability, restlessness, and/or increased anger
- Reduced school performance
- Enhanced drug use and/or alcohol consumption
- Decreased interest in performing normal activities

☐ **A Diagnosis of Any of the Following Conditions:**

- ADHD
- Bipolarism
- Schizophrenia
- Personality Disorders
- Conduct Disorders
- Mood Disorders
- Oppositional Defiant Disorders

☐ **Feelings of Hatred**

Hatred is the extreme dislike of a group of people one perceives to have uniformly negative traits. This sort of prejudicial thinking can lead to attempts to injure and intimidate other people due to their ethnicity, religion, sexual orientation, or disability.

ENVIRONMENTAL FACTORS

☐ **Growing up in a Public Housing Project or a Shelter**

Youngsters growing up in an inner city housing project are subjected to a set of environmental conditions unrelated to any intentional purpose on their part.

Sometimes, those growing up in the "projects" are closely identified with those projects. Teenagers living in one project may seek to assault residents in neighboring projects. There doesn't have to be a solid reason other than, let's say, the Washington projects seeking to dominate the Jefferson project. Merely being associated with a particular project is reason enough to be hunted down as "the enemy." It is easy for teenagers to feel in a state of constant danger in the "hood." Consider Kevin's experience below:

**Kevin Explains How Living in a Homeless Shelter Can Place
A Boy at Risk of Violent Behavior
(As told by one of our teenage clients)**

What 14-year-old wants to go from having everything, a beautiful home, loving parents, amazing friends and having the freedom to do certain things to a year later having all that taken away from them and having to go into the shelter with their parent(s). How embarrassing is that?

I'm sad to say that that happened to me. I was living in Atlanta, Georgia, with my mother in a beautiful 2-bedroom apartment, going to an amazing school, and having friends who loved me and my mother dearly. One day my mother decided it was best that they move back to New York to be closer to our family since it was only the two of us living in Atlanta. Once I finished my last year of junior high school, my mother told me that in a month or so, I would be back in New York. That shattered my world. I didn't want to leave. Why did I have to? My mother insisted it would be for the best.

Relocation to New York

On August 9, my mother packed up everything, put it all in a U-Haul truck, and drove to New York. I knew this wasn't going to be good. I didn't get along with my aunt, who stayed in New York—and that's exactly who we were going to end up staying with. When we reached New York, I was disgusted. The air smelled horrible. The roads had too many potholes, and the streets were jam-packed with people. I cried for about a month, wanting to go back down south, but my mother made it clear that we were not going back.

My mother and I stayed with my aunt for a few months. With tension in the air every day, my mother decided it was best to go into a shelter. A shelter? I was devastated, embarrassed, and outright angry. I couldn't believe that my mother was really putting me through this. Once again, my mother packed all our clothes, put them in our car, and drove to the nearest shelter (PATH) located in the Bronx. When we entered, we were asked to go through a metal detector. No outside food was allowed, and only a certain number of bags could be brought in. We were told to take a number and be seated.

We waited for our number to be called. This process seemed to last forever but was actually a mere seven hours.

Life in a Shelter

We were placed in a shelter near Hunts Point in the Bronx. It looked like an apartment—one bedroom with two beds, a bathroom, and a kitchen. The apartment, however, contained absolutely no heat and was full of mice. My mother and I tried our best to make do with it. It was our temporary home, but both of us hated it.

Shelter residents had to sign in and out each time they entered and left the building. There was also an 11 pm curfew. If we were late, that was a violation, and it could get us kicked out of the shelter and back to Step One all over again.

Things worsened when my mother was arrested. As a result, I was kicked out of the shelter and forced to stay with my grandmother for the time being. I would much prefer that to being in a shelter flooded with mice. As soon as my mother was released, we were back at Square One.

Home, Sweet Home!

After my mother was released, we were both in the shelter for a year before finding a place to call "home." The last shelter we lived in wasn't bad at all—except for our having to share a bathroom with all the others on our floor and having to eat what the workers cooked in the kitchen. The experience wasn't as bad. And we finally inched our way toward the top of the Homeless Department's eligibility list for being awarded our own home.

On September 1, 2011, my mother and I were given keys to our brand-new home. We were placed in a newly built development. Both my mother and I cried with joy when we saw our new two-bedroom apartment in the Bronx.

Not all shelters are scary. You meet a lot of amazing people. When doing so, you realize, "I'm not the only one going through this dilemma, so I shouldn't be ashamed." Think of it as a stepping stone. In life, you must overcome certain obstacles. I overcame most of these obstacles. But for many who have undergone the shelter experience, the scars of bitterness and frustration can lead to a life of criminal and violent behavior.

☐ Unsanitary Living Conditions
(The experience of SCAN-Harbor's client Roger)

Not all youngsters can cope with their living environment like Kevin did. Consider the example of our client Roger:

Thirteen-year-old Roger has grown up in a subsidized apartment rented by his mother. Roger is surrounded by filth, garbage, and unneeded items strewn all over the apartment, and countless bugs populating the floor and walls.

Roger had long been resigned to his mother's neglect of her house-keeping responsibilities. He sensed that she was a hoarder, unable to distinguish between needed items and garbage. But the overall impact of the environment on Roger is regretful resignation. His mother's lack of acceptance of her responsibilities has contributed to his laziness and his poor personal hygiene. Roger cut school regularly. He has acted disrespectfully toward his mother, cursed her out, lied often, and peed on his clothes without changing them.

Three Strikes and Roger's Out

There are services that provide deep cleaning—and, in fact, one was hired. Roger's mother, however, soon allowed the apartment to revert to its former state. SCAN-Harbor's caseworker was revolted every time he set foot in the apartment, but he decided to oversee a re-organization of the possessions and debris. That effort, too, failed. Roger's mother seemed content in her horrific environment.

Fortunately, Roger's paternal grandmother agreed to invite him to live with her. But the case is a testament to how the environment can affect a youngster's behavior. If parents resist maintaining an acceptable environment, all options must be explored to remove their children.

FAMILY-RELATED FACTORS

☐ **Being a Witness to Domestic Violence Within the Family**

A child who grows up in such an atmosphere may develop the feeling that violence is an acceptable way to solve problems or release emotions.

☐ **Having Someone in the Home Abusing Substances**

This circumstance may mean that the youngster may have access to the substances and begin experimenting with using them. It also makes the child feel that substance abuse is an acceptable way of dealing with life's stress.

How Jessie Coped with a Drug–Addicted Mother
(as told by one of our teenage clients)

No child or teenager wants to hear that their parent(s) struggle with drug addiction—or any addiction for that matter. That has got to be the most heartbreaking thing to watch—your mother or father strung out on drugs knowing there is nothing you can do to help.

At the age of 13, I found out that my mother was an addict. I should probably say "is an addict" because no one can ever say they have permanently conquered addiction. Once an addict, always an addict, I learned that while attending Narcotics Anonymous (NA) meetings with my mother. Every day drug addicts have to fight the urge to use, whether they are one day clean or 20 years clean.

A Disturbing Discovery

One day, we were on our way to visit my brother (he was incarcerated at the time), and we stopped off at a gas station to grab some snacks and fill the tank with gas. I'd fallen asleep and woke up when I noticed we had stopped. My mother was leaning against the back door where I had rested my head. I tapped the window to get her attention, and when she turned towards me, that's when I witnessed the worst. My mother's nose was filled with cocaine powder. Instantly, I knew then all those stories my family told me about my mother were true. MY MOTHER WAS INDEED A DRUG ADDICT.

Witnessing was the worst because I never wanted to believe it. How could I sit my mother down and ask her not to do drugs? What would she say? How would she react knowing that her baby girl finally knew her secret? The entire visit with my brother had come and gone—and I hadn't said anything about what I saw.

Opening up a Dialogue

When we finally reached home, I asked my mother if we could talk. We were both still very excited about the visit with my brother. I didn't want to ruin the moment, but I knew I had to bring it to her attention right away. Sitting on my mother's bed, I looked at her and said, "I know what you were doing at the gas station. I saw you snorting cocaine."

At that moment, my mother knew her secret was no longer a secret. She broke down and cried. She was hurt but even more embarrassed. She must've wondered how she could have been so careless. But it was certain that I never looked down on my mother because I loved her— whether she was doing drugs or not. She promised me that she would stop, and I believed her. I had never known anyone close to me to be on drugs, so for it to be my mother was devastating.

When I heard about drugs as a child, I thought about death, and that's all I thought of. I believe that if my mother continued using, she would die. Every day I tried my best to convince my mother that she didn't need drugs. I told her I was her drug and that she should be addicted to me, her daughter. I was wrong. Since the late '80s, my mother had been using it. It seemed like everyone except me knew the truth, which hurt the most. While my family bashed my mother, called her names, and talked down about her, I was always praising her. "Not my mother. She would never use drugs." Seems as though I didn't know my mother as well as I thought I did.

Trips Across Town

Months passed, and my mother had gotten comfortable knowing that I knew her secret. She would bribe me to ride across town with her to get her "medicine." She used the term "medicine" to refer to the drugs. I always agreed to go. I felt that knowing where she was and who she was with would put me at ease. I would sit in the car and wait for her to finish up and come down from her high before we would go back home. I agreed almost every day to drive across town with her. Some people would ask, "Why would you ever agree to go with her?" I'll tell you why. My mother was in too deep—and knew that she needed me. I always thought that if I left my mother alone, something horrible would happen to her. I would feel as if it was my fault. So I tagged along. It was comforting. We would come back home, and I would tuck my mother into bed and kiss her forehead. I made sure my mother knew I didn't judge her and that I would never turn my back on her.

Honestly, I hurt inside. I hated that my mother was on drugs. I cried often, and I wondered what would happen if my mother ever went too far and overdosed. That was always a thought in the back of my mind. But my mother was a functioning addict—one who did drugs but maintained a healthy life. My mother had a great job as a cook in a detention center. Every morning she would go to work, and I'd take the bus to school. When I got home, she was always waiting for me, with dinner cooked and all. She helped me with my homework and came to all of my school functions, and made sure I lived the life of a pre-teen. On Fridays, she would drop me off at the skating rink, where my friends and I would meet and skate until closing. Then she would come back and pick me up. On Saturdays, it was the mall or the movies. Overall, Mom was a great mother. I was never hungry, and I had everything I needed and wanted. Despite her addiction to drugs, my mother was amazing.

Some Angry Times

But then there were a few days when my mother would get angry—not at me but at her significant other. That's when things got bad. They fought often. My mother was hurting because she was in a relationship with a partner who was unfaithful. That made my mother spiral out of control. At times, I noticed her abuse of drugs increased. She would disappear for days at a time, and I wouldn't hear from her. That's what worried me. I could remember one of many occasions when my mother wouldn't show up for two days. I called her phone, and it went straight to voicemail. I called police stations, hospitals, and anywhere I could think of. But there was no sign of her, and I panicked. I had no choice but to call her partner so we could go look for her. We drove around, and I asked her partner to drive across town just to see if we might have spotted her car. I knew that if I spotted her car, I would know where she was and that she was okay. Luckily, I did spot her car. I never brought it to her partner's attention because it just would have caused a ruckus—and no one needed that.

The Unfriendly Boyfriend

I never realized how badly my mother was hurting inside. The person she was madly in love with broke her heart—over and over again. One morning, I woke up, and things were different. The vibe in the house was bad. I looked out the window and realized my mother's car was still parked. It was weird because that particular day, I knew she was supposed to be at work. I walked downstairs, hoping to smell coffee being brewed, but I didn't. It was quiet. I called my mother, and she didn't respond.

When I walked into her room, my heart stopped. I ran toward her, yelling and screaming her name, but she didn't move. I dialed 911. I knew for sure my mother had overdosed. She lay there naked, foaming at the mouth, and her eyes were in the back of her head. There were suicide notes written in lipstick on the mirror in the bathroom and notes on the kitchen table. My mother wanted to die because of her lover. I stayed by my mother's side until the EMS came. When they took her pulse, it was at 3. Her heart rate was at 11. I almost lost my mother that particular day. If I had waited another 10 minutes, we would have lost her. That was a day I will always remember. Up to this present day, my mother is still an addict. Every day she struggles, and every day I tell her I love her.

To those who have a parent or both parents who struggle with drug addiction, I advise you to never turn your back on them. Try to give them love and affection. Never talk down to them—and if you see that they want to get clean, attend some meetings with them.

It's important because they won't feel that they're alone. I went to every meeting with my mother after the incident happened. I realized this is a disease my mother is struggling with.

☐ Having an Incarcerated Parent

For starters, the youngster is missing out on the advantages of having two available parents. Children in this situation may also become ashamed of their parents—which may lower their self-esteem and cause them to exhibit risky behavior.

How His Father's Incarceration Affected Edward
(as told by one of our teenage clients)

Edward Thompson's father was convicted of armed robbery when Edward was six years of age—and served ten years behind bars. Edward had been attached to his father—and so he was not happy about the prospect of rarely seeing him during his crucial developmental years.

Edward was placed in a position where he had to fend for himself. He felt angry and hurt by his father's situation. Edward considered his father to be inconsiderate of his feelings.

Spiraling Downhill

Edward's mother was not a particularly communicative parent, so he didn't have anyone at home to discuss problems with. As a result, Edwards's increasingly uncontrolled temper led to his involvement in fights. For protection, Edward joined a gang. His fellow gang members pressured Edward into participating in numerous assaults and thefts.

Eventually, Edward was sentenced to a prison term of five years. Thus, Edward Thompson became a classic example of how the imprisonment of one family member lays the path for the all-too-familiar cycle of incarceration in subsequent generations of the same family.

☐ Having Access to Weapons in the Home

In 2019, 37% of U.S. households had at least one gun in possession (Statista Research Department, November 19, 2019, "Gun ownership in U.S.; p.2). An estimated 4.6 American children reside in households where at least one gun is kept loaded and unlocked (thetrace.org/newsletter/study. P.2.).

Unfortunately, parents who choose to maintain weapons in their homes often are not discreet about hiding the means of access from their children. As a result, there are numerous instances each year of teenagers taking guns from their supposed hiding places into the streets. If a youngster has a weak self-image, "packing a pistol" may provide the youngster with at least a momentary sense of power.

☐ The Loss of a Loved One

When a key family member dies, a youngster's emotional ties are disrupted. Often the diseased person provided activities and structure to the teenager's life. Until the youngster has grieved over and adjusted to the loss, he/she will be at risk of antisocial behavior.

Our 15-Year-Old Client Martin Deals with the Loss of a Loved One

At some point, just about all of us are confronted with a family tragedy. Many people think that we live forever—instead of coming to the realization that we are living only to die. Our time on this Earth isn't forever.

In 2012, my grandmother was diagnosed with stage three pancreatic cancer, an aggressive form of the disease that develops in the tissues of the pancreas. Located in the abdomen behind the lower part of the stomach, the pancreas aids in digestion. When my mother came home and broke the news to me, I felt as if someone had kicked me in the stomach. I couldn't breathe. All I could do was drop to my knees and cry. Over and over, I asked God why it had to be my nana.

Nana was a vibrant, energetic, beautiful woman. She went to church every Sunday—and each day, she went outside for a walk. She loved shopping and eating. My nana would stay in one store for 3 hours at a time and eat an entire five-course meal like it was her last. She enjoyed going to Riverbank Park to walk the track and to the beach—just to watch everyone else build sand castles and splash in the water.

Troubling News

Once the news broke out to the immediate family that Nana was sick, they all came together. The doctor stated that with the cancer that my grandmother had, she would probably only live for six months—if even that. We vowed to make sure my grandmother's final days were spectacular. Six months had come and gone, and my grandmother was still alive. Thanksgiving and Christmas came and went. But, day by day, Nana was shrinking more and more. She was going to chemotherapy, but all that did was make her even sicker.

Fast forward to August 2014. My family had come from Delaware to celebrate my nana's birthday. They threw her a big party in Pelham Bay Park. She had a blast. Just seeing her smile and watching her dance and laugh proved how strong a woman she was. She never let that cancer get her down. She always said to me, "Leave it to God, and he will always take care of you." And that she did.

A few weeks after her birthday party, she was admitted to the hospital. Her stomach had grown to the size of a six-month pregnant woman— and she wasn't even eating. The doctors told her she needed to have surgery, but my grandmother didn't want that. She let them know that she sensed her time was coming to an end—and she wanted to be at peace with herself. After a month of being in the hospital, she was released, and we brought her home. She had a small incision in her stomach where a tube was placed because her bowels were not moving —and the little food she ate was not being digested. It was all stuck inside of her. Each day, her family would have to drain her tube and clean it. She was also hooked up to a feeding tube. Because my grandmother wasn't eating, the doctor gave her a liquid supplement that was injected through her veins. Anything she would try to digest by mouth would be thrown up.

Chemotherapy Stopped

My grandmother had a nurse who came to see her twice a week to change her medicine bag and to talk to her. Her family knew for sure that Nana wouldn't live to see Christmas. That was heartbreaking. The chemotherapy was stopped because the cancer had spread throughout her body. There was nothing left to do for her. My grandmother was 97 pounds and was unrecognizable.

She was tired. All Nana kept talking about was how she was ready to go home (to heaven). She suffered. She was in a lot of pain. In the middle of the night, my grandmother would wake up hollering because she hurt badly. The only thing that was keeping Nana alive at this point was the medicine bag.

On November 27, 2014, my grandmother decided to discontinue her medicine bag on the evening of Thanksgiving. Her nurse came to see her, and he let my entire family know that once she discontinued her medicine bag, that would be it. He gave us a heads-up about what to expect from that point on. Believe me when I say nothing good came out of it.

Thanksgiving Day came, and my grandmother had an apartment full of family and church members. We prayed, sang her favorite church songs, and prepared for when her medicine bag ran out. That was a good day. We all laughed, we all cried, we reminisced. It was a beautiful day.

Grandmother Passed

The morning after my grandmother's medicine bag finished, I woke up early in the morning to check on her. Her nurse had told us that she might go blind, and she did. In less than 24 hours, my grandmother's eyes were cloudy and gray. Also, my grandmother could barely talk. How did it go from my grandmother telling me the night before how much she loved me to this? My family was heartbroken. The apartment was silent—with nothing but my grandmother's music playing. We prayed. She loved prayer. Thankfully she was able to hear us. Her nurse told us she would live for maybe 48 hours after the medicine bag was finished.

On December 4, 2014, at 7:48 am, my grandmother took her last breath. She was at peace now. As I entered her bedroom and looked at her face, she smiled. My grandmother passed away with a smile on her face. I laid next to my grandmother's lifeless body, kissed her beautiful face and hands, and kept telling her I loved her dearly.

It hadn't hit me that she was gone until the coroners arrived. I watched as they wrapped her body in a sheet and placed her in her blue body bag. As soon as they zipped her up, that's when it all hit me, I would never see my grandmother again. I cried hard. That was the worst image. I followed the coroners out of the apartment and down to their van, where they placed her.

Fond Memories

My heart ached. My grandmother was my best friend. We talked about everything. The fact that I would never see her again broke me into pieces. Her funeral had come and gone—and I was distraught. Life wasn't fair; never in a million years would I think I would have lost my grandmother.

My grandmother once said, "Martin, you are so handsome. Live and love life to the fullest. Tomorrow is never promised, so always live every day as if it is your last one."

Not a day goes by when I don't think about my grandmother. I believe she is watching. I talk to her every day and ask for her guidance. I know she is very proud of me. To this day, I cry not sad tears but happy tears. Happy knowing that my grandmother left this world with a sense of fulfillment.

Dealing with a loss of a loved one is never easy. But it becomes much easier knowing that the deceased person is no longer suffering.

EMOTIONAL FACTORS

☐ Having an Uncontrollable Temper

Many criminal acts stem from the inability of youngsters to manage their angry feelings in a positive manner. There is nobody who doesn't feel angry now and then. In order to prevent one's temper from contributing to criminal behavior, it is first helpful to understand what sort of events trigger such acts. Youngsters often let their anger spill overboard for the following types of reasons:

- Someone makes nasty comments about one of their family members or their ethnicity.
- Someone invades their personal space.
- Someone disrupts a boyfriend-girlfriend or a friend-friend relationship.

- A child is told "no" by a parent when they are determined to get a "yes."

And so, what are some of the ways that angry feelings can bring out the temper in a teenager and may lead to antisocial or even criminal behavior

- Taking personal property as a form of revenge.
- A slap in the face—no big deal in itself—but it could lead to a greater level of violence.

☐ Low Self-Esteem

When people don't feel good about themselves, they are prone to taking risks because they don't feel they have much to lose.

☐ An Extreme and/or Continuous Anxiety and Stress

All human beings undergo periods when they experience anxiety and stress. If it is extreme in nature and refuses to fade into the background, the youngster would be at risk of antisocial behavior.

☐ Lack of Empathy

Empathy is the capacity of an individual to put oneself in somebody else's shoes to understand how they would likely react to a particular situation. An example from our program is when one of our teenage clients, Tom, called in a false report to the police about a criminal act supposedly committed by a peer named Oscar. This deed created a huge disruption in Oscar's family beyond what Tom intended. If Tom had a greater degree of empathy, he could have refrained from committing such a devastating act.

BEHAVIORAL FACTORS

☐ A Tendency to React to Situations Impulsively

There are youngsters who cautiously contemplate the consequences when they are about to commit an illegal act. And then there are other youngsters who have established few boundaries for their behavior and simply allow their worst instincts to prevail when given the opportunity. All of us act impulsively at times, but those who do so often are at risk of getting into serious legal trouble.

☐ Patterns of Lying and/or Stealing

Just about every youngster has lied, and many have shoplifted at least a candy bar or helped themselves to the contents of their parent's wallet. Dishonesty is a major risk factor—especially when it is permitted to continue without strong consequences established by parents. Youngsters who lie their way out of situations will go on to commit worse deeds with the confidence that a bigger lie will help them avoid significant consequences.

A particularly dangerous attitude is that of entitlement. A youngster might rationalize that "When I want something, I expect people to provide it for me. This sort of thinking can lead to committing crimes such as theft, burglary, or assault.

☐ Refusal to Adhere to a Curfew

Unless youngsters are held to strict guidelines as to when they are permitted to leave the home, they will feel free to roam the streets at later and later hours. It is no secret that a high percentage of crime occurs under the cover of darkness.

☐ Being Consistently Absent from School

When youngsters cut school or classes, it is important to find out where they go and what they do instead. It is often likely that they are up to no good. Beyond that, such behavior indicates that there is little regard for how education impacts the quality of their entire life. If youngsters devalue education, they are unlikely to set goals for themselves or to be held to behavior which leads them in a positive direction.

☐ Poor Choice of Friends and Acquaintances

Some youngsters surround themselves with peers who genuinely care about what happens to their associates and will even caution them against ill-advised behavior. Those teenagers who are less selective about what will happen to their friends and associates may well suffer the consequences.

☐ Membership in a Gang

It is difficult enough being a teenager dealing with various problems which come your way. But when you join a gang, you also can become responsible for helping other members extricate themselves from the situations they have created for themselves. Not to mention possible requests of fellow members to engage in criminal activity.

How Gang Members Ruined Alexis' Pajama Day—Probably Only One of Many Such Victims
(as told by one of our teenage clients)

We all know that the last few days of school are always the best—moving onto new challenges and meeting new people. The best part for me was "Spirit Week." Spirit Week might include Twin Day, '80s Day, Crazy Hair Day, or Tacky Day.

I participated in all of the above events, but Pajama Day was my all-time favorite. After all, who wouldn't want to wear their favorite, most comfortable pajamas to school? I decided to wear my red Minnie Mouse pajamas, which my grandmother had given me as a Christmas gift. I never thought I would have to deal with the consequences of wearing the color red. But when you live in New York, if you wear certain colors, you're most likely associated with a gang (so I was told).

I enjoyed my day at school; everyone came in with pajamas or maybe slippers. Even some of the teachers participated.

An Attack from Behind

At the end of the day, as I walked home, I noticed a group of kids behind me. Being in my own world, I was not really thinking the worst. In less than a minute, I was attacked. I knew for sure I was being attacked by gang members only because when I glanced at them, they all wore blue bandanas. I was attacked by members of the "Crips Gang." The Crips wore the color blue, and the color I wore that particular day, red, was affiliated with their enemy, the "Bloods Gang." Now I'm not sure if it was a gang initiation and they had just picked out someone to jump, but I assumed it was because of the color that I was wearing. Who knew Pajama Day would end with me trying to fight off three guys and two girls? With blows to my face and my being kicked over and over in my stomach, the attack seemed as if it would never end.

That day, I learned a valuable lesson. If I'm going to participate in another Pajama Day, I will either never wear red pajamas, or I'll just take extra clothes with me to school to change into.

☐ Not Taking Responsibility for One's Behavior

All of us, at times, make poor decisions that result in anti-social and regrettable behavior. We are unlikely to learn from such experiences and decrease the risk of future such behaviors unless we take responsibility for past transgressions. To set the stage for better future behavior, we must understand the point we are starting from.

☐ Social Isolation

Social isolation often indicates a teenager has difficulty relating to people. It can often be a result of rejection by peers. This can create resentment and a desire to strike back at others.

☐ Boredom

We caseworkers have often seen how youngsters with little to do will fill the time with anti-social activities. For example, Luke would fill bags with stones and throw them out the window. This continued until he hit a passerby causing his family to be ejected from the building where they lived.

Please notice the boxes that precede the numbers assigned to the above risk factors. If you're reading this book with a particular teenager in mind, check off how many risk factors apply. A highly unlikely zero would signal amazing risk aversion. Scores of 9 to 15 would indicate a moderate presence of risk factors. A score approaching 23 should ring the alarm bell. This would appear to be a situation where a time bomb is ticking.

Child _____
Number of Risk Factors _____

CRIMINAL BEHAVIOR AMONG YOUTH: MORE PREVALENT IN BOYS

About 70% of the arrested teenagers in our program have been male. Certainly, such biological factors as the existence of testosterone and serotonin in boys' systems have some impact on their predisposition toward aggressive behavior. A scientific link between testosterone levels and susceptibility to violence has, however, not been established.

How Boys' Future Is Shaped

What has a greater impact on the amount of violence perpetrated by males is the interactions from an early age that boys have with their parents, other adult authority figures, and their peers. The way these persons communicate with boys and especially the love shown towards them has a permanent effect on boys' brains and their social behavior.

The life a boy will lead is shaped from the earliest stages—how he is cuddled, reassured, taught, and comforted. A boy must be shown how to identify and express feelings in order to become a healthy emotional person. It is impossible to spoil a boy by providing him with too much love and affection—if appropriately displayed.

Some Myths To Lay To Rest

In order to provide the emotional support that boys need to lead non-violent lives, we adults need to dispel the following stereotypes that persist with regard to young males:

1. Real boys should act macho. In other words, "Real" boys should carry around a tough image and should demand respect from all others. On the contrary, boys should develop the

capacity to relate to their peers in various ways (maybe even sensitively) as the situation dictates.

2. Boys are prisoners of their masculinity. This myth states that there is something inherently dangerous about boys and that they are unable to act civilized and socially responsible. Clearly, there are plenty of admirable males walking the planet to provide evidence to the contrary. Boys—even those raised by single fathers—can show the same degree of empathy as girls.

Boys should be self-sufficient and not overly rely on others for help. When boys suffer from disappointments, they indeed need to know adults and/or peers they can go to for help. They must realize all humans have vulnerabilities and weaknesses—and that they can be overcome by being open to receiving help from others. As the saying goes, "Going solo is dodo."

A parent's life with teenagers of either gender will often feel like a tug-of-war. Is that a feeling you experience when you are with particular adolescents? Hopefully, this chapter will help you as a parent or professional better understand the forces swirling around their youngsters and that this illumination will help make the tug-of-war seem less necessary.

Chapter 4

Some Ways to Keep Kids Out of Trouble

Skills: Dealing with Changed Circumstances

As a parent, it's important to know what you do best and when you need to call on others for assistance. There are simply youth who are born into circumstances or who have mental health conditions that make our program ill-equipped to have a significant positive impact. Our program proceeds on the assumption that it is not possible to prevent violent and criminal behavior in every instance, but that steady support for youngsters over time can substantially reduce the volume of kids who find themselves in legal trouble.

In order to do so, our program has had to set some boundaries in terms of the type of children with whom we have a reasonable chance of a successful outcome. For that reason, we have thought twice before committing resources to the following sorts of situations:

Mentally Retarded or Bipolar Children – We are able to refer them to specialists.

Pathological Liars – Successful violence prevention casework is dependent on honesty and trust.

Youngsters who have ADHD (Attention Deficit Disorder with Hyperactivity) when they are not receiving medication.

Children with Severe Conduct Disorders – especially those with marked anti-social tendencies;

Drug-Using Children with Massive Denial and/or Without a Commitment to Go Clean.

Children with Severe Learning Disabilities - examples being speech, language, hearing, and visual problems.

Children Who Have No Parent or Guardian Willing to Demand Accountability – Caseworkers are, at most, temporary parent role models who can only be effective if someone is ready to step in and make the child accountable to him/her.

When the Parents Don't Want Help or Don't Want the Treatment to Succeed – ("know-it-alls," "control-freaks," etc.).

When the Parents Lack the Capacity to Absorb Training.

Overwhelmed or Self-Absorbed Parents Who Are Unable to Focus on Learning New Behaviors.

When the Parents and Children Have Such Irreconcilable Culturally-Based Values That They Are Already in a "Divorce Mode." You may simply have entered the case too late to save the situation. Examples of this syndrome are immigrant parents from authoritarian countries who try fruitlessly to superimpose another nation's values where they don't apply to the child's daily reality in the United States.

* * *

When deciding whether to admit a particular youngster into the program, the presence of one of the above obstacles does not automatically disqualify a candidate. The severity of the obstacle must be weighed—as well as any positive factors that may be conducive to a successful outcome.

As part of the process for evaluating whether a particular candidate is appropriate for our program, we ask that the referring party complete the following form. (Appendix 4A):

Appendix 4A

SAMPLE FORM FOR REFERRING YOUTH TO DELINQUENCY PREVENTION PROGRAM

(This form can be used by a parent, caseworker, or educator)

Client Being Referred Mr. Ms. (circle one) _____ Date_____

Address of Client_____ Telephone_____
Date of Birth_____ Date Probation Ends_____
Client's email address_____
Mandated?_____

Agency Making the Referral _____Email address _____
Person Making the Referral _____ Telephone _____

Who Client Lives With_____ Cell Phone_____
Siblings _____ Telephone _____
Other Parent _____ Telephone _____

Client's School Attending _____
Guidance Counselor at School _____ Telephone _____

How did you initially become involved with the client?
_____
Lawyer _____ Phone: _____ Email _____
Do you have a written report(s) on the client?

What is the primary reason that you feel that the client is susceptible to committing violent acts?
_____
_____
_____
_____

Please check applicable behavior demonstrated by client and give example (if possible) or explanation:

Behavior	Example/Explanation
__ Aggressive Tendency	_____
__ Difficulty in controlling anger	_____
__ Recruitment attempts by gangs	_____
Or actual gang involvement	_____
__ Strong interest in weapons	_____
__ Major preoccupation with violent	_____
Films, TV programs, or video games	_____
__ Biases towards other cultural or	_____
Social groups	_____
__ Potential abusive dating behavior	_____
__ Battering of family member	_____
__ Other behavior	_____

Initial Engagement with a Client Family

After one of our caseworkers have obtained as much available written information as possible regarding the client's case history, an initial appointment is scheduled. The first session is often at home since that environment usually yields the most information.

The discussion between the caseworker and client family is usually focused on the following objectives:

- Providing client families with an "Overview of the chosen Delinquency Prevention Program. Please see at the end of this "Initial Engagement" section.
- Outlining requirements in order to graduate from our program; see after overview below.
- Building a rapport as much as possible with all family members.
- Helping the family understand that conversations with us are confidential—except in life-threatening cases or when a future crime can be averted.
- Demonstrating an even-handed approach to disagreements between family members without condoning unacceptable behavior.
- Eliciting what changes each family member wants in the future regarding the child's or parent's behavior—without dwelling unnecessarily on touchy past events.
- Establishing a caseworker role that is strictly delineated from law enforcement and is clearly that of an advocate for the client.
- Finding as much common ground as possible between the aims of the client and those of his/her parents.
- Beginning to perceive any discrepancy which exists between expressed and underlying parental motives.
- Helping the client understand the importance of two-way trust and truthfulness in the client-caseworker relationship.

- Getting clients and their parents to see involvement in the program as an opportunity to turn the child's life around— not just punishment.
- Avoiding having the parents feel that they're failures in their role and motivating them to take charge of their parental responsibilities.
- Asking parents to call us if they detect even a minor worsening of behavior on the part of their child.

Some Potential Requirements to Graduate from a Delinquency Prevention Program

Individual and Family Counseling — weekly sessions

Weekly Peer Groups — emphasis on Anger Management, Relationships, Attitudes Toward Authority, etc.

Weekly Self-Defense Session — focusing on 12 defensive skills in order to make our young clients feel that carrying weapons is unnecessary

Prison Visit — to see harsh conditions and talk with specially trained inmates

Challenge Trip — one example is a visit by parent and child to a climbing tower, which facilitates in bonding

Bad Habits — parent identifies those which child has — follow-up provided by our program

Apology Letter — addressed to a victim of misdeeds by youngster

Socialization Trips — ice skating, "Laser Tag," visit to an amusement park, etc.

DELINQUENCY PREVENTION CURRICULUM CATEGORIES

Our curriculum containing over 350 exercises, is based on the situations that teenagers must cope with as they either get into or stay out of trouble. We refer to the many methodological vehicles we have developed as our "tools." Most of these tools can be used with adolescents alone, with family members, or with groups of peers.

Our tools can be found under the following categories:

ADD/ADHD	Family
Accepting Responsibility	Gangs
Anger Management	Goal-setting
Anxiety/Stress	Impulsivity
Attitudes Toward Authority	Leadership
Bad Habits	Media Usage
Bullying	Peer Mediation
Communication	Positive Reinforcement
Consequences	Prison Visits
Curfews	Problem-Solving
Dating/Sexuality	Relationships
Dealing with Conflict	Self-Defense
Decision-Making	Self-Esteem
Delinquency	Sleep
Depression	Substance Abuse
Diversity	Trust
Education	Weapons
Executive Functioning	

Many of the exercises from the curriculum have been included within the various chapters of this book.

During the intake session, we usually ask the parent(s) to sign an agreement delineating certain expectations we have regarding their participation in our program. We explain to the parent(s) that though we are meeting with them because of the unacceptable behavior of their child, our work with the child can only have a successful outcome if the child is accountable to his/her parents for future behavior. When asked by parents about the amount of their time they would be required to devote to the program, we can't provide an exact number of hours per month. We tell them that we will call on them only when we need them. Here is the agreement we ask the parents to consent to. (Appendix 4B):

Appendix 4B

WHAT PARTICIPATING PARENTS SHOULD EXPECT

(This agreement is usually provided by a caseworker to newly participating parents.)

1. Parents/Guardians will be liable and responsible to comply with your programmatic requirements—including getting photo ID.
2. Parents/Guardians will participate in family interventions and other treatment activities requested by your child's caseworker.
3. Parents/Guardians will implement disciplinary techniques which are suggested by the clinician.
4. Parents/Guardians will engage the child regularly in active communication--daily or more often.
5. Parents/Guardians will monitor academic performance, school attendance, completion of homework. Grades will be shared in a timely fashion with your caseworker.
6. Parents/Guardians will work with the caseworker toward developing a policy regarding mobile phone usage which does not have negative consequences for the child's family relationships, education, and socialization.
7. Parents/Guardians will enforce their child's curfew.
8. Parents/Guardians will inform their clinician when their child's behavior is unacceptable.

Agreed to: _____

      (Parent/Guardian)

_____

(Parent/Guardian)

_____

(Teen Client)

_____

(Date)

While on the topic of expectations, it is also important to be clear about what we expect from the entity referring the youngsters to us. We request that they adhere to the following procedures:

1. We Offer a Package of Activities:
We ask them to inform the youngsters that when they are referred to our program, they are expected to participate in a range of activities (individual and family counseling, a peer group, self-defense, field trips, etc.)

2. No "Picking and Choosing":
We emphasize that there is a reason for the required range of activities we offer. Clients should not expect to be able to "pick and choose" which ones they prefer.

3. Compliance and Attendance:
When youngsters do not comply with the requirements of our program, they will be expected to do community service. We request that the referring party support us on this.

4. When the Teens Complain:
When this happens, the true reasons for complaints are usually that the youngsters don't like to be held to our standards of compliance. We ask of the referring source that they not be too quick to side with them or give them too much power in this situation. They may not be sending them the right message.

Finally, our program, even at this early stage, tries to induce our teenage clients to start thinking about those personal changes they are committed to making while in our program. In order to facilitate this process, we use the following "Change Plan Worksheet" (Appendix 4C):

Appendix 4C

DEALING WITH CHANGED CIRCUMSTANCES
(A caseworker should lead a teenage client through this process.)

The changes I want to make are:

The most important reasons why I want to make these changes are:

The steps I plan to take in changing are:

The ways other persons can help me are:

Person	Possible ways to help
•	
•	
•	

Some things that could disrupt my plan are:

I will know if my plan is succeeding if:

Participant's signature_____

Date_____

Clinician's signature _____

Date_____

_____

Hopefully, readers of this chapter will have an understanding of who would be the best candidate for a Delinquency Prevention Program, who would not be, and how to enroll the bonafide candidates.

Chapter 5

Addressing Risk Factors

Skills: Home Visits, Program Evaluation

Selecting multiple interventions

In this chapter, Brian, Thomas, and Robert will be presented as receivers of the most unusual home visits. Also, you will be introduced to Giselle, Stephen, Frank, and Danny, who had problems fitting into groups.

We have seen in Chapter Three how various risk factors may contribute to delinquency. Due to the multitude of potential factors, a single intervention conducted in isolation is not likely to solve the problem. The most effective programs include several types of interventions and strategies that complement one another. For example, a mentoring program to help teens avoid gang membership may be complemented by an intervention that offers alternative after-school activities. Instruction in nonviolent conflict resolution for school children may be complemented by an intervention that teaches families how to foster nonviolence at home.

Someone designing such a program should carefully consider their available resources, community support, and level of caseworker experience when selecting interventions. And they should make sure that the interventions chosen are complementary to each other.

Ways Client Families Can Progress Through Our Violence Prevention Program.

Our teenage clients alone participate in some of the activities we offer; they join their parents as co-participant in other activities, and then there are a couple of activities exclusively designed for parents. The following flow chart portrays how a family progresses through our program:

Referral

Intake /Pre-Test

Children's Activities	**Parent-Child Activities**	**Parent Activities**
Individual Counseling	Family Counseling	Parent Training
Anger Management Groups	Crisis Intervention	Crisis Parenting
Peer Leadership Sessions	Parent-Child Communication	
School Visits	Curfew Management	
Prison Trip	"Challenge Trip"	
Court Visits	Addressing Negative Attitudes	
Apology Letter		
Mentoring		
Self-Defense		

Termination /Post-Test

SEEKING MULTI-GENERATIONAL POSITIVE CHANGE

When the anti-social behavior of youngsters is discussed, how often do we hear "He/she is just like his parent(s)? Like father, like son, or like mother, like daughter." There are many instances when negative conduct is repeated in the next generation.

How refreshing it is then when staff members of a program find that it has generated positive behavior in more than one generation of the same family. As an example, here is our teenage client Linda, who describes how what she learned in our program influenced how she approached her role as a mother:

"I entered your program when I was 16 years old. That was 14 years ago. What I appreciate is that after all these years, my caseworker checks in periodically to see if I'm still on the right track.

When I first came to your program, I was defiant, disrespectful, and angry at the world. I was ready to chew anyone's head off. I didn't listen to my mother. School wasn't important to me. I didn't listen to my mom. It wasn't that I didn't love her. I just felt I knew better than her.

I entered your program because I had been in a number of fights and, in one of them, broke a girl's jaw. I had also been disruptive in school.

Even though I gave my caseworker a hard time, she kept coming to my house. She didn't focus on my past mistakes as much as on rebuilding my relationship with my mom—to pay more attention to her and help her out. She taught me to focus on important issues, such as school, and let go of the things that didn't really matter.

When I was part of your weekly group, one of the memorable events was the trip to Arthur Kill Prison, where we saw the horrible conditions and talked with specially trained inmates about their teenage years and the lives they had thrown away. Your staff took me on ice-skating trips and to Coney Island. The other kids, I think, saw me as a leader. My relationship with my mother also improved—even though I stumbled along the way. I actually came to see her as an amazing person—somebody I could always turn to. Your program helped me see the ties between my education and achieving the life I wanted.

Here is the life I've created for myself after my time in your program:

My college degree is in Therapeutic Recreation. I am looking forward to a Master's Program in Occupational Therapy. I have also been enjoying working with the elderly.

Most important are my two children—Nancy and Hector. As I think about my role as a parent, I often remember the issues which we discussed while I was in your program.

I took away the following lessons:

- You have to pick your battles.
- Try rewards before punishment
- When talking with both my children, don't compare them. Every child is different.
- When you want your children to change a certain behavior, ask them to repeat what you said to make sure they are listening.
- Then, give them a chance to speak without interrupting them.

In conclusion, what I learned in your program has remained with me 14 years later. "MUSIC TO OUR EARS"!

Careful readers will note that on the flow chart described on Page 51A, they find the words "pre-test" and "post-test." These events refer to our efforts to evaluate the impact of our program on the future behavior of our teenage clients. The pre-test is administered as part of the intake process. The post-test is conducted immediately before the youngster leaves our program.

Social service programs—and particularly prevention programs—are often criticized because their success is seldom evaluated. Doing so enhances not only the program itself but also the whole credibility of the field.

In terms of Violence Prevention, our program has developed pre-and post-tests, which **track the following behaviors** listed below, among others.

- Physical confrontations
- Threats of violence
- Arrests
- Weapons usage
- Gang involvement

The pre-test covers the period before the referral to our program. The post-test covers the period from referral to six months out or termination, whichever occurs last. The format of the pre-and post-tests is as follows (Appendix 5A):

PRE-POST INVENTORY OF VIOLENCE-RELATED FACTORS

Client _____ Pre- Test Date _____ Post- Test Date _____

Person Questioned Regarding Client_____
Relationship/Position _____
Person Administering Questionnaire_____

I. **AGGRESSIVE BEHAVIOR**

♦ Family Member: Major _____ #Minor _____

  #Threats _____

  Describe:

_____

♦ Outside Authority Figure: Major _____ #Minor _____

  #Threats _____

  Describe:

_____

♦ Peer: [CIRCLE ONE] student, camper, rival gang member, neighbor

  Major _____ #Minor _____ #Threats _____

  Describe:

_____

♦ Boyfriend/Girlfriend: Major _____ #Minor _____

  #Threats _____

  Describe:

_____

♦ Destruction of Property: Number_____

  Describe: _____

II. **REACTION TO POTENTIALLY VIOLENT SITUATIONS:**

#Settled Verbally (a) _____ #Settled Physically (b) _____
#Removed Self Physically from Situation (c) _____
#Sought Adult Assistance (d) _____
Describe (cite letter- a,b, etc.) _____

\#

Usage of Anger Management Technique- Describe (cite letter – a,b, etc.)

_____

_____

____

Where Technique Was Learned _____

III. **ARRESTS:** Number _____ Describe: _____
IV. **WEAPONS:** Seen Carrying (a) _____ Threatening Usage (b) _____
     Actual Usage (c) _____ Describe (cite letter – a, b, etc.)
V.   **GANGS** (formal or virtual) – (check one) Membership _____
                                          Participation_____
VI. **WHO'S AT RISK OF BEING THE VICTIM OF A VIOLENT ACT COMMITTED BY
     CLIENT?** _____or nobody_____

Home Visits are Crucial

Some family service programs have personnel wait around their offices in expectation of the arrival of their clients for scheduled appointments. There are a couple of problems with this approach. One is that this method of operation is favored by some because it is convenient for the social worker—but not necessarily for clients. Clearly, many more office visits fail to materialize than home visits.

At least as important are the advantages that home visits have over office visits. Clients are more likely to be open with their feelings at home rather than in an office, where they feel more like guests.

Our program has relied heavily on home visits because of the essential information they yield—and because the home is where future plans can be most graphically laid out. The entire cast of characters is most likely to be accessible. In many cases, the most candid and helpful information has come from extended family members or friends whom we were not even planning to see during our visit.

Home-visiting interventions should also help parents tie into support networks. By linking them to community organizations, churches, medical-care providers, and other services, home visitors can help parents obtain assistance with finances, emotional problems, and other needs.

Each visit should have a clear agenda. To keep activities on track, it is best to focus on long-term goals. At the end of each visit, it is helpful for an evaluation to be conducted. Creating a "contract" with participants can be useful in determining what the agenda of visits should be. Visits should not be driven solely by crises.

Youngsters Need to Monitor Their Decisions

Every day, we all make hundreds of decisions. They range from the meaninglessly routine ones that require no thought (such as blowing one's nose) to the highly significant ones (such as saying "no" to drugs).

Obviously, our caseworkers try to distinguish the routine from the significant decisions and help our teenage clients focus on the latter. We want them to notice and learn from the following sorts of situations:

- New behaviors
- How others react to both old and new significant behaviors
- The consequences of all such significant behaviors
- New forms of communication with others
- The results of depending on adults for advice.

If youngsters notice these situations, they will realize that they are based on significant decisions which they have made. It is our hope that in the future, such decisions are made thoughtfully with regard to the consequences.

Our caseworkers encourage our teenage clients to consider every day of their lives to be an opportunity to learn and grow. At the beginning of every counseling session, we ask the youngsters if there was a significant situation since we last saw them that they either "handled well or could have handled better."

Some kids will regularly be able to recall such situations (an argument, a case of being disrespected, etc.). Others have difficulty doing so. Because of the importance of this issue, we are persistent in our efforts to get youngsters to identify significant events in their lives and distinguish them from routine occurrences. What follows is an exercise we use to assist them with this sorting out process (Appendix 5B):

SORTING OUT SIGNIFICANT EVENTS FROM ROUTINE

(This exercise is administered by a caseworker early on in the program)

Place an S by those events in your life that you consider SIGNIFICANT and an R by those events which you consider ROUTINE:

1. When a kid who has in the past drawn you into fights, tries again, for the first time you ignore him. _____

2. You continue your policy of never letting adults know when you are being threatened or bullied. _____

3. You have tried "I" messages before, but it worked the first time recently. _____

4. You curse out a teacher who annoys you. _____

5. You are invited to join a gang and again decide not to join. _____

6. Instead of arguing with a teacher during class, as usual, you ask to speak with her after class. _____

7. Something has been bothering you about your relationship with your boyfriend/girlfriend, and rather than ignoring it, you finally start a discussion. _____

8. You walk down the street with someone you hardly know, and he starts a fight. _____

9. You finally tell a negative friend that you can't see him anymore. _____

10. A kid calls your mother a bad name, and, as usual, you snuff him. _____

11. You have an early curfew, but you come up with something new that you enjoy doing at home. _____

12. You're offered weed, and you turn it down, as usual. _____

ANECDOTES FROM OUR 20 PLUS YEARS OF HOME VISITS

The 300-Pound 14-year-old:

Early on, our program took on an unusual case—not one where the youngster Brian was at risk of harming others, but rather of having a suicidal lifestyle.

When we first met Brian, the visual setting immediately yielded clues as to the problem and possible remedies. Brian's life was almost entirely played out within a 25-square-foot area of the living room. He almost never left a bed where, during his waking hours, he would sit (with legs crossed like a Buddha). Brian's basic needs were met without his having to leave his home base. To the left was his video set, and to the right was his TV, while his meals and snacks were provided by his doting entourage (mother, live-in mother's girlfriend, and grandmother). These three women, it became clear, were helping drive Brian's express suicide vehicle.

Seeing Is Believing

Only when we viewed Brian's environment did it become evident which case approach would be needed. Our behavior modification approach was to be focused on finding ways to reward Brian for physical movement, exercise, and dietary control. The eventually successful treatment plan would, of course, require the cooperation of the three women and on-site monitoring. The key point here is that only when the home was visited could we begin to understand the nature of Brian's problem.

Teen Manipulation: "The Lost Shoes"

I'd like to say that experienced caseworkers can consistently outsmart our teenage clients, but it seems as if their manipulative tactics are becoming increasingly more creative.

One example occurred the day I arrived to bring the truant Thomas to school. His mother had bought him an Xbox, which meant that he was determined not to leave home—for fear that she would take away his beloved Xbox. The last place Thomas wanted to go was school.

So Thomas did not actually relish my appearance on a sub-freezing day. As part of a plot to prevent our leaving for school, his shoes mysteriously disappeared. His family and I looked frantically for them while Thomas went through the motions. After a 30-minute hunt, I concluded that Thomas was not equipped to leave the house, so I left with my suspicions.

But before leaving the building, I waited for five minutes outside the door to Thomas' family's apartment. Then I knocked on the door, and when I re-entered the apartment, the first thing I noticed was Thomas' shoes. Victory for me. So off to school, we went!

The Shortest Home Visit Ever

Despite the belief of our staff in the overriding value of home visits, sometimes unexpected developments short-circuit even the best-laid plans. On one such occasion, I had just begun to do family counseling when police sirens permeated the Bronx neighborhood. Mother and son raced to the window to see the older son being arrested by police officers. As they immediately flew down the stairs to the aid of the older boy, I realized that the counseling session, after 30 seconds, had run its course. I would return on another day.

The Isolated Youngest Sibling Discovered During a Home Visit

When we met Robert, he was the 14-year-old youngest of four siblings. The older children of Betty and Jim were all living out of the house but in the neighborhood.

If our caseworker had insisted that Betty, Jim, and Robert come into our office for family counseling sessions, much useful information would have been unseen. Even though Robert's three older siblings lived out of the house, they visited often. Their visits almost always took on a similar script. The parents and the older siblings who were present angrily ganged up on Robert with a string of denunciations regarding his behavior. The effect was that Robert was boxed into a corner to the extent that he was hard-pressed to get a word in—much less to discuss any possible behavioral changes.

If our caseworker had not witnessed these lop-sided exchanges, the case plan might have looked very different. What was needed as a first step was for the older siblings to lay off Robert and make it clear that he had one functioning parent—Betty. Once the siblings laid off Robert, and Robert felt he could get a word in, and once Betty listened to Robert expressing his feelings, Robert's behavior underwent a dramatic change for the better. His school attendance and grades improved—and he was home when he was supposed to be.

TEEN GROUPS

Weekly teenage groups have been an essential part of our Delinquency Prevention Program. Normally we have had a mix of more positive and more negative types in terms of their attitudes and past behaviors. A major goal of the groups is for the more positive types to have a healthy influence on their less positive colleagues.

The agenda of the group sessions is taken from the "Delinquency Prevention Curriculum" categories, which can be found in Chapter Four. In reality, a good percentage of the time is usually spent on Anger Management, Relationships, and Media Usage. The Teen Group is described below:

Teen Groups only work if there is an agreement by the participants to abide by certain rules. These rules are summarized in the "Teen Contract," which can be drawn up as follows (Appendix 5C):

The following are rules designed to keep Teen Groups both productive and civilized:

TEEN GROUP CONTRACT
(The contract is to be presented to new group members when they are enrolling in the group.)

General Rules:

1. Participants must conduct themselves in a respectful/responsible manner at all times when on our premises.
2. When a group participant breaks a rule, he/she will be given a "pull-up," which is a final warning. A second pull-up will result in an "absence" and a community service assignment of a particular number of hours in duration.
3. Participants must be on time to group. Two latenesses equals one absence.
4. When attending leadership skills groups, participants will dress appropriately. No gang colors, beads, hats, durags, headbands, cell phones, I-pods, etc.
5. Seating placement will be at the discretion of our staff.

Participation:

1. Participants are expected to share their experiences after the first session and to respond to questions directed to them.
2. If, in the opinion of the group leaders, a member does not participate, the whole group may be kept over at the end of the session. Also, a non-participant shall be marked absent on the attendance sheet.

Unacceptable Behaviors:

1. Refusal to carry out instructions of the program staff;
2. Using abusive or profane (cursing) language;

3. Stealing, fighting, gambling, or destroying someone else's property.

When in Group:

1. No "put-downs." Affirm others' good points.
2. Do not interrupt staff or each other. No side discussions.
3. Volunteer yourself only.
4. Maintain confidentiality.
5. Help group leaders enforce group rules.

Agreed to: _____

Date: _____

Considerations Regarding the Composition of Groups

If group leaders decide to include both violent and nonviolent young-sters, caution is suggested when designing intervention activities. While negative teenagers may be impacted for the better by more positive participants, aggressive adolescents need special attention. A treatment plan intended for a general population may not succeed. And if the proportion of violent to nonviolent teenagers is too high, the nonviolent ones could be negatively affected. Some examples of how groups can go wrong follow:

When a Violence Prevention Group Itself Turned Violent

When arriving late for a group session one day, one of our teenage clients, Giselle, was searching for a seat. One chair was empty except for the presence of Stephen's bag, so Giselle, with no acknowledgment, took it upon herself to remove the offending accessory. Stephen reacted by directing one of the most disrespectful-looking grills at Giselle.

In the world of teenagers, the wrong sort of glance can be all it takes for all hell to break loose. On this occasion, Giselle bounded from her seat and charged Stephen. He responded by dragging her out of the building by her hair with one hand and punching her with the other. Fortunately, our staff intervened to prevent the worst from happening. Certainly, this episode provided a reality-based backdrop for the following session's discussion of Anger Management techniques.

Long Memory – Short Fuse

When they were 14, two members of a group had been involved in an incident on the streets of the Bronx, with familiar details. One of Frank's crew had jumped Danny. Frank had boasted about the incident on YouTube. Now, some 18 months later, here was Frank entering the same group as the one Danny was in. The memory of the incident had lengthened Danny's memory and increased his sense of embarrassment. So upon the sight of Frank, Danny leaped out of his chair and, seeking revenge against Frank, chased him. Fortunately, other group members intervened so as to prevent serious injury. But the incident demonstrated how the Internet has expanded the statute of limitations on revenge situations. It has a way of keeping angry feelings from being extinguished.

Appendix 14B

It is helpful to start the sessions by having participants share what is happening in their lives, with reactions and support from the others in attendance. The sentence completion exercise below, which helps bring current problems into the open, is often helpful:

SOME ANGER MANAGEMENT SENTENCE COMPLETIONS AS OPENERS FOR GROUPS

1. The last time I felt like hitting someone was ...
2. The hardest person for me to deal with at school is ...
3. Kids often get in trouble during the summer because ...
4. The last time a kid disrespected me, I ...
5. In school, I feel most disrespected when ...
6. The most frequent reason I have arguments is...
7. The quickest way to get me angry is ...
8. The last instigator I had to deal with was ...
9. A time recently when I needed help from an adult was ...
10. The biggest beef I have with my parents is ...

Chapter 6

Addressing Risk Factors Related to Mental Health

Skills: Dealing with Various Forms of Disorder

In this chapter, you will be introduced to our teenage client Tiffany, who went to the brink of committing suicide.

Even the most competent people cannot be expected to solve every sort of problem that comes their way. It is important for caseworkers to recognize that the level and focus of their training may not have equipped them to treat all mental health conditions to be found in their clients. Sometimes the most which can be expected of a clinician is to develop the ability to make educated hypotheses regarding the presence of certain mental health conditions. At that point, the client will, in most cases, be referred to a specialist for treatment.

Starting with the less severe and working our way toward the most severe mental health conditions are the following:

Youngsters With ADHD

When structuring a delinquency prevention program, it is necessary to consider the particular nuances of the target population. ADHD (Attention Deficit/Hyperactivity Disorder) is prevalent among many youngsters who exhibit impulsive, negative behavior. ADHD is an illness caused by an imbalance of brain functions. If not treated by the age of 14, ADHD can lead to a state of extremely aggressive conduct disorder, then criminal behavior.

Teens with the hyperactive type of ADD look very different from those with the inattentive type. In fact, teens with the hyperactive or combined forms often have high energy levels, while teens with the inattentive form are almost the exact opposite.

The Official Diagnostic Criteria for ADHD (DSM-IV)

The official criteria for a diagnosis of ADHD is found in the Diagnostic and Statistical Manual, 4th edition (DSM-IV), published by the American Psychiatric Association in 1994. The DSM-IV criteria:

- Describes the current diagnosis for attention deficit disorders;
- Presents symptoms under the category of inattention;
- Presents symptoms under hyperactivity and impulsivity.

According to the criteria, an individual must exhibit six or more (out of the nine) symptoms in the inattention category and/or six (out of the nine) symptoms of hyperactivity and impulsivity.

The following are the symptoms found in youngsters with ADHD:

Inattention

1. Does not give close attention to details or makes careless mistakes in schoolwork, often leading to poor academic results.
2. Frequently distracted by outside stimuli.
3. When spoken to, does not appear to listen.
4. Often does not carry out directions nor schoolwork, chores, or duties in the workplace.
5. Often has difficulty organizing and finishing tasks.
6. Often avoids tasks requiring sustained mental effort, such as schoolwork or homework.

7. Often misplaces objects necessary for activities such as school assignments, pencils, books, etc.
8. Is often bored.
9. Often forgetful in daily activities.

Hyperactivity/Impulsivity

1. Often fidgets with feet or hands or squirms when seated.
2. Tendency to leave a seat in the classroom or in other situations in which remaining seated is expected.
3. Often roams in situations in which such behavior is inappropriate.
4. Has difficulty engaging in leisure activities quietly.
5. Often talks excessively.
6. Often provides answers before questions have been completed.
7. Often have difficulty waiting their turn.
8. Often interrupts others during conversations.
9. Takes unnecessary risks.

Some Consequences of Having ADHD

To understand what the consequences are, it is helpful to look at what some of the developmental demands of adolescence are and how ADHD impacts youngsters' ability to respond to these demands successfully.

Major teenage concerns include the following:

1. Achieving a sense of independence from what seems to be a stream of authority figures

Because teenagers with attention deficits often have difficulty following rules and are impulsive, they are likely to have conflicts with their parents, teachers, and other authority figures. Conflicts most often arise when they don't do their classwork, homework, or chores. Power struggles between teenagers and parents are common. Many teenagers have problems with stubbornness, defiance, refusal to obey, temper tantrums, and verbal hostility. Many chafe for independence from their parents, typically before they are ready for this independence.

Parents have long observed that youngsters with attention deficits are more difficult to parent and discipline. They simply do not respond to rewards and punishments like other youngsters do. This behavior may help explain why they receive more criticism, rejection, and punishment than other children their age.

2. Developing Rewarding Friendships

Youngsters with ADHD often do not develop effective social skills. They can be bossy, offend their peers without realizing it, interrupt conversations, and not pick up on subtle social cues. As a request, they may have more difficulty making and keeping friends. Talking back and arguing with adults may also be a problem. Teens with ADHD also may inherit a gene that makes them more likely to be impulsive risk-takers.

3. Achieving Reasonable Success In Education and/or Job Training

Parents and teachers may be puzzled because teenagers with attention deficits may be bright but often underachieving academically. Frequently, teachers comment that these teenagers are not doing well in school mainly because they don't pay attention, don't complete class-work and homework,
forget to do make-up work, and sometimes, sleep in class. Even when they do their homework, they may forget to turn it in. Students with attention deficits often have tremendous difficulty getting started on schoolwork and may turn in assignments late. At times, teenagers with attention deficits must be baffled by their own behavior.

Some days these students can do the work; other days, they can't. This unevenness in performance is extremely confusing to both parents and teachers. On the surface, it looks as if they can do the work but choose not to. The unevenness of schoolwork is one of the primary problems of youngsters with ADHD.

Although elementary school children with attention deficit disorders also have problems with inattention and impulsivity, the challenges facing teenagers are more complex. During the teenage years, the risks of school failure, school suspension or expulsion, or dropping out of school are greater. Because of their academic struggles, many teenagers develop an aversion to school. Yet school success is critical for developing healthy self-esteem.

4. Staying Out of Trouble

Unfortunately, a few of the more impulsive and aggressive teenagers may have problems with law enforcement agencies. These "brushes with the law" are usually minor and not the result of any malicious or criminal intent. Instead, they result from poor impulse control, risk-taking behavior, and/or failure to anticipate the consequences of their actions. For example, teenagers with attention deficits have been known to receive speeding tickets, talk back to police officers, shoplift inexpensive items, sneak out of the house after curfew, indulge in underage drinking, and experiment with drugs.

Parents are understandably frightened by these impulsive behaviors and may fear that this kind of acting-out behavior may become more serious. Fortunately, parents can often prevent more serious problems from happening by learning to intervene when their child misbehaves, imposing appropriate yet reasonable consequences, and continuing to believe in and support their child.

Treatment Options for ADHD

When ADHD is not treated by the mid-teen years, severe behavioral problems may develop, which could well result in a permanent conduct disorder.

Once a youngster is identified and diagnosed with ADHD, there are many ways to help him/her and the family. The most effective approach is a multifaceted treatment that might involve the following types of interventions:

- Medical
- Psychological (behavioral)
- Educational
- Medical/pharmacological intervention – Pharmacological treatment involves the use of medication to manage ADHD symptoms.

It is important to consider the medication issue by asking: What are the side effects of not taking medication? Unless the ADHD is very mild, youngsters with attention deficits who do not receive treatment are at high risk of developing the following serious problems:

- Increased risk for behavior problems
- Increased risk of school failure and family turmoil
- Increased risk of drug abuse

What if a Teen Resists Taking Medication?

In many states, a youngster has the right to resist such medication unless the judge orders an intramuscular injection. If parents interfere with this process, they can be charged with medical neglect.

Parents need to be educated about ADHD and treatments and their legal rights in the educational system, so they can effectively advocate for their youngsters—in both the educational and healthcare systems.

Youngsters should be included as active partners in the entire treatment program. They need to understand the reason for various interventions and how those treatments are intended to positively affect their daily lives. Youngsters must be included in this process so that they will be motivated to cooperate and participate in (not sabotage) the treatment.

The Challenge of Treating ADHD

Treating a youngster with ADHD poses a formidable challenge when the behaviors are most apparent in the school setting. The youngster's parent(s), a school official, and a mental health professional must all communicate with and cooperate with each other, normally over a substantial period of time – in order to fine-tune a successful medical response.

One of a family of psychostimulant medications is usually prescribed, but the particular pills, the dosage, the timing, etc., may all have to be manipulated in order for ADHD to be effectively treated. Needless to say, not every youngster can rely on an effective parent, educator, and mental health professional who are motivated to cooperate with each other. For this reason, woefully few cases of ADHD are successfully treated.

Parents are the youngster's primary care managers. They need to find appropriate professionals and build a team to help with the care and management of their ADHD youngster.

Most positive outcomes are achieved when collaboration occurs between:

- Parents
- School personnel
- Physicians
- Mental health professionals
- The youngster

Since ADHD often lasts throughout one's lifetime, a person may need some support and interventions at different times in his or her life (assistance from educators, mental health professionals, physicians, tutors, and coaches).

What follows is the discovery by one of our client's mother about "how she could effectively deal with her son Jamie's case of ADHD:

"Before Burt was diagnosed with ADHD, six years ago, my husband and I shouted at him several times a day. His behavior seemed defiant to us. We thought he was being disobedient in order to get a rise from us. We were punished and screamed, making our home life terrible. We didn't seek other ways to parent Burt because <u>we didn't understand him</u>.

After the pediatrician diagnosed him, I read every book on ADHD that I could find. The more I read, the more I understand my son's strengths and weaknesses. The more we discussed Burt with behavioral and occupational therapists, the more I learned about the causes of his different behaviors. I no longer viewed his negative behaviors as willful disrespect. They were caused by his ADHD wiring.

I was punishing Burt for behaviors that he had no control over. So now I try not to let him get me upset. But I may have shifted too far in the other direction. I began to use ADHD as an excuse when he misbehaved. He came to believe that whatever he did, he could blame it on ADHD and that he would be forgiven. That created a different "sort of problem."

In his book "The Explosive Child," Ross Greene, Ph.D., advocates that parents show calmness and take care not to overreact to their children who have ADHD. The calmer the parent is, the calmer the child is likely to be.

Attitudemag.com ("Learn the Right Reasons for Your Child's Wrong Behavior") has done a good job of suggesting how a parent should respond to ADHD-related behavior. The suggestions are:

1. **Recognize that what looks like willful disobedience could have other causes.** First, parents must try to understand their children with ADHD and the reasons for what seems to be disobedience. A child with ADHD may disobey on purpose, like any other child, but those instances of disobedience are likely to be no more frequent than is the case with other children. They do, however, suffer from frequent periods of frustration.

2. **Try to steer a child through their moments of frustration.**
   Often, meltdowns by teenagers might seem hard to fathom.
   Parents may seek to impose their will and be firm, and yet the
   child goes out of control. It may appear that the reason is that
   the child didn't get his/her way. But it's not. They are not
   throwing a fit to force you into giving them what they want. It
   may not be a tantrum at all. They are emotionally out of control
   because they don't see that there's more than one way to react.

3. **Don't confront children when they are melting down;**
   stay detached. Remember that your child's behavior is not
   meant as a personal attack on you. By not reacting on a
   personal level, you are more likely to stay calm.

4. **Work together to teach your child skills.** Particularly
   important are problem-solving skills, where several options are
   created. View everything as a problem that can be solved.

5. **Reassure yourself that you have control of the situation,
   even if it appears that the child is in the driver's seat.**
   Appeasing your child can make matters worse. Seek other ways
   of maintaining control other than shouting. Yelling or
   threatening to punish your children when they act up will only
   prolong the outburst; remaining calm will shorten it.

Calm is Crucial

The key to calm parenting is to understand the triggers and functions of
your child's unwanted behaviors. Use one or more of the following techniques when you feel yourself getting angry or frustrated. They have
worked well for Moms and Dads:

- Remind yourself that your child is acting like a child because
  he or she is one.
- Put yourself in his or her shoes.
- Give yourself a timeout.
- Take a walk around the block.
- Turn on some music.

- Hum a tune.
- Start singing a silly song.
- Close your eyes and take relaxing belly breaths – in through your nose and out through your mouth.
- Speak to your child in a whisper.
- Clean something.
- Find something to be grateful about.

The stress of parenting a child with ADHD is heavy enough without yelling. Kids with ADHD are perceptive – the calmer you are, the calmer they are likely to be, and vice versa.

When Feelings of Hatred Fuel Anger

Youngsters with feelings of hatred often see themselves as victims wronged by a group or class of people who are considered to be dangerous foes.

In order to help teenagers overcome feelings of hatred, parents might be advised to do the following:

- Say positive things about the ethnic, religious, or other groups that your child seems to hate.
- Talk about positive experiences you have had with diverse groups.
- Create and explore a rule that it is not permissible to lash out at people because they are part of a different group.
- Refer to examples of persons who are different in entertainment or public life who have made positive contributions to our country.

CLINICAL DISORDERS WHICH CAN LEAD TO ANTISOCIAL BEHAVIOR

Personality Disorder (Develops before birth from genetic factors and reaches full state in adulthood. If it develops after birth, environmental factors including family, religion, cultural values, or education – play a role.)

Some Symptoms:

- Little respect for authority
- No sense of morality beyond what's good for oneself
- Inability to form relationships with strong bonds.

Behaviors Often Displayed

- Antisocial
- In violation of social standards
- Manipulative
- Self-serving
- Often intelligent
- Limited in regard for others
- A lack of emotional connection

It is important for parents to realize that personality disorders cannot be treated; only the associated behaviors can be.

Mood Disorder — A psychological disorder characterized by an elevation or lowering of a person's mood—as exemplified by depression or a case of bipolar disorder.

Mood disorders are characterized by the following symptoms:

1. Impulsive behavior
2. Poor judgment
3. Manipulative behaviors
4. Anti-social behavior
5. A usually high level of intelligence

Treating persons with a mood disorder requires mood-stabilizing medication.

Oppositional Defiant Disorder (ODD) — as defined by the American Psychiatric and Psychological Association (APPA) in their Diagnostics Statistical Manual (p.219):

A pattern of angry/irritable moods, argumentative/defiant behavior, or vindictiveness lasting at least six months as evidenced by at least four symptoms from any of the following categories, and exhibited during interaction with at least one individual who is not a sibling. It affects about 10% of American youngsters.

The APPA goes on to outline some of the symptoms associated with a case of Oppositional Defiant Disorder, including the following:

Angry/Irritable Mood

1. Often loses temper
2. Is often touchy or easily annoyed
3. Is often angry and resentful

Argumentative/Defiant Behavior

4. Often argues with authority figures or, in case they are children or adolescents, with adults.
5. Often actively defies or refuses to comply with requests from authority figures or with rules.
6. Often deliberately annoys others.
7. Often blames others for his or her mistakes or misbehavior

Vindictiveness

8. Has been spiteful or vindictive at least twice within the past 6 months.

The following are suggestions about how to reduce the extent of ODD Behavior in teens:

- Set clear limits and household rules.

- Create structure by adhering to a regular routine for your teen.
- Serve as a role model for your child by effectively managing your negative emotions.
- Work with your partner to strive for consistency in your parenting styles.
- Look for opportunities to provide positive feedback for your teenager.
- Limit your number of rules to ones that are especially important.
- Provide consistent and appropriate consequences (e.g. loss of privileges) for aggressive and otherwise negative behaviors.
- Seek out other adults (e.g. teachers, coaches, etc.) in your teen's life to provide positive reinforcement as well.

Conduct Disorder – Affecting about 4% of American youngsters, this condition can develop in children as young as seven years of age. Conduct disorder in teenagers refers to someone with a serious inclination toward aggression directed at others. It is marked by bullying, violence, and cruelty.

Children and adolescents with this disorder experience great difficulty following rules and behaving in a socially acceptable way. They are often seen by other children, adults, and social agencies as "bad" or delinquent rather than mentally ill. Among the factors contributing to a child developing conduct disorder are brain damage, child abuse, genetic vulnerability, school failure, and traumatic life experiences. The child does not see anything wrong with his behavior. There is no guilt or remorse, which leads to manipulation in order to confirm his own sense of his reality (often compounded with ADHD).

Youngsters with conduct disorder may show the following sorts of behaviors:
Hostile behavior toward human beings and animals:

- Bullies or threatens others
- Often causes fights

- Has used dangerous weapons (bat, brick, broken bottle, knife or gun)
- Is physically cruel to people or animals
- Steals from someone during an assault
- Sexually aggressive behavior

Destruction of property:

- Sets fires with the intention of causing damage
- Deliberately destroys property belonging to others

Deceitfulness, lying, or stealing:

- Highly manipulative
- Breaks into someone else's building, house, or car
- Lies to obtain goods or favors
- Shoplifts

Children who show these behaviors should be given a comprehensive evaluation. Those with a conduct disorder may have other conditions, such as mood disorders, anxiety, substance abuse, learning problems, ADHD, or thought disorders, which can be more easily treated. Research shows that teenagers with conduct disorder are likely to have continuous problems if they are not treated early on and comprehensively. Otherwise, many young persons having conduct disorder may be unable to adjust to the challenges of adulthood and may have ongoing problems with relationships and with maintaining employment. They may well indulge in anti-social and criminal behavior.

Who is at risk for conduct disorder?

Parents of children with conduct disorder often lack many important parenting skills. Such parents often are more violent and critical in their use of discipline and more inconsistent and erratic in monitoring their children's behavior. Cases of conduct disorder may start as early as three years of age. In fact, some infants who seem "fussy" appear to be candidates for conduct disorder. Other factors that could be conducive to conduct disorder include:

- Early rejection by one's mother
- Being separated from one's parents without an adequate substitute caregiver
- Being institutionalized early on
- Neglect by family
- Abusive or violent behavior in the home
- Having parent(s) with mental illness
- Constant parental bickering
- Being ignored in a multi-child family
- Living in crowded conditions
- Growing up in a poor family

A Bipolar Condition

The bipolar condition can affect 4% of the population at some point and can emerge at any age from 5 years of age on. If it becomes evident between the ages of 5 and 18, it tends to take the form of a Schizophrenic or Thought Disorder. A youngster may be angry or depressed at a particular time and happy and outgoing the next moment. Often, more than one member of the same family may experience bipolar disorder. Symptoms include rapid speech, distractibility, and impulsive behavior.

Normally, the Bipolar condition occurs in two phases. The first is the Manic Phase which takes the form of ADHD symptoms. The second phase, as described earlier, is depression, when sadness and anger take over. The timing of the phases depends on how long the bipolar condition has existed. The longer it is untreated, the quicker the transition from one phase to the other will occur. Our program refers most bipolar cases to specialized treatment agencies.

It is important for Delinquency Prevention caseworkers to be able to identify the possibility of bipolar disorder. A bipolar youngster may be bright and achievement-oriented but may be haunted by hallucinations of all types. When a youngster's anger turns into an enduring rage, intense emotion can dominate his/her life. Anger can override the capacity to reason. A separation from reality may emerge. When there is a bipolar condition, there can be alternative periods of rage and calm. Youngsters will often not be able to exercise sound judgment, nor will they be able to analyze the consequences of their behavior. Among the symptoms will be impulsivity, racing thoughts, intense emotions, and distractibility.

Bipolar youngsters will often seek isolation and usually rebel instinctively against social service programs and activities. They often require a more intensive program and restrictive setting if they are to re-enter a state of relative full-time reality. Lithium is one medication that can help moderate the extreme nature of bipolar associated emotions.

Schizophrenia

This thought disorder usually appears early in life in children with a low I.Q.

As is the case of bipolar youngsters, there can be a separation from reality. This condition, however, is caused by a lack of organization in thinking. This breakdown in the thought process can make progress in counseling and positive behavioral change difficult. Again, our program refers most cases exhibiting schizophrenia to specialized treatment agencies—including mental health institutions and appropriate departments of hospitals.

Depression

Depression is a significant condition in Americans of all ages. Among 10 to 19-year-olds, it is the leading cause of illness and disability. Suicide is the third leading cause of death among teenagers. Studies have shown that about 14% of teenagers are clinically depressed at a particular time, with 20% of those at some point being classified as having major depression. Having a blood relative with depression can increase the risk of someone suffering from depression.

The Three Forms of Depression:

Situational Depression:
Normally, this form of depression is brought on by major stressors in life, such as divorce, the death of a loved one, or the loss of a job. Emotionally healthy persons will usually grieve over these situations until they have learned to adjust to the event. Often this form of depression lasts from three to nine months. It is more common in adults than teenagers.

Cumulatively Developed Depression:
This form of depression is not caused by a catastrophic event but a series of rejections which, over time, erode the self-image of a youngster and create increasingly severe bouts of depression. Such rejections could include not being chosen by the captain to be on a pickup team, having no one respond to your phone calls or texts, or having nobody accept the invitation to your birthday party.

Clinical Depression:
Usually, clinical depression is the more severe type, causing more substantial obstacles to normal functioning. It may be caused by biological and/or genetic factors. Furthermore, it doesn't generally disappear when the stressor is removed. Typically, a person who is clinically depressed may have suicidal thoughts. Antidepressant medication may be necessary to treat the likely chemical imbalance.

Some Causes of Depression Felt by Teenagers

- Mental health conditions such as bipolar disorder, untreated ADHD, schizophrenia, etc.
- Ongoing or severe physical health problems
- Being abused or neglected
- Being rejected by friends or persons of romantic interest
- Inability to reach out for assistance regarding feelings of depression

- Tragic or disturbing events—the death of somebody close, the ending of an important relationship, etc.
- Inability to handle pressure

Being a persistent target of bullies can be a major cause of depression.

More should be said about bullying since it is so often a core cause of cumulatively developed teenage depression. Bullying does not have to be of the physical variety. It more often takes the form of the following sorts of unkind comments: ridiculing how somebody walks, rude comments about one's sexual preferences—whether the comments have any validity are not—comments about one's physical appearance or clothes, or ethnic or religious slurs.

What a teenager needs to be told is that bullying is a reflection of the character of the bully and not the person being bullied.

The inability to handle pressure can be another major cause of depression. More should be said about this topic since it is another frequent cause of cumulatively developed teenage depression. Life is full of various forms of pressures of one kind or another. Some particular forms of pressure include the pressure to excel academically, the pressure to be invited into honor classes, the pressure to be admitted to a prestigious college or a demanding post-high school alternative, or the pressure to be an accomplished athlete, artist, musician, etc.

Reducing the Pressures Felt by Youngsters

Parents wishing to reduce the amount of pressure their children are experiencing may consider a number of initiatives. They can reduce the amount of time that their kids are scheduled, ensuring that they have some "downtime." They can provide their children with opportunities to verbalize their feelings and sense that they're being listened to. They can give their children positive feedback on their present status rather than merely promising them accolades for future accomplishments. They can emphasize to their kids that they should feel good about what type of person they are instead of only what they are able to achieve.

Some Symptoms of Depression:

- Spending time alone
- Tiredness and lack of energy
- Neglect of personal hygiene
- Diminished interest in school work and activities;
- Having difficulty concentrating, making decisions, and remembering important things
- Angry outbursts, irritability, or frustration, even over small matters
- Frequent fixation on past failures and self-criticism

The Connection Between Depression and Laziness

Clearly, depression is a mental health problem that, by its very nature, cuts into the quality of life of individuals. Beyond that, it leads to laziness which affects a person's productivity which others may require. Depressed persons often have feelings of loneliness, a lack of energy, and few interests to look forward to.

On the home front, parents cannot surrender entirely to their depressed children. They need to insist that chores be done. They must also be able to hold themselves up as examples of hard workers to be imitated.

How Parents Can Assist Depressed Youngsters

Many parents feel that it is their duty to monitor and ask questions about their children's grades, eating habits, or physical activity. They are less likely to monitor their children's emotions. One reason is that they imagine—perhaps incorrectly—that youngsters resent their parents prying into their emotional life. The result is that too seldom are teenagers asked about whether they are happy or sad or angry or why that might be. So the next step might be a therapist's office or an emergency room. A call to 911 or your local emergency number may be needed. The National Suicide Prevention Lifeline is (800) 273-TALK or (800) 273-8255. An opportunity for preventive intervention by parents has been lost. The result may be more extensive therapy or medication, or even hospitalization.

How Depression Led Tiffany to Thoughts of Suicide
(In the words of one of our teenage clients)

Do you ever feel as if you're alone? That nobody understands you. Do you feel as though you must portray yourself as a happy individual? But in reality, you're hurting—mentally, physically, and emotionally—and you think the only way out is to end it.

I know that feeling well. Everyone around you thinks you have such a good life—as nothing could be wrong. You walk around with your big beautiful smile, covering all the hurt and pain that you're really feeling. No one really knows what's going on behind closed doors. They don't see the tears, the anger, and the depression.

I struggled to keep all my demons to myself. Like finding out that my mother is an addict and knowing that she wanted to die. Being homeless and some days hungry, sexually assaulted, and not having anyone to talk to. Every day I prayed. I wanted my life to go back to normal—to the time I was really happy, when everything was "perfect." But that couldn't be. I would wake up and look in the mirror, and I hated myself and everyone else.

Drugs Took Over My Life

My mother was more strung out on drugs now than ever. She disappeared more often—and made it clear drugs were now "her life." I would go to school and fake smiles, laugh with friends, and make it look like I was okay. Nobody knew that I lived in a shelter or that my mother was an addict, or that I had considered killing myself. In their eyes, I had a good life.

When I was raped one night, things changed. I was stripped of everything in an instant. Bombarded by a man who took everything I had—physically, mentally, and emotionally. I was hopeless. I fought as hard as I could, but he overpowered me. I cried for days. I had nightmares. Why did this happen to me? Why did this man force himself on me? Why hadn't I gone to the cops? I didn't deserve this.

No one deserves this. I was angry. I felt so alone. I felt disgusted. I still remember how he smelled—and for days, I could smell him. His scent just lingered. I was 16 years old. Every detail of that night I remembered.

Pretending Life Is OK

I went on with my everyday life. Going to school and work. Keeping a smile on my face. I tried my best not to show the other side of me—the side no one knew—my "demon." I can remember thinking about how I was going to "do it." Still, no one knew about the attack.

My mother and I argued a lot these days. She would always tell me how she wished she never had given birth to me. That hurt a lot. My mother hated me. She didn't care if I went to school anymore. She didn't care where I hung out. Half of the time, she had no idea who I was or what I was doing. So my thoughts were, "Nobody is going to miss me when I'm gone."

After weeks and months of contemplating, holding on to my pain and this "demon," I knew I had to let go of it all. My mother had been on medication—a lot of medication. I didn't care what it was. I knew that once I took the whole bottle, it would only be moments until I was gone. I was scared, I cried, but still, I took each pill, one by one—and then a handful. I walked back to my bedroom. I called my boyfriend and told him I loved him. I called my mom and got no answer. I wanted to hear her voice one last time. I needed my mom to know it wasn't her fault. I wanted her to know that I loved her. And then I drifted off to sleep.

Regaining Consciousness

How I was found, I didn't know—but I woke up in a hospital. My stomach was being pumped. My boyfriend was there crying. My grandmother was there also praying. My mother was there. I felt weak. My body ached. My head pounded. Doctors kept asking me if I could hear them, if I knew where I was. They placed me in a suicide ward, wanting to keep me there for a few days. I refused. I wanted to leave; I didn't want to speak to anyone. I cried about being raped. I wanted the man to be dead.

Months went by—and I opened up about the ordeal to two of my closest friends, Raj and Toni. We skipped class one day and stayed in the stairwell. Raj asked me if I was okay. She and my friend Toni noticed I hadn't been myself lately. I asked both of them if I could trust them. Without hesitation, they both said yes. I asked them to promise that they would never tell anyone about this. They promised not to. I started from the beginning—when I witnessed my mother sniffing coke to when I saved her life, from moving from New Orleans to New York and ending up in a shelter, being raped, and trying to kill myself. I spoke the truth. As I finished sharing my story, Taj and Jay broke down and cried hard—and then embraced me. That was the first time in a long time I felt someone cared for me. Those two seemed like my family. At that moment, I felt fine. Having held onto my "demons" for so many years is what had pushed me to the brink.

Learning to Appreciate Life

Years later, I am able to speak about "demons." I have opened up to my mother about what took place the night I was attacked and about how I felt about my life in general. It was hard. For years I hated my life and felt I had only one thing to do—END IT! But God had other plans for me. I'm healthy now. My mother and I have a wonderful relationship now. As for the attack, I have learned to put it all behind me. I couldn't let that malicious night alter my future. My life today isn't perfect, but it's worth every breathing moment.

Depression and suicide are both nothing to take lightly. If you or anyone you know is suffering from either or both, have them talk to someone—a close friend, a family member, or a mental health professional. Life is precious—and I believe we were all brought into this world for a reason.

* * *

Tiffany's experience is a vivid demonstration of how family members can and should be on the lookout for the signs of depression and suicidal ideation and intervene appropriately to prevent a tragedy from happening.

The Two Major Ways Depression Can Be Treated

Medication: Brain chemistry may be a factor in causing depression. Anti-depressants are often prescribed in order to alter one's brain chemistry. This process can take a few months. But, if there is no improvement in the level of depression after a few weeks, the psychiatrist should consider modifying the dose of the medication or substituting a different antidepressant.

Psychotherapy: Talking about depression in the company of a therapist can be a stand-alone treatment option, or it can be used in concert with the prescription of antidepressant medication. One promising form of psychotherapy is Cognitive Behavioral Therapy (CBT) which is aimed at solving specific problems contributing to the client's depression.

How Depression Can Lead to Thoughts of Suicide

Verbal Warning Signs that Suicide May Be Contemplated:

- "I feel always left out of everything by people."
- "I don't ever seem to figure out how to solve problems."
- "Do you see me as a burden on the family?"
- "I wish I could deal with all the challenges of this world."
- "I feel as if nothing matters anymore."

Behavioral Warning Signs:

- Taking risks (speeding while driving, jumping recklessly, etc.)
- Neglect of personal hygiene

- Becoming isolated from family and friends
- Unloading possessions which had previously seemed important
- Demonstrating lack of interest in schoolwork and/or activities to an unprecedented degree
- Difficulty concentrating, making decisions, remembering important things

Children suspected of having suicidal thoughts need professional help, but meanwhile parents can ask questions, which can establish that suicide indeed is being contemplated. Among the questions are the following:

- "Are you thinking of hurting yourself?"
- "How would you do so?"
- "What is keeping you from hurting yourself

A parent might also be advised to ask:

- "Are you thinking of hurting someone else?

Some Reasons Why Suicide Might Be Contemplated

- Feelings of hopelessness
- No way out of a problem situation
- Retaliation against someone who will feel the loss
- Total removal from reality
- Lack of support system

Signs Indicating That Suicide Is Being Contemplated

- Hiding marks derived from cutting or other forms of self-injury — as demonstrated by wearing long sleeves or turtlenecks even when it is warm, or coming up with excuses for injuries

- Reckless Behavior — (drinking Clorox, walking on high window ledges, careless street crossing, etc., which could be conscious or unconscious suicide attempts.)
- Talking or writing about death or suicide
- Giving away prized possessions
- Saying goodbye or talking about not being around

Questions to Ask of Depressed Youngsters

Testing for Suicidal Thoughts (Do they envision a future for themselves?):

- When you finish growing up, what do you want to do?
- If a genie could grant you three wishes, what would you ask for?
- (Home, clothes, food answers indicate they don't feel they have them—signs of depression)

Some Questions to Ask of Youngsters Who Might be Contemplating Suicide:

- When do thoughts of suicide occur? (Time of day, what are you doing at the time);
- What would suicide accomplish for you?
- What are other ways of accomplishing that?
- What are early recollections you made? Are they all negative?

Find out who the key people are who are close to youngsters contemplating suicide so that they can be asked to be on the lookout for the warning signs.

Through a series of questions, enable the youngster to verbalize the feelings that have caused their depression:

- Are there times when you have feelings of hopelessness?
- On what sort of occasions does this tend to happen?

- Do these feelings cause you to take unnecessary risks with your life?
- What are examples of these risky behaviors?

Through a series of questions, help youngsters see the positives in their lives which will carry them through their depression:

- What are your greatest strengths?
- How have you been able to get through hard times in the past?
- Which are qualities of yours that make people admire you?
- What can you do to avoid any risky behaviors you are contemplating?

Failed Suicidal Attempts

When a youngster indulges in self-mutilation or in what appears to be a genuine but failed attempt at suicide, the act usually represents an attempt to produce other sensations. Often the individual is trying to confirm that he/she is alive and can feel pain.

It is most important for a youngster's family and close friends to take self-mutilation and failed suicidal acts seriously. They must take note of the events and the youngster's behavior which preceded the act. It is helpful to monitor the youngster's apparent level of happiness or sadness. When such youngsters exhibit feelings of sadness or depression. It is especially important to monitor what's going on in their lives and refer them for professional help—if necessary.

Positive Parental Pearls

- "Are you thinking of hurting yourself"
- "How would you do so?"
- "What is keeping you from hurting yourself?"
- "Are you thinking of hurting someone else?"
- "What would suicide accomplish for you?"
- "What are other ways of accomplishing that?"

Chapter 7

Addressing Risk Factors Related to Emotional Health

Skills: Anger Management, Anxiety and Stress Management, Building Self-Esteem

Discouraging Impulsive Behavior

You likely know one or more adolescents who are capable of committing unpredictable and self-defeating acts.

It is known that impulsiveness can be a dangerous trait, but where does it come from? A teenager's impulsive personality is an outgrowth of a need for immediate gratification. But the good news is that the need for gratification can be channeled into a different form. Behavior can be changed. It is essential that impulsive youngsters must connect behavior to consequences.

One reason that youngsters can be impulsive is that they feel the pressure to make a decision immediately - - when often they can make the best decision after considerable thought. As an example, when Jane and Sally have an argument at school, Jane is so angry that she decides within five minutes to spread a malicious rumor about Sally. If she had reflected a little on the incident, she might have come up with a less inflammatory response. Jane might have come up with a better response if she had taken the time to weigh the costs and benefits of various different responses. Our caseworkers practice these problem-solving skills with our young clients.

Helping Teenagers Manage Their Angry Feelings

Anger is a natural emotion that is part of everyone's chemistry. It must be seen by youngsters as neither good nor bad. Anger must be viewed as something to be talked about rather than acted upon physically. However, some of us have an anger-laden personality which can develop at an early age. One cause can be poor responses by a parent to toddler tantrums.

Many youngsters first experience anger through bodily sensations. It is helpful for them to recognize the following sorts of symptoms: muscular tightness, a racing heart, heavy breathing, sweaty palms, or feeling your face is getting hot.

It is also important for teenagers to recognize the following types of negative feelings, which may soon turn into anger: sadness, feelings of failure, frustration, confusion, loneliness, and inadequacy.

Only with the acceptance of negative feelings is a youngster in a position to deal with them in a productive, problem-solving manner.

How Anger Can Lead to Fights

If a youngster has an uncontrollable temper, there is a good chance that he will develop a reputation as a fighter. Many teenagers see fighting as the normal way to resolve conflict. They become so focused on the inevitability of fighting that they don't see all the options—using verbal skills, involving adults, etc.

An example is that many children at an early age come to believe that the only appropriate response to somebody who trash-talks your family (e.g. "your mother ain't nothing but a ho") is to hit them. Of course, this can be an extremely risky behavior—inviting the possibility of an arrest on an assault charge.

But before that happens, youngsters need to learn how to respond to other persons' anger. To start, they need to try to understand what the angry person is saying or feeling—and how to best deal with the situation. They need to stay calm and ask questions which will help them develop an appropriate non-violent response. Among viable options are to listen empathetically, to ignore the situation, or to offer a solution.

The first step would be to find out where this belief on how to deal with family-directed trash talk came from. (It is often from a discredited source long ago.) Secondly, ask the subject of the trash talks (e.g. the mother, whether she needs her child to start a fight in order to defend her name.) When the inevitable "no, thanks" is uttered in the presence of the teenager, this usually goes a long way toward breaking down this misguided belief. The adolescent comes to realize that this line of reasoning carries with it a risk much greater than any reward.

Anger as Related to Invasion of Space

Some youngsters have an especially short fuse when another person is "in my face." It is unclear why some people need more or less space before "feeling invaded." It may result from a lack of nurturing or physical expression of affection within the family.

Generally, American culture says that two feet is the acceptable distance for two people in an argument to approach each other. (Latino culture accepts a distance closer to one foot.)

In any case, youngsters who are overly sensitive to space invasion must understand how their standards relate to the norm—and recognize that their rigid standards may put them at risk of being drawn into fights, resulting in possible assault charges.

Tracking How Angry Moments Are Handled Going Forward

It is important for adolescents to be aware of how their methods of dealing with anger evolve as they become older. Our clients are asked to keep journals in order to monitor whether their anger is expressed through aggression or in an assertive manner. The journals are reviewed and discussed at counseling sessions.

Examples of other impulsive behaviors might include cheating or raiding one's parents' liquor cabinet. It is just these sorts of dishonest behaviors that can set the stage for criminal acts as the youngster grows older. Three of the most frequent causes of arrests of our teenage clients are assault, spontaneous thefts, and illegal sexual activity—all of which can occur as a result of impulsivity.

First, it is important for all of us to understand what circumstances make us angry. Here are some of the **common anger-inducing "triggers"**:

- Being accused of something you didn't do
- Someone telling lies about you
- Being told by a parent you can't do something
- When someone invades your personal space
- Being looked at in what seems to be a disrespectful manner
- Being rejected by a sought-after girlfriend/boyfriend
- When someone takes one of your possessions without your permission

Showing Empathy When Youngsters Are Angry

When youngsters get angry, they often are unable to control their emotions and can evade them, unable to empathize with their peers' feelings. Some ways parents can reduce the likelihood of having their children engage in cruel, violent, and criminal acts are by modeling the following sorts of behaviors:

- When people or entertainment characters are suffering, demonstrate a concern for what they must be going through.
- Emphasize the importance of preventing the suffering of others or helping them in their time of distress.
- When someone appears to be upset, try to find out the reasons in order to try to assist them.

- Demonstrate that you listen keenly to others and try to understand what their feelings and predicament might be.

As important as modeling the above behaviors is, ambitious parents must also discuss the reasons for them and allow their children to react.

When you're angry, there are some behaviors to avoid if you're in the process of reacting:

- Assaulting the person who angered you
- Making threats
- Damaging property
- Cutting or self-harming
- Pretend nothing has happened
- Cursing out the person who angered you

Anger management training (A.M.T.) is the core process by which our caseworkers help youngsters gain control over their tempers. Our program has been conducting A.M.T. activities during individual counseling sessions, family sessions, parent groups, and peer groups. In all of these settings, our primary goals are:

- To help the participants understand what their particular anger-inducing triggers are
- To help the participants understand what the unsettling underlying conditions are
- To help participants understand what options are available to persons who are angry in terms of how to react to the situation
- To help participants understand what behaviors they should avoid in reacting to the situation

Our Anger Detection Instrument

An uncontrollable temper is a major factor in assaults, domestic violence, and other criminal behavior, which could cause youngsters to be referred to our program. An uncontrollable temper can be found in a child who responds to specific behaviors which trigger angry feelings.

On the other hand, there are some people who have angry personalities which are shaped by personal, historical, and environmental factors, which make them "a time bomb ticking." Near the beginning of a youngster's participation in our program, we ask them to respond to a forced choice agree/disagree questionnaire titled "Thoughts About My Life." This exercise seeks to identify which life circumstances and attitudes may have created ongoing, pervasive angry feelings. "Thoughts About My Life" zeroes in on a number of major areas of youngsters' lives, including the following: feelings regarding family, extra-familial relationships, and uncontrollable circumstances (race, gender, physical attributes, family finances, etc.) (Appendix 7A):

THOUGHTS ABOUT MY LIFE

(This process can be used with individual teenagers or groups of them.)

For each statement, circle one of the following:

SA – strongly agree   DS – disagree somewhat
AS – agree somewhat   SD – strongly disagree

1. I dislike the control my parent(s) has (have)
    over my life.   SA   AS   DS   SD

2. I am upset that my efforts to succeed
    in life do not pay off.   SA   AS   DS   SD

3. I am blessed with all the physical
    advantages I could want.   SA   AS   DS   SD

4. I have experienced rejection by a
    romantic interest of mine.   SA   AS   DS   SD

5. In my family, I feel ignored.   SA   AS   DS   SD

6. My efforts in school have paid off with   SA   AS   DS   SD
    good grades.

7. I feel my friends are there when I need
    them.   SA   AS   DS   SD

8. I am upset that my parents have not
    played much of a role in my upbringing.   SA   AS   DS   SD

9. I consider myself to be a fortunate person.   SA   AS   DS   SD

10. Probation has been one of the most
    upsetting experiences of my life.   SA   AS   DS   SD

11. I get treated just as well as my brothers
    and sisters.   SA   AS   DS   SD

12. I can't stand people who have different
    sexual preferences than me
    (heterosexual, homosexual).   SA   AS   DS   SD

13. I feel as if I'm continually discriminated
    against because of my race.   SA   AS   DS   SD

14.	It bothers me that our family has so little money.	SA	AS	DS	SD
15.	I'm satisfied by the love and affection I get from my family.	SA	AS	DS	SD
16.	I have never been physically abused by adults/parents.	SA	AS	DS	SD
17.	I have had a death in the family which has been difficult for me to get over.	SA	AS	DS	SD
18.	I am ashamed about what my parents have done with their lives.	SA	AS	DS	SD
19.	I often feel lonely.	SA	AS	DS	SD
20.	I feel the adults at school mostly treat me fairly.	SA	AS	DS	SD
21.	I'm glad that I'm the gender I am (male/female).	SA	AS	DS	SD
22.	My parents are available when I need them.	SA	AS	DS	SD
23.	I am optimistic about my future life.	SA	AS	DS	SD
24.	I have been sexually abused by another person.	SA	AS	DS	SD
25.	I am mad at how my teachers treat me.	SA	AS	DS	SD
26.	I'll find a way to get back at anyone who disrespects me.	SA	AS	DS	SD
27.	My feelings are considered important by my family.	SA	AS	DS	SD

Responses Most Indicating Unsettled Attitudes Conducive to Anger

SA – strongly agree AS – agree somewhat DS – disagree somewhat SD – strongly disagree

#1. SA (4 Points) AS (3) DS (2) SD (1)
#2. SA (4 Points) AS (3) DS (2) SD (1)
#3. SD (4 Points) DS (3) AS (2) SA (1)
#4. SA (4 Points) AS (3) DS (2) SD (1)
#5. SA (4 Points) AS (3) DS (2) SD (1)
#6. SD (4 Points) DS (3) AS (2) SA (1)
#7. SD (4 Points) DS (3) AS (2) SA (1)
#8. SA (4 Points) AS (3) DS (2) SD (1)
#9 SD (4 Points) DS (3) AS (2) SA (1)
#10 SA (4 Points) AS (3) DS (2) SD (1)
#11 SD (4 Points) DS (3) AS (2) SA (1)
#12 SA (4 Points) AS (3) DS (2) SD (1)
#13 SA (4 Points) AS (3) DS (2) SD (1)
#14 SA (4 Points) AS (3) DS (2) SD (1)
#15 SD (4 Points) DS (3) AS (2) SA (1)
#16 SD (4 Points) DS (3) AS (2) SA (1)
#17 SA (4 Points) AS (3) DS (2) SD (1)
#18 SA (4 Points) AS (3) DS (2) SD (1)
#19 SA (4 Points) AS (3) DS (2) SD (1)
#20 SD (4 Points) DS (3) AS (2) SA (1)
#21 SD (4 Points) DS (3) AS (2) SA (1)
#22 SD (4 Points) DS (3) AS (2) SA (1)
#23 SD (4 Points) DS (3) AS (2) SA (1)
#24 SA (4 Points) AS (3) DS (2) SD (1)
#25 SA (4 Points) AS (3) DS (2) SD (1)
#26 SA (4 Points) AS (3) DS (2) SD (1)
#27 SD (4 Points) DS (3) AS (2) SA (1)

Scoring Guidelines for Anger Detection Instrument

82-108----------------- angry person
69---81 ---------------- moderately angry person
55---68----------------- not very angry person
27---54----------------- not angry person

Our Anger Detection Instrument can be scored in order to estimate the level of ongoing and pervasive anger a youngster may be experiencing. In any case, since our caseworkers started using "Thoughts About My Life," they have been able to zero in on those circumstances which are causing the anger. This instrument has often enabled our caseworkers to cut much more quickly to those anger-related factors which can lead to impulsive violent behavior.

And yet, if youngsters feel that anger is a bad thing that has gotten them into trouble, they may try to camouflage any evidence of angry feelings. In order not to be labeled as an "angry kid," he or she may use their "street smarts" to answer the questions as if no problems causing angry feelings exist.

In most situations, we therefore also use chronologically oriented attempts to detect sources of anger. In order to do this, we ask the youngsters and their parent(s) to go back in time in order to identify critical events which may have led to an underlying angry personality. Hopefully, the information gleaned from such an instrument can lead to frank discussions between caseworker and teenager about such topics as bereavement and social, familial, and environmental frustrations.

Appendix 7B

Below are anger management options that can be discussed with individual teenagers or groups of them. They are responses that can be used selectively:

Some of the Options Available to Persons Who Are Angry:

1. Ignore the precipitating comment or incident.

2. Move away from the person you're angry at.

3. When verbally expressing anger, use the "I –message" format:

  ☐ I am angry.....
  ☐ When you (their upsetting behavior)...
  ☐ Because (the reason this has made you angry)...
  ☐ In the future, could you please (alternative behavior you would prefer).

4. Take five deep breaths.

5. Count backward from ten to one.

6. Consider the long-term consequences of letting your anger lead you to act inappropriately.

7. Keep your voice low and calm.

8. Let off steam through physical activity (do exercises, run, bicycle, etc.)

9. When your temper or desire for revenge is about to result in a poor decision, get help from an adult (parent, teacher, counselor, etc.).

10. Find out why the person who is making you angry feels as he does.

After going over anger management options with our teenage clients, we then check to see how well they are able to apply them appropriately to the situations described in Appendix 7C:

_____

NON-VIOLENT RESPONSE MATCH

Teenagers can then take the following test in order to evaluate to what degree they are able to apply the anger management options appropriately:

Enter a letter of the most appropriate response after an angry trigger. The same letter can be used for more than one number.

1. You're alone at school. Somebody thinks you are a member of an opposing gang and wants you to go out to the staircase to settle things. _____

2. A teacher unfairly identifies you as having thrown a spitball in class. _____

3. Your brother is playing Netflix so loud that you can't hear your favorite music. You want him to know how you feel about the situation. _____

4. Your body tightens as you become angry with your mother's constant criticism of you. _____

5. A bully tries to provoke you into a fight by calling your mother a bad name (even though he's never met her). _____

6. You are continuously angry with your girlfriend but are confused as to the reasons. _____

7. All day, your mind has been so filled with anger that you can't study for a test. _____

8. You have a history of fighting your older, big brother. He starts shouting at you. You feel like shouting even louder back at him. _____

9. A student you've had run-ins with gives you a disrespectful look. _____

10. You plan to get revenge on a kid at school tomorrow by planning an ambush.

11. You are angry with your mother and wish you had something to say to her other than to call her a bad name. _____

   a. Ignore what happened.
   b. Take a walk or run or ride your bicycle around the block.
   c. Keep your voice low and calm.
   d. Wait until the end of the class period and explain your case.
   e. Use an "I-Message."

> f.   Get help from an adult.
> g.   Write a letter, but don't actually send it
> h.   Take five deep breaths.

The developer of the "Non-Violent Response Match" considers the most appropriate answers to be as follows:

> 1-F   4-H   7-B 10-F
> 2-D   5-A   8-C 11-E
> 3-E   6-G   9-A

Being disrespectful is one "trigger" precipitating violent reactions. A discussion of this dynamic can be found in Appendix 7D below.

Some questions our caseworkers ask of younger adolescents who feel the need to act older than their age can be found in Appendix 7D.

Appendix 7D

RESPONSES TO PROVOCATIVE SITUATIONS

(This exercise can be used individually or with groups in order to help youngsters decide how to respond to potentially explosive situations.)

Think of a **non-violent** response to each of these situations. Your response should be aimed at **reducing the tension.** If you select a verbal response, **insert the exact words you would use.**

Situation	Non-Violent Response
1. You look at a gang member-type in the street who angrily asks, "What are you looking at?"	_____ _____
2. A kid who is brand new to the neighborhood starts flirting with your boyfriend/girlfriend.	_____ _____
3. A kid who has never even met your mother calls her a bad name as a means of drawing you into a fight.	_____ _____ _____
4. A kid accidentally bumps into you on the subway.	_____ _____

5. A kid bumps into you on the subway –
seemingly on purpose.   _____

6. A kid your age is beating up another kid,
to the point where there's bleeding. You don't
know either one of them.   _____

7. You are walking with a friend, who suddenly
attacks another kid. A ferocious but even fight
breaks out.   _____

8. You're in the lunchroom when someone
accidentally spills juice on your sandwich.   _____

9. Same situation—but it appears to be on
purpose.   _____

10. You're waiting in line for a popular movie,
and another kid cuts in front of you.   _____

11. An apparently gay student of your gender
hints that he/she is interested in you.   _____

The following exercise contrasts assertive vs. aggressive verbal styles. Can it be used with teenagers individually or in groups?

Appendix 7E

ASSERTIVE VS. AGGRESSIVE COMMUNICATION

The following exercise can be used individually on in groups in order to help youngsters avoid overly aggressive, provocative statements:

Assertive communication is positive speech that expresses your needs, feelings, and point of view in respectful and non-threatening ways.

Aggressive communication is forceful, attacking speech that is meant to hurt and provoke someone through putdowns, threats, or coercion.

People often respond to situations with aggressive speech because they have not learned other ways of communicating strong feelings or ideas. Assertive communication combines anger management techniques and "I" statement skills contained in this book.

Put an X beside each statement that you think is aggressive and an O beside each statement that you think is assertive. Be ready to explain your choices to the group.

_____ 1. Hey, let's stop this and talk about it later when we both cool down.

_____ 2. You're crazy, but you can't help yourself because your whole family is that way.

_____ 3. You're just dead wrong, and you're going to get what's coming to you, jerk!

_____ 4. You are the one who started all this, and I've had enough.

_____ 5. Look who's talking.

_____ 6. I really did not see it that way. Let's talk about it.

_____ 7. I can see why you are mad, but there are some other facts I'd like to tell you.

It is helpful to give youngsters an opportunity to practice being assertive. To view our process for doing so, see Appendix below.

Appendix 7F

TRYING OUT ASSERTIVE RESPONSES

The following exercise can be used individually or in groups in order to help youngsters formulate assertive responses:

Situation:

#1. Your brother is using the telephone and you want to use it.

Aggressive Response: "Give me the phone."
Assertive Response: _____

#2. Your girlfriend wants to go to a movie you don't want to see.

Aggressive Response: "That's a dumb movie."
Assertive Response: _____

#3. You buy a new shirt but find a stain on it, so you return to the store.

Aggressive Response: "Give me another shirt."
Assertive Response: _____

#4. You're standing in line for a rock concert, and somebody tries to push ahead of you.

Aggressive Response: "Get the hell back where you belong."
Assertive Response: _____

#5. Your teacher has made a mistake grading your test.

Aggressive Response: "You cheated me out of ten points."
Assertive Response: _____

#6. A girl new to the neighborhood is flirting with your boyfriend.

Aggressive Response: "If you don't leave my boyfriend alone, your face won't be too pretty."
Assertive Response: _____

#7. You heard that a member of some gang is planning to beat you up at school.

Aggressive Response: "If you come near me, I'll kick your ass."
Assertive Response: _____

#8. You are falsely accused of stealing a bicycle.

Aggressive Response: "You're dead wrong, you jerk."
Assertive Response: _____

All persons have "hot-button issues" which make them feel angry or annoyed. I think that it's important for youngsters to be able to demonstrate some control over their emotions and to be able to prioritize which issues are more or less urgent. In order to see how we assist youngsters in doing so, see the exercise below. (Appendix 7G)

Appendix 7G

In order to help teenagers sort out which irritating situations they most urgently need to address, we offer the following exercise which can be used individually or in group:

CHOOSING WHICH BATTLES TO FIGHT

Teenagers are upset or disappointed at the many limits which parents and other authority figures place on their lives. But some limits have a greater effect on teenagers' daily lives than others. So it is important for every youngster to decide which battles are most important to fight.

Of the issues listed below, put **1** before the issue you consider most important to pursue with authority figures, **2** before the next most important issue, etc. **9** should be placed next to the least important issue to pursue.

_____ Whether you should have to show your parents your completed homework.

_____ Getting back at a kid who makes a rude comment about your family.

_____ Challenging your school's dress code.

_____ Whether your parents should have a say in who you hang out with.

_____ Whether you keep your bedroom clean.

_____ What your curfew should be.

_____ Whether you should be allowed to attend a particular party.

_____ Getting back at the school security guard who may have treated you a little disrespectfully.

_____ Where you can go when your parents say safety is an issue.

How do you decide which battles to fight?

_____

_____

_____

If you pick the <u>wrong</u> battle to fight, what do you lose?

_____

_____

_____

It is helpful for youngsters to see the importance of having a positive self-image and to understand to what degree their own self-image can be considered positive and strong. Appendix 7H below presents questions aimed at providing clarity around the issues.

Appendix 7H

STRENGTHENING YOUR SELF-IMAGE

Feeling good about yourself can contribute to your happiness and success. On the other hand, feeling bad about yourself can lead to laziness and lack of achievement.

Elements of one's self-image include the following:

- One's level of achievement at school;
- One's participation as a team member of his/her family;
- The quality of one's social life;
- One's level of achievement in non-classroom activities; and

- Positive and negative aspects of one's character.

Some Questions:

1. What is the most important factor in whether or not you feel good about yourself?

_____

_____

_____

2a. On a scale of 1(lowest) to 10 (highest), how would you rate your academic achievement?

_____

_____

_____

2b. What school subjects need improvement?

_____

_____

_____

2c. For each subject, is improvement needed with regard to
• Classroom attendance and focus?

_____

• Homework?

_____

• Asking for Help?

_____

3a. Do you feel valued as an important member of your family?_____
If not, why not?

_____

_____

_____

3b. By your actions, do you help provide for the needs of other family members?

_____

_____

_____

3c. By your words and actions, do you create a number of problems for your family?

_____

What type of problems?

_____

_____

_____

4. Who do you feel most valued by?

_____

_____

_____

5. Do you have any special abilities as an athlete, artist, musician, or actor, or do you participate in any other activities not required by your school?

_____

Which activities?

_____

_____

6a. Are you happy with who your close friends are and how they treat you?

_____

_____

6b. Do you feel happy with your romantic life?

_____

_____

7. If an event were arranged in your honor, what good things would

people say about the kind of person you are (honest, responsible, caring, etc.)?

_____

_____

_____

8. What criticisms are made about your character (dishonest, selfish, irresponsible, etc.)?

_____

_____

_____

9. When you feel a low sense of worth, how does it affect your behavior?

_____

_____

_____

10. Do these feelings and behaviors cause you to take unnecessary risks with your life?

_____

_____

_____

11. What are examples of these risky behaviors?

_____

_____

_____

Youngsters increase their self-confidence by getting in touch with positive aspects of their lives which their family and friends may see. Appendices 7I and 7J below present questions aimed at boosting youngsters' self-confidence.
The following exercise can be used individually and in groups in order to increase the level of youngsters' self-esteem.

_____

BOOSTING YOUR SELF-CONFIDENCE

Respond to the questions that follow by writing down all the amazing things about yourself. You probably have more great qualities than you even realize! When you finish, bookmark this page and revisit it when you're feeling down. If you need more space, you can use a separate sheet of paper.

What would your family say are the five best things about you?

1. _____
2. _____
3. _____
4. _____
5. _____

What is your strongest character trait?

_____

If you asked your friends to describe you, what is the most positive thing they would say?

_____

_____

_____

Write about a time you did something kind for a friend.

_____

_____

_____

Write about a time you made a mistake and overcame it.

_____

_____

_____

What are you really, really good at?

_____

_____

_____

Appendix 7J

BEING MINDFUL OF THE POSITIVES IN YOUR LIFE

What is your greatest strength?

_____

_____

_____

What is one obstacle that was hard to overcome but you did it?

_____

_____

_____

What helped you through such obstacles in the past?

_____

_____

_____

What is one thing others admire about you?

_____

_____

_____

What words of wisdom would you offer a struggling friend or sibling?

_____

_____

_____

Pick at least one role model who has overcome adversity. Why do you admire that person?

_____

_____

_____

What is at least one important positive event that has contributed to your becoming the person that you are?

_____

_____

_____

Appendix 7K, Our "Strength Training Instrument" (see below). Designed to help create a positive self-image by providing adolescents with an opportunity to talk about people and things they are proud of.

_____

Appendix 7K

Our Strength Training Instrument provides an opportunity to talk about those aspects of their life you are proud of. It can be presented individually or in a group.

Our Strength Training Instrument

1. A friend who has had an important positive impact on your life.
2. A family member who has had an important positive impact on your life.
3. A role model you hold in high regard.
4. An adult in school whom you have a good relationship with.
5. Something you enjoy doing in your spare time.
6. If an event were arranged in your honor, what good things would be said about you?
7. A new skill you have learned within the last month or year.

8. A recent problem that you handled very well.
9. A decision that you made that required considerable thought.
10. The completion of a task that was very time-consuming but which you stuck at.
11. A family tradition that you are especially proud of.
12. Something you refrained from doing, about which you are proud.
13. Something you've done for an older person.
14. A time when you said something when it would have been easier to remain silent.
15. A time when you didn't say something important when it would have been a mistake to share your thoughts.
16. An athletic feat you accomplished recently about which you are proud.
17. Something you did in art, music, or acting that you are proud of.
18. A bad habit you worked to overcome and succeeded.
19. Something you did to resist going along with the crowd.
20. A time when you pleasantly surprised yourself.
21. The person who values you the most.
22. A way in which you helped your family.
23. Something you did to contribute to racial understanding.
24. Something you did to uphold your religious beliefs.
25. Something you've done to make the world more beautiful.
26. A funny thing you did or a joke you created about which you are proud.
27. A time when you were an important example for a younger child.

All people go through periods of stress. The secret is to understand what is causing the stress and to devise ways to control it. Appendix 7L below raises questions pertinent to these issues:

___

UNDERSTANDING STRESS AND TO WHAT DEGREE YOU CAN CONTROL IT

If you could control everything that happened in your life, there would be no reason to get stressed out because things would work out just the way you would like them to. Unfortunately, no one has that much power, and the things that stress people out are often beyond their control.

You undoubtedly realize you can't control certain things, like the weather, how much math homework you get, and what time you have to be at school. Then there are things you can control, such as other people, places, things, or situations.

On the lines below, describe the specific issues which bother you.

School, work, or extracurricular activities

_____

_____

Physical or Mental Health

_____

_____

Family

_____

_____

Friends

_____

_____

Risky Behaviors (sexual behavior, drugs, alcohol, etc.)

_____

_____

Looking at your answers in the different categories, circle the problems you have some control over and are able to change. Cross out the ones you have no control over.

Focus your effort on the problems you have control over and can possibly solve.

* * *

SEVERE VULNERABILITY TO ANXIETY AND STRESS

Do you know one or more teenagers are consumed by anxiety and/or stress?

Anxiety is a normal emotion. It is a by-product of your brain sensing that there's potential danger ahead and sounding an alert. For instance, students may experience anxiety right before a test they feel unprepared for. Occasional anxiety is normal. When the anxiety is constant and overwhelming, it becomes an anxiety disorder.

It is estimated that 25% of American teenagers have symptoms of an anxiety disorder.

In the book *Stress Survival Guide for Teens*, (2019), Jeffrey Bernstein, Ph.D., has identified four main triggers that cause heightened stress among teenagers:

1. Academic Triggers — some examples:

- Being placed in a difficult class
- Falling behind on homework
- Feeling unprepared for a test
- Receiving disappointing grades

2. Social Triggers — such as:

- Feeling pressure to fit into a particular group
- Being overly sensitive to negative feedback from peers
- Feeling excluded from particular social situations
- A romantic disappointment

3. Body Image Triggers — including:

- Feeling that one's peers have "superior" bodies
- Believing that others have better clothes
- Placing undue emphasis on physical appearance
- Forgoing desired foods in order to diet religiously

4. Family Triggers — some examples

- Feeling pressured to measure up to parental standards;
- Wishing more money were available;
- Caught up in family disputes;
- Being compared unfavorably to siblings.

5. Panic Disorder — When people have recurring bouts of a panic anxiety attack, they may find it difficult to breathe. Not everyone who experiences panic attacks has a panic disorder. Those who have panic attacks without prior warning are likely to suffer from a panic disorder.

How our Daily Lives Can Be Affected by Stress

- Which of the above stress triggers do you experience most often?
- Are there other triggers that you experience from time to time?
- How is your life affected and the lives of others around you affected by your stress?
- How do you tend to respond to stressful situations?
- Have you managed certain types of stress effectively? If so, how?

Which of the following personal symptoms do you currently have which might indicate that you are undergoing an especially stressful period? If so, how?

- Fast Heartbeat
- Chronic Tiredness

- Back or Neck Ache
- Shortness of Breath
- Sleeping Problems
- Loss of Appetite
- Poor Concentration

Exercise can help alleviate stress. What forms of exercise would you be willing to do?

- Swimming
- Basketball and Other Team Sports
- Weight Training
- Martial Arts
- Cross Country Running
- Tennis
- Rock Climbing
- Yoga

Non-athletic activities can also help reduce stress. What are activities you would consider engaging in?

- Get a hug from someone
- Do some cooking
- Get together with a friend
- Play with an animal
- Meditate
- Watch Funny Videos
- Sing or play an instrument
- Read a book

Which of the above athletic or non-athletic activities have worked best for you?

_____

_____

_____

Appendix 7M

Another precipitating event for teenage violent behavior is their perceived need for revenge in retaliation for a prior "wrong."

What follows is a process our caseworkers use individually or in groups in order to find non-violent alternatives to address a perceived need for revenge:

UNDERSTANDING THE FUTILITY OF REVENGE

Revenge: to inflict harm or injury in order to retaliate for "a wrong."

Directions: Describe a situation with siblings or friends when you felt the need for revenge. Explain what you did then and how you might react differently now using a strategy that does not cause further problems:

1. REVENGE SITUATION:

_____

_____

2. HOW I REACTED THEN:

_____

_____

3. HOW I WOULD REACT NOW:

_____

_____

What feeling causes a person to seek revenge?

_____

_____

What types of "wrongs" might a person think deserve revenge?

_____

_____

How does a person expect to feel after getting revenge?

_____

_____

How could getting revenge create other, more serious problems?

_____

_____

Does revenge usually end when the wronged person retaliates?

_____

_____

What could be a better way of handling the feelings that cause you to seek revenge?

_____

_____

For a youngster, some of the elements which will create a higher or lower level of self-esteem include the following:

- One's level of achievement in school
- One's participation in and acceptance by one's family
- One's level of achievement in non-classroom activities
- One's popularity with peers
- How much one's character is seen by others as positive or negative
- Physical attractiveness and maturity, height, muscular development, etc.

Signs of a Healthy Self-Esteem

- Confidence
- Being able to say "no"
- Bouncing back from negative experiences
- Being able to express one's needs

Signs of Low Self-Esteem

- Lack of Confidence
- Tendency to focus on one's weaknesses
- Abnormal fear of failure
- Difficulty accepting positive feedback

Youngsters with positive self-images feel valued. Those whose characters and behavior are constantly criticized are likely to have low self-esteem. This negative self-image affects future behavior. Teenagers come to feel that their life doesn't count for much, and so they take increasingly large risks.

Some ways Youngsters Can Improve their Self Confidence

- Start working out
- Try doing things that used to make you feel uncomfortable
- Upgrade dress and/or appearance
- Participate in activities in the community beyond what is available at home and at school.

Our goal is for our teenage clients to feel better about themselves. Also important is for parents who may be focusing on negative behavior to be more aware of their child's good side. This greater awareness can help them provide the all-important positive reinforcement, which fosters more consistently positive behavior.

What follows are some questions we ask of our teenage clients in order to clarify how good they feel about themselves:

The Connection Between Low Self-Esteem And Teen Antisocial Behavior

A major goal of adolescents is to develop a sense of identity. Most importantly, having a positive self-image can lead a person toward a life of happiness and fulfillment. To feel good about themselves, youngsters need to feel lovable, valuable, capable, and worthy of being treated with respect. Parents can assume one of their most important roles by making their children feel loved by the following sorts of expression: words of affirmation, acts of kindness, acts of support, and appropriate touching.

On the other hand, low self-esteem can lead to patterns of anxiety, depression, and low productivity.

PERSONAL QUALITIES WE MAY SEEK AS WE PURSUE A HIGH LEVEL OF SELF-ESTEEM

We ask our teenage clients:
"What are some of the character traits that you are striving for?"

We wait to see what responses they come up with. If certain key qualities are not mentioned, we may suggest some of the following:

Honesty — telling the truth.
Patience — to be able to wait for things without becoming upset.
Courage — to remain strong even amid frightening circum-stances.
Self-Respect — confidence and belief in oneself.
Enthusiasm — throwing oneself into situations and activities with intense emotion.
Loyalty — being there for a friend or family member in good times and bad.
Kindness — showing a concern for the well-being of others.
Responsibility — fulfillment of duties that you take on or others expect of you.

Motivation — an inner desire to accomplish things for oneself or on behalf of others.

STRATEGIES FOR IMPROVING SELF-ESTEEM

Physical Activities:

Running	Basketball
Swimming	Yoga
Jogging	Boxing
Hiking	Weight Lifting
Team Sports	Scuba Diving
Biking	Walking your dog
Ballet	Soccer
Kickboxing	Softball
Frisbee	Wrestling
Lacrosse	Martial Arts
Handball	Rollerblading
Stretching	Jumping Rope

Non-Physical Activities:

Reading	Eating Out
Family Time	Music
Going to a Movie	Housework
Computer Games	Crafts
Puzzles	Watching Sports
Drawing	Photography
Renting Movies	Playing Cards
Socializing	Cooking/Baking
Painting	Writing
The Headspace APP	The Calm APP
(with its focus on stressful relationship)	(with its focus on sleep and meditation)

Volunteer Activities:

Environmental	Literacy Programs
Organizations	Hospitals
Food Banks	SPCA or Animal Programs
After-School Programs	Nursing Homes
Disaster Relief	Retirement Communities
Parks and Outdoor Areas	Homeless Shelters
Museums	Libraries
Tutoring Programs	Political Organizations
Boys and Girls Clubs	Aquariums
Mentoring Programs	Special Olympics
Community Cleanup Projects	Volunteering Daycare Centers
Writing to a Military Person	

There is much that parents can do to diminish the amount of stress their children feel. They can share with their kids the ways they deal with stress. They can teach problem-solving skills and see if their children are willing to apply the skills to current problems they are facing. They can also encourage their kids to get enough sleep at night (8 to 10 hours) and sufficient exercise (at least 60 minutes a day.)

Selective Mutism

Selective Mutism (SM) is an anxiety disorder that goes further than mere shyness. It causes a youth to feel unable to communicate effectively in some, but not all, venues. As an example, children with SM may be adequate communicators at home but not at school. They may have difficulty initiating or joining conversations when the situation is anxiety-provoking. Children with SM may want to talk but are unable to enunciate words due to a form of vocal paralysis.

A parent, teacher, or social service provider who regularly interacts with children with SM should not apply pressure for them to speak. There should be no assumption that the child has below-average intelligence. Because children with SM suffer from anxiety, they may indeed not test well. A mental health provider with behavior therapy skills should be sought out. If psychological methods do not work, medication may ultimately be needed. Children with SM can be cured, but only with a treatment process that reduces their level of anxiety.

* * *

I hope that readers of this chapter will feel better equipped to understand the often complex emotions of teenagers they have responsibility for and to respond appropriately. Without the assistance of qualified adults, emotional factors can elevate the level of risk adolescents face.

Positive Parental Pearls

- "Hey, let's stop this and talk about it when we both cool down."
- "I really didn't see it that way. Let's talk about it.

Chapter 8

Addressing Risk Factors Related to the Family and Home

Skills: Dealing with Bad Habits, Grief, Lack of Communication, Potential Runaways

Growing Up in a Home with Abusive Behavior

Life stressors, such as poverty, unemployment, overcrowding, and ill health, are known to have an adverse effect on parenting and, therefore, to be related to the development of conduct disorder. The presence of major stressors in the lives of families with conduct-disordered children has been found to be much greater than in other families. These stressors will be the focus of this chapter.

Of course, the greatest form of abuse that impacted children is when they are the actual victims of physical or sexual abuse. The impact can be felt physically, emotionally, and psychologically. Victims of child abuse often will have behavioral and mental health issues. Sadly, in recent years, according to state registries, there has been an annual national average of 685,000 victims of these two types of abuse.

Physical abuse is direct harm inflicted on a child's body. It can take the form of a single act or repeated acts. Types of physical abuse include hitting a child, cutting a child's skin, or burning the skin.

Sexual Abuse occurs when an adult engages in a sexual act with a child. It can range from actual sexual penetration to inappropriate touching or kissing.

When there is an indication that the youngster has been a victim of physical or sexual abuse, the caseworker should seek answers to the following questions:

- What form did the abuse take?
- How often did it occur?
- What was the profile of the perpetrator?
- To whom was the offense reported?
- Was an arrest made?
- Did child protective authorities become involved?

Once these questions are answered, caseworkers should try to identify the most urgent problems the abuse is likely to cause going forward— and to work with the youngster at problem–solving. What follows is the eight–step process we teach them:

1. Identify the problem.
2. Define your goal.
3. Think of as many solutions to the problem as you can.
4. For each potential solution, consider all the consequences— pro and con.
5. Choose your best solution.
6. Rethink your solution a few more times.
7. Make a decision.
8. Act upon your decision.

Beyond these forceful acts are the following aggressive forms of child maltreatment:

Emotional Abuse — This occurs when ignoring or dismissing children's expressed feelings or by shaming or humiliating them.

Child Neglect — This is probably the most common form of child maltreatment. It may involve failure to provide essential food, clothing, or shelter for a child. In extreme cases, it can lead to disease, mental retardation, or even death.

Domestic Violence — another stressor that has a huge correlation with children's negative behavior is chronic conflict and abusive behavior among the adults within the family. These circumstances tend to make the parents irritable and less effective as disciplinarians and problem-solvers. What's worse is that in families where there is domestic violence, children are estimated to be physically abused or neglected at a rate that is 15 times greater than the national average.

Sadly, state agencies focusing on domestic violence have shown that 28% of teenagers have reported witnessing an inter-parental assault at some time. Witnessing marital abuse often has the effect of spurring similar behavior in the next generation. On display for youngsters to watch and possibly view as normal are the typical characteristics of abusers—disregard for the rights of others, a lack of empathy, unstable relationships with all family members, impulsivity, a need for admiration, and an inflated sense of self-importance.

Marital separation and divorce take an especially great toll on youngsters, particularly when those events are accompanied by intense conflict and discord. Most damaging is when children witness actual physical abuse and violence in the home. Caseworkers serving such a family would be advised to help youngsters understand what the effects of such incidents are and how they can best deal with those effects.

Not only should well intentioned parents try not to constantly argue and yell in front of their children, but they should also teach their children non-aggressive conflict resolution. Usually, the lesson in conflict resolution is best delivered after two or more people in the family have been upset over an issue and have had the opportunity to calm down. The lesson is most effectively presented in a conversational manner than as a lecture. Some of the points to cover include the following:

Our Efforts to Break the Cycle of Incarceration

Having positive role models is one of the most important resources a child can have. Best of all is when they have two accessible parents who serve in that role. Unfortunately, too often, at least one parent is absent from the child's home.

Obviously, one consequence is that the youngster has fewer family members available when in need of limits or advice. Even more distressing is how adolescents may react to having an incarcerated parent. Some examples include the following:

First, youngsters in this situation will feel ashamed of what such parents have done with their lives. They will perhaps subconsciously transfer this sense of embarrassment onto themselves. They may well shroud their lives in secrecy, making it difficult to have open relationships with their peers.

Secondly, incarcerated parents may find themselves trying to whitewash the image they project to their children. In their attempt to justify their misbehavior, they may be providing a rationale for criminal deeds in the next generation.

When our caseworkers have young clients with incarcerated parent(s), they face a challenge. They must help the teenager separate the importance of the relationship with their parents from the circumstances which led to their incarceration. In other words, it would likely be helpful for youngsters to separate the positive intentions their parents might have had from their bad behavior. By doing so, we might help the adolescent understand what led to their parent(s)' arrest. Was it an uncontrollable temper, a sense of entitlement to others' possessions, or perhaps not having clear sexual boundaries? If the youngster understands these character flaws clearly, they may be able to avoid their being present in their own evolving lives.

Identifying the Bad Habits of Teenagers

One of the techniques that we use in our program when working with families is to have parents identify several of their child's habits that have potentially serious consequences. Though there are innumerable bad habits found in human behavior, we will concentrate on the following four more serious ones for illustrative purposes—bad temper, disobedience, dishonesty, and impatience:

1. Bad Temper — exhibited by angry outbursts and physically aggressive behavior.

In order to attempt to reduce the instances when a youngster's bad temper occurs, the following steps should be followed by a parent or other authority figure:

a. Identify when the bad temper surfaces For example:
•Acknowledge that certain family members are upset.
•Allow those who are upset to explain why without being interrupted.
•Show empathy for your children's feelings.
•Search for compromise solutions so that everyone in the family has their feelings acknowledged.
•If further anger erupts, discontinue the conversation until everyone has calmed down.

Does the temper tantrum occur after the parent says "no" to a teenager's request? Perhaps the youth's desire to attend a particular party has been denied due to the reputation of the would-be host.

b. What is going on in the life of the teenager which would contribute to an angry outburst?
Perhaps the youngster has few friends, so when one includes him/her in a social occasion, it seems enormously important to attend.

c. Parents should explain clearly what their expectations are with regard to their child's bad temper.
For instance, the parent will "only listen to you when you speak with a calm voice."

d. Parents should try to identify what the warning signs are which indicate a temper tantrum is about to happen. Perhaps their child's heart is pounding faster, or their hands are clenched in a fist position.

e. Parents should teach their children anger management techniques.
Some include leaving the room, taking five deep breaths, and considering the long-term consequences of a physical attack.

f. Parents should reinforce non-violent behavior.
They might say to their child, "I noticed you were really angry, but I saw that you walked away from the situation in order to avoid physical conflict."

2. Disobedience — exhibited by defiant and rebellious behavior. Steps toward reducing instances of disobedience include the following:

a. What circumstances seem to bring out disobedience? With whom is he most often disobedient? Does that person not listen to the child?

b. Identify the sorts of occasions that seem to lead to disobedient behavior. Is the parent's brand of discipline at times overly harsh? Is the youngster feeling stressed out due to being over-scheduled? Is more expected of the child than he/she is capable of delivering?

c. Parents should state what their expectations are when it comes to obedience. They can impose a time limit on disobedient behavior. They can offer the child choices on how their expectations can be met. They can seek a compromise between their expectations and the youngster's expressed needs.

d. Parents should demand respect and explain what it means to them. It usually involves being polite, considerate, and sensitive to one's wishes and feelings.

e. If the disobedience continues, a consequence may need to be imposed. There can be a loss of privileges—usage of a smartphone or skateboard or setting an earlier curfew.

3. Dishonesty — This can involve lying, cheating, stealing, failure to accept responsibility for one's behavior, etc.

a. Identify the source of the dishonest behavior. Do the adults in the family exhibit honest behavior? Does the child feel too much parental pressure to be a success at all costs? Do the parents impose such exorbitant punishments on the youngster that it becomes difficult for him/her to own up to mistakes?

b. Make sure that the youth understands why lying, cheating, and stealing are wrong. Parents might cite examples from the moral choices they have made in their own life. (e.g. how they handle income taxes or how they address a situation when they have been given too much change in a financial transaction.)

c. It is important for youngsters to understand the consequences that dishonest behavior can have on their life. Once a youth tells "minor" lies or starts cheating on a limited scale, the stage can be set for progression to major acts of dishonesty, which can have legal consequences. Also, once people have earned a reputation for being dishonest, they will find fewer persons will be interested in friendships, romantic relationships, or business associations with someone they cannot trust.

d. When their child exhibits dishonest behavior, the parents should express their concern as soon as possible.

e. Consequences set by parents for their child's dishonest behavior should also be immediate.

f. Parents should point out when their children make an honest decision when a dishonest one could have been simpler.

4. Impatience — When youngsters can't wait for something they desire, they may become the victim of unreasonable expectations.

a. Where is the impatience coming from? Is the youngster accustomed to getting his/her way upon demand? Does he/she feel considerable pressure to connect with friends or witness an entertainment event? Do the parents demonstrate patience?

b. Reacting to a child's impatient behavior — Don't give in too quickly. Make the child wait, and parents should explain the reason why they must do so.

c. Setting the stage for future impatient episodes — Parents should stretch their youngster's patience level by extending the waiting time gradually.

d. Helping the child understand the difference between necessities (" I truly need") and wants (" I would like").

e. Refusing to allow interruptions by the youth to gain for him/her what they are seeking. Parents should make it clear that interruptions will only be tolerated in the case of a true emergency. Parents should make it clear that children should almost never interrupt a parent's live or telephone conversation or wake up a sleeping parent for a "want."

There will inevitably be differences of opinion between family members, but it is everyone's responsibility to find creative ways to limit the magnitude of the conflict—including the following:

Some Suggestions For De-Escalating Conflict

1. Try to avoid arguments when the participants are heated over an issue and unable to have a calm discussion.
2. Keep your voice at a reasonably low volume.
3. Talk slowly enough to make sure that what you have to say is understood.
4. Avoid pointing your fingers, invading the other person's space, or using other threatening body language.
5. Take the time to digest what the other person is saying before responding.
6. Do not interrupt the other person.
7. Show that you are listening to the other person and understand what they are saying, even if you are not in agreement.
8. Talk about how you feel and what you need.
9. Try to focus on current issues instead of past issues or conflicts.

Some Rules Which Harmonious Families Observe

1. No hitting or kicking. No one is allowed to physically strike anyone else.
2. No swearing. No one is allowed to use vulgar, profane or obscene language.
3. No temper tantrums. If someone becomes upset, the person is to go to his or her room until he or she is calm.
4. No threats. No one is allowed to threaten another person, either verbally or physically.
5. Do something nice. Each family member must do something nice for at least one other family member every day. (This may

not be possible when a family member is away from home for a few days.)

6. Don't talk back. Children must listen without interrupting when a parent or another adult is talking. If a child wants to respond, he or she must ask permission and then talk in an appropriate voice tone (no yelling, whining, etc.)

7. Cooperate. Family members should do chores, solve problems and make decisions together. (Some decisions should be made only by parents, but many can involve the whole family.)

8. Show respect. Everyone in the family should treat each other with respect. This means remembering that Mom, Dad, Sister, Brother and any other family member who lives in the home are the most important people in the world.

9. Show love. Everyone should take time each day to tell other family members how much they're loved. Affectionate gestures like hugs, kisses and pats on the back are always a good idea.

10. Live the Golden Rule. The Golden Rule tells us to treat others the way we want to be treated. This is the key to getting along with others.

Having Guns in the Home—and Accessible to Teens

A parent may keep a gun in their residence for possible use against intruders or additionally for recreational reasons. Responsible parents will explain the purpose(s) to other family members and see that the guns are not accessible to their children.

Inner city youngsters, in particular, may feel that walking the streets can be dangerous. Even if they're not in a gang, they may face harassment from adolescents living in rival housing projects or as a robbery victim. They may even boast of "packing heat" to their peers.

For this reason, our caseworkers find themselves trying to discourage our teenage clients from carrying weapons. Our Self-Defense Program, which will be described in Chapter 14, is our attempt to provide our clients with practical techniques for defending themselves without the need for a weapon.

Beyond that, youngsters who are contemplating carrying a gun, a knife, or a box-cutter and who have tempers and an impulsive personality face special challenges. When they feel threatened or angry, they may, without considering alternatives, reach for their weapon. What they do next could change their whole life.

So, our program helps our young clients understand why they sense a need to carry a weapon. Having done that, we try to get them to realize that the dangers of doing so outweigh the benefits. Finally, we provide them with alternative methods of protecting themselves by either learning self-defense techniques or using "street smarts" and strong communication skills to de-escalate a threatening situation.

Helping Youngsters Deal with the Loss of a Key Person

Children form personal attachments to a variety of persons who enter their life- - parents, grandparents, uncles, aunts, teachers, guidance counselors, clergy, activity directors, etc. They also count on these mentor types for a variety of enforcement to their lives, love, advice, knowledge, skills, etc.

These "key persons" play a vital role in the lives of youngsters. Subconsciously, youngsters come to see them as almost an extension of themselves, a resource that will always be there for them. Of course, mortality is a concept that eludes children until they are confronted with a death that has an impact on their lives.

How Teenagers React to Death

- It represents the complete opposite of everything that is at the core of this stage of their lives.
- Because adolescents are often convinced of their own invincibility, they find it difficult to accept death.
- The death of a loved one may generate a confusing mix of emotions—anger, shock, denial, and guilt.

- They may see a loved one's passing as depriving guidance, affection, and support. There may be a feeling of helplessness.
- They may fear the loss of their remaining parental figure, raising the issue of potential abandonment.
- Death in the family can cause a teenager to become attached to a gang as a response to the need for protection in the face of trauma.

The first step of someone talking with a youngster who has suffered the loss of a key person is to acknowledge the feeling they must be experiencing. This is not a time for "you'll get over that." When the emotional pain and sadness begin to level off, the youngsters may be ready to consider future adjustments.

It is important that a child in that situation be given the opportunity to clarify what the special contribution the departed one made to their life. Was it emotional support or spending time or good home cooking, teaching a sport or skill, or providing advice? Hopefully, the end result is that the youngster will identify someone to whom they have access who can make a contribution in the area where there is now a void. Youngsters may not feel comfortable approaching someone to join their inner circle. The assistance of a parent or caseworker in that regard may prove invaluable.

Some Questions to Ask of Grieving Teens

1. What was the cause of death (natural, provoked by HIV, etc., a prolonged disease, a sudden passing due to neglect, murder, suicide)?
2. "How did you feel when you first knew about the loss of such a loved one."
3. "Are you sorry that you didn't have a chance to say goodbye?"
4. "What do you wish you'd had a chance to say to him/her but did not?"
5. "Were you able to tell him/her how important they were to you?"

6. "Were there any disagreements you had with him/her that remained open at their time of death?"

Follow-up:

Encourage a youngster to use the information from the above questions in a letter or verbal message to the deceased.

Other Approaches For Use With Grieving Adolescents:

1. Keep a Journal:

- Some youngsters may prefer to write about their emotions.
- If the death was sudden and unexpected, the youngster might write a letter to the deceased -- a way of saying "goodbye."
- Drawings, photo albums, and poems about the deceased also provide opportunities for maintaining memories of the departed one.

2. Foster Peer Support:

- Grieving adolescents may need time with their families. They may find the peer support system comforting.

3. Create a Sense of Structure and Security:

- Even if youngsters are in denial of their loss, have them realize that you will be there for them and that time will heal their pain and insecurity about the future.

4. Let Youngsters Grieve in Their Own Way:

- Let go of preconceived notions of how children "should" grieve. Each child is unique and should be allowed to express their emotions as they choose, as long as they're not destructive.

5. Try to Convert to Positive Behavior:

- Get youngsters to see the importance of their positive behavior, so that the deceased parent would be proud of them.

6. Have the Youngsters Consider Joining a Support Group:

- Children often interact better with their peers than they do with adults. Support groups for children who have suffered the loss of a family member can provide an opportunity to hear feelings expressed which are similar to what they are experiencing.

7. Encourage Youngsters to Visit the Cemetery:

- This will help bring closure.

Though the above approaches used in some combination may be helpful, their usefulness in a particular situation must be constantly re-evaluated. The impact of grief on a youngster's life is highly unpredictable.

Preventing Teenagers From Unnecessarily Creating Pitfalls

When confronting challenging situations, youngsters can view them as just problems ready to be solved. But too many times, they attribute to the situations overwhelming obstacles which make solutions seem unimaginable. It is this latter type of perception of a challenging situation that our caseworkers address in Appendix 8A.

Creating Family Activity Nights

Some parents attempt to bring their family members closer by scheduling regular family activity time—often once a week. These occasions might provide opportunities to play games, watch movies, or dine out. Family activity nights are best implemented when the children are young so that a teenager won't perceive this tradition as a form of punishment. It is advisable for parents to make family nights feel inclusive by having each family member select an activity on a rotating basis.

CHALLENGING DISTORTED THINKING

1. All-or-Nothing Thinking — a distorted thought process that involves perceiving a situation using extreme language rather than a more balanced description of the various components. All-or-Nothing thinkers tend to use words such as "always" or "never" rather than less extreme words such as "sometimes" or "usually."

   In order to help our teenage clients view situations in a more balanced way, we provide them with a few situations and ask them to select the most balanced interpretations as follows:

   a. You're entering a new school and starting to think about how you'll approach situations when you're meeting students for the first time:

   ___ 1. I'll find out who the athletes are. They're probably the only ones I can relate to.

   ___ 2. I'll pretty much know who my friends will be the first week and stick with them.

   ___ 3. I'll try to meet as many students as possible, and over time I'll find out with whom I share common interests.

   Check off the strategy above, which represents the most balanced way of thinking.

   b. Another example relates to family reunions:

   ___1. Although I find most of the people boring, there's good music, and Julia is a cousin I look forward to seeing each year.

   ___2. It'll probably rain like last year, and there will be no fun activities.

   ___3. We have the most unlikable family members imaginable.

   Again, check off the above thought that represents a balanced attitude.

2. Extreme Magnification of Situations — Everyone, especially youth, is capable of "making mountains out of molehills." More helpful to one's decision-making capacity is to view situations through the lens of a proportionally realistic framework. In order to encourage this, our program presents situations that can be viewed differently as follows:

Situation	Extreme Thinking	Proportional Thinking
a. Eric fails a science test	"I'm a failure as a student"	"I just need to study harder."
b. Rhonda's best friend is angry with her.	"She'll never talk to me again."	"After a while, we'll discuss what happened and repair the relationship."
c. Ralph loses a tennis match to a lesser player.	"I'm a total loser."	"I had a bad day and will do better next time."

3. Avoiding Impulsive Decisions — Youngsters who make impulsive decisions on a routine basis, often find themselves in trouble. Our program encourages our teenage clients to take the time necessary to make thoughtful decisions aimed at achieving better outcomes. They are asked to identify both impulsive reactions and thoughtful reactions as follows:

a. You're playing a tennis match and spectators favoring your opponent call you derogatory names out loud.

Impulsive Reaction:

_____

_____

Thoughtful Reaction:

_____

_____

b. A teammate you've had run-ins with spreads mud on your Jersey during practice.
Impulsive Reaction:

_____

_____

Thoughtful Reaction:

_____

_____

c. You have loaned your sister a sweater, and this becomes one more item borrowed from you that she loves.

Impulsive Reaction:

_____

_____

Thoughtful Reaction:

_____

_____

One of the underlying factors of violence in the home is the lack of regular communication between family members. When parents and children don't communicate about the everyday occurrences in their lives, they find themselves in the middle of stressful and confrontational events.

Appendix 8B

<u>DAILY PARENT-CHILD COMMUNICATION</u>

In order to make daily communication occur, our program has created a structure for participating family members to engage in regular daily communication. The ground rules and guidelines are described below.

<u>Time</u>: When the latter (or last) of the participating family members comes home — a minimum of ten minutes.

<u>Location</u>: A spot in the home that provides some privacy and where interruption is least likely.

<u>Ground Rule</u>: Both (or all) participants must stay seated during the entire conversation.

<u>Some Suggested Questions</u>: (Best are questions without yes/no answers)

- Describe what happened today.
- What were the high points?
- Did you have any disappointments or angry moments? What were they?
- Do you have much homework? Can I be helpful?
- What can we do together tonight—a TV program, a game, etc?
- What can we do over the weekend?
- What family problems do we need to discuss?

Place in Home for Daily Conversation_____

Time Conversation will Start_____

Date and Time for Observation by your caseworker_____

In order to make daily parent-child communication a useful learning experience, we have created the following process:

PARENT-CHILD COMMUNICATION PROCESSING GUIDELINES

1. How did each of you feel doing this?

_____

_____

_____

2. What was the most difficult part?

_____

_____

_____

3. What does it take to keep the conversation going?

_____

_____

_____

4. What behaviors were helpful?

_____

_____

_____

5. What are the best subjects to talk about?

_____

_____

_____

6. What benefits do you see in doing this?

_____

_____

_____

The frequent culmination of a stressed-out youngster's frustration is when thoughts of running away from home present themselves. In Appendix 8C below, we present a series of questions that are usually asked to individual teenagers.

Appendix 8C

When Teens Are Considering Running Away From Home

Our adolescent clients occasionally discuss in our weekly groups the possibility that they could run away from home before actually doing so. When running away seems to be on a participant's mind, we use the following questions to help sort out the issues:

1. Have you ever thought about running away from home? _____

2. How did you deal with that thought?

_____

_____

_____

3. What problems led to your thinking of running away?

_____

_____

_____

4. What would you imagine life would be like without being at home with your family and the love and money they provide?

_____

_____

_____

5. What would be possible negative consequences of running away?

_____

_____

_____

6. Would running away solve problems or create additional problems?

_____

_____

_____

7. When you have a problem with your family, how do you try to solve it?

_____

_____

_____

8. What results do you usually get?

_____

_____

_____

9. What is a particularly annoying problem you have right now?

_____

_____

_____

10. How can you deal with that problem in a new way?

_____

_____

_____

I hope that readers of this chapter will feel better equipped to identify some of the risk factors family members face in their homes and to respond to them appropriately.

* * *

Positive Parental Pearls

- How did you feel when you first knew about the loss of such a loved one?
- Are you sorry that you didn't have a chance to say goodbye?
- What can we do together tonight—a TV program, a game .....?
- What family problems do we need to discuss?

Chapter 9

Addressing Risk Factors Related to Teen Behaviors

Skills: Dealing with Lying, Stealing, Drug Usage, Curfews, Consequential Thinking

Lying, stealing, substance abuse. To a great degree teenagers make the bed which they go on to sleep in. This chapter will explain how this process occurs and what can be done about it.

Lying

When we were children, many of us were introduced to the concept of lying by hearing of a George Washington myth. Our first President reportedly cut down a cherry tree, but would not allow things to get worse by lying about the incident.

It is difficult to conceive of anyone who hasn't lied at some point in their life. The issues center around how often one lies and under what circumstances.

Characteristics of Liars:
Liars may make an untrue statement which are either:

- A simple reversal of the truth
- An exaggeration (magnification of the truth)
- A fabrication (creation of an untrue story)

- A confabulation (development of a story that is partly true and partly false)
- A wrongful accusation (blaming on someone else)

Underlying Causes of Lying:

- Liars may be trying to avoid being punished for a misdeed.
- Lying can be an index to a youngster's feelings of being unloved or from feelings of inadequacy or pressure.
- Liars may seek to enhance themselves in front of others by claiming to have done things which actually may not have occurred.
- Liars may be attempting to gain the attention and approval of others.
- Liars may strive to maintain friendships with their peers.
- Liars may be attempting to escape dealing with painful memories or occurrences from the past.

SCAN-Harbor's Approach to Encouraging Truth-Telling:

Getting teenagers to discuss their personal history of lying is difficult. It is important for parents not to overreact. The child must feel safe enough to see admitting the truth as a better alternative to lying. But parents must avoid being too lenient about lying—or children may see lying as a habit they can get away with.

Our caseworkers also elicit the reactions of our teenage clients to the following consequences of developing a pattern of lying:

First, teenagers who lie habitually and get away with it will gradually assume that they will never be caught in a lie. For this reason, they will tell increasingly outrageous untruths, taking greater risks of being caught in more serious situations.

Secondly, teenagers who lie often will find that this habit erodes their personal relationships—with their families, friends and romantic interests. After all, persons seeking close relationships feel a sense of trust. Why would they trust liars?

Telling the truth also is important when youngsters are trying to put negative behavior behind them. It is critical to take responsibility for one's behavior before trying to make significant behavioral changes.

It is important that parents let their children know that we all make mistakes, but the consequences parents will impose will be less severe if the youngster admits the mistake.

Youngsters must understand what sort of lies they are capable of, and compare the long-term consequences of telling or not telling the truth with regard to those subjects.

Preventing Stealing and Shoplifting

Youngsters who have developed a habit of stealing often start with taking items from their parents' purse or wallet. From there, they may go on to shoplifting and thefts on the street.

If our teenage clients are to eliminate stealing as part of their criminal behavior, they must, of course, understand what the underlying causes of their propensity to steal are. Some of the motivations might include:

- Feelings of entitlement to what other peers or persons in the media have
- Feelings of entitlement to "my fair share of what my parents have"
- Feelings of boredom which can lead to a desire to "get away with it"
- Feelings that "I need more stuff to feel like I'm part of the group"

In order to uncover further motivations for stealing, it is important to explore the following:

- Attitudes toward money
- What it is like to feel poor
- Whether one's parents are giving their children their "fair share"

- Whether stealing is done alone or as part of a group or criminal enterprise
- What type of person the victim is

The Insanity Of What a Teenager Will Steal

Sad to say, I have seen youngsters in our program who have surrendered their freedom for stealing cell phones or iPods. In tragically extreme examples, more than one teenager in the Bronx is serving a life sentence for murdering another youngster in an attempt to steal a cheap electronic device.

If the would-be thief would think for a moment of the extremely limited benefit of stealing a cell phone, there would be many fewer incidents of this type. Clearly, the provider of cell phone service can, upon request, suspend service, thus making the stolen item essentially worthless. Youngsters must be made to understand that stealing a cell phone or iPod is not worth the risk.

The Relationship of Entitlement to Stealing

All the focus in the media on expensive LeBron James sneakers and super-smart iPhones have sent the message that we are all deserving of such. It is important that youngsters be aware of the extent their desire for these material possessions are manipulated by the media, regardless of whether such items are affordable to the family. Youngsters who steal usually are not having their non-material emotional needs met.

The challenge of a parent or caseworker is to help the teenager see that he/she is really entitled to little more than a place to live, food, education, medical care, adequate clothing, and emotional nurturance. Beyond that, a youngster must either earn or be given the money to purchase other material goods.

What Parents Can Do When Their Children Steal

1. Correct the Behavior:

- If a youngster takes a candy bar from a store, require him/her to return to the store and give it back (if not half eaten) or pay for it.
- If a youngster has no money to pay for what has been taken, parents can loan money and then subtract it from an allowance, or require that the youngster earn money to pay for it.
- An apology should be made to store personnel.

2. Tightened Supervision:

- In order to provide less opportunity for stealing, the curfew and permitted whereabouts of the youngster should be adjusted.

3. Seek Causes of the Behavior:

- Look at what's going on in the youngster's life. Is stealing a substitution for some sort of loss, possibly abandonment, separation, illness or death within the teenager's family or circle? Find a way to discuss or deal with such a loss.

4. Develop an Alternative Source of Income:

- Try to set up a system where the youngster can earn money by doing chores for the family. If youngsters have money of their own, they are less likely to steal.

5. Find Out What Might Be Bought with Stolen Money:

- If the money might be used for drugs or alcohol, you must verify that and deal with those problems as well.

6. Parents Must Question Feelings of Entitlement:

If we are all, to some extent, victims of the message of entitlement sent out by the media, responsible parents must make their children aware of the dangerous consequences of certain messages. By the age of 7 or 8, children must hear corresponding issues raised by their parents along the following lines:

- Do you realize how much emphasis the media places on the importance of having material possessions?
- Do you understand the importance of hard work in acquiring possessions which are either necessary or important to you?
- Can we work together so that you can develop talents, interests and skills which can lead to your becoming an income producer?
- You may be smart and come from a fairly wealthy family, but do you realize that you will still have to work in order to get what you want in life?
- Does my shopping behavior put an emphasis on necessities or trendy items?
- Do you realize that you may have to wait for treats until there is a special occasion or when the budget allows rather than right after you ask for them?

If feelings of entitlement go unquestioned, teenagers will often manipulate other people in order to satisfy their perceived needs. Manipulation can take the form of lies, intimidation, angry fits, and playing parents off against each other.

What follows in Appendix A is a process we use with our teenage clients individually or in groups in order to encourage teenagers to re-think any feelings of entitlement that they may have:

Appendix 9A

STEALING FROM PARENTS, STORES AND OTHERS

1. Have you ever had something stolen from you? _____

If so, how did you feel?

_____

_____

2. What are the reasons people steal?

_____

_____

3. Which of those reasons might lead you to steal?

_____

_____

4. The first opportunity to steal is often from your parents. When do you remember first being tempted to do so?

_____

_____

5. When did you actually do it?

_____

_____

6. Why did you take the money – or not take it?

_____

_____

7. Knowing how hard it is for parents to make money, how did you feel about what you did or did not do?

_____

_____

8. What were the consequences? (Change in your relationship with your parents, punishment, etc.)

_____

9. Studies show that more than 35% of Americans shoplift at least once. When did you first consider taking something from a store?

10. When did you actually shoplift for the first time?

11. Why did you decide to do so or not do so?

12. What were the consequences?

13. If you need more spending money or personal items, what can you do to acquire them legally?

14. Have you ever been caught with anyone who was stealing or riding in a stolen car?

15. What might be the consequences if the car should be stopped by a police officer?

16. Other than for money, what are the reasons why people steal?

_____

_____

Growing Up in a Home Where Substances are Abused

Excessive alcohol and marijuana consumption causes a loss of inhibition and awareness of one's surroundings. The usage of drugs and alcohol has a strong correlation with the incidence of violent behavior. Studies indicate that chronic juvenile substance users are 1.6 times more likely to be victims. Even more alarming is the research which shows that chronic juvenile substance users are 2.6 times more likely to be perpetrators of violent crimes.

Adolescents whose parents use drugs and alcohol literally may feel that such habits are just a part of living in the 21st Century. Many imagine that within a few years, they'll be indulging in this rite of passage. Some teenagers will not wait long at all. If they learn where their parents are stashing drugs and alcohol, they may feel entitled to help themselves to a batch.

Keeping Teen Drug and Alcohol Usage to a Minimum

Youngsters who have a substance abuse problem fortunately have a number of highly regarded treatment alternatives available, Phoenix House and Odyssey House to name a couple. But sometimes it can take a while for a teenager to agree to participate in a drug program. So while waiting for this to happen, our program has the following approach to substance abuse prevention:

When an underage teenager seems to be experimenting with drugs or alcohol—whatever the source might be—our caseworkers try to expand their consciousness about the subject in the following ways:

1. Straight out information based on research:

- For those under 25 whose brains are still developing, there are long-term negative effects of marijuana usage.
- For teenage students, the usage of weed decreases the ability to concentrate on tasks and to memorize information.
- For would-be adolescent athletes, reactions and muscular coordination are reduced.
- 81% of heroin and cocaine addicts used marijuana before going on to harder drugs.
- Studies have shown that smoking weed can lead to infertility, depression, and thoughts of suicide.

2. When it comes to substance usage, parents should make drugs—not themselves be the bad guy. The focus should be on the impact of drugs and alcohol on teenage brains and bodies. Since marijuana is now legal in many states, such discussions have become trickier. Adolescents should be advised to make decisions regarding substance abuse based on factors pertaining to their personal health and safety.

3. We try to develop a greater degree of awareness among our teenage clients about why they might use drugs. To accomplish this we use the following process:

Whether or not our teenage clients are currently using drugs, our case-workers find it important for them to understand what their actual or potential reasons for drug usage are. Toward that end, we have developed the following process, see Appendix 9B:

SOME REASONS FOR DRUG USAGE

I recognize that you may or may not have used drugs. To the extent that you have or might someday do so, place a 1 next to the most likely reason, a 2 next to the second most likely reason, and a 3 next to the third most likely reason.

____ Relieve Boredom

____ Feel Good

____ Forget Your Problems and Relax

____ Have Fun

____ Satisfy Your Curiosity

____ Take Risks

____ Ease Your Pain

____ Feel Grown-Up

____ Show Your Independence

____ Belong to a Special Group

____ Look Cool

Question:

- What are alternative ways of meeting the above needs?

* * *

For those of our young clients who may be using drugs or alcohol, what changes in their lives have they experienced?

- Are there changes in your physical appearance?
- Have you stopped doing things which you used to enjoy?

- Do you feel you need drugs or alcohol to get through the day or week?
- Are you becoming more isolated from friends and family?
- Has your school attendance and/or grades declined?

Helping Parents Enforce Curfews

Establishing a curfew for their children is one of the ways a responsible parent sets limits. Once a youngster feels that there are no limits to their whereabouts, there may be an accompanying sense that there are no limits to delinquent behavior. Since parents have a legal responsibility to ensure the safety of their children, a curfew is an important enforcement tool.

Curfews first involve setting the times when a child is expected to be at home. Most parents feel that their children are able to walk the streets unsupervised at around the age of 11. A parent who is setting a curfew has to consider the following factors:

- How should daylight and darkness considerations affect the curfew?
- What would be the difference between setting a curfew on days before a school day or before a non-school day?
- How responsible is the child we are setting a curfew for?
- Have they previously been home at the times when they have been expected?

Of course, one of the images that defines the teenage years is the tug-of-war between parent and child as to how much freedom will be allowed. It is incumbent for the parent to tie the demonstration of responsible behavior to the granting of more freedom. Doing so should provide an incentive for youngsters to toe the line.

Beyond the issue of setting curfew times are the connected concerns about where teenagers may go and who may accompany them. A well-informed parent must be aware of what parts of the town are safe and which are not—and act accordingly.

So, must youngsters just accept their role as human prey, or is there anything that can be done to increase their level of safety? Here are some issues parents and caseworkers can bring to their attention:

- Routes used to arrive and leave school
- Routes used to approach their home neighborhood
- Times arriving and departing in school and home neighborhoods
- Places youngsters choose to hang out
- Whether people who youngsters hang out with are magnets for trouble
- Images youngsters are trying to project
- Clothes worn by youngsters (are they provocative?)
- Visual and vocal habits (do others find them intimidating?)

The challenge our caseworkers face is to instill in our teenage clients the sense that they have some control over how much violence saturates their young lives. We want the youngsters to recognize that the decisions they make about the above issues will largely—though not necessarily totally—determine the level of their future personal safety.

Furthermore, it is important for parents to know who their children spend time with and what they think of them. It is helpful that before a parent allows their children to visit another child's home, to gather relevant information.

Get on the Same Page as the Parents of Your Child's Friends

- Find out who your kids hang out with by asking guidance counselors, Deans, etc. at school. Get the telephone numbers of the families of their friends.
- Inviting your child's friends to your home instead of having your child visit other families helps you keep control over the situation.
- Make a pact with parents of friends of your kids that your kids will meet certain conditions in order to have permission to go out, such as:

- Make sure your children let you know where they are going, supply a telephone number; and provide you with an opportunity to meet any friend with whom they wish to spend a night at their family's home. In addition, before parents grant permission to their children to visit the home of another youngster, they should have the contact information of the host parent(s) and have an acknowledgment that they are expecting the visit.

When asked to be home for what seems like excessive amounts of time teenagers often claim that "being at home is boring." Our program attempts to encourage parents to work on creating a less boring environment in the following ways:

- What are activities their children can do at home which would cut down on the boredom (drawing, games, exercise routines, etc.)?
- Are there any kids in the immediate neighborhood who can be invited over more often?
- Are there activities which various family members can share in? ("Charades" and "Twenty Questions "are oldies but still "goodies."

Teenagers bear some of the responsibility for organizing their schedules so that they both participate in out-of-home activities and have social time that is acceptable to their parents.

Our program tries to facilitate in-home activities feasible for financially strapped families. Upon occasion, we have purchased art supplies, board games, and exercise equipment.

In Appendix 9C (below) is a process we use with teenagers in order to help them clarify some of the issues around curfews:

COPING WITH EARLY CURFEWS AND LONG HOURS AT HOME

1. What is your curfew? _____

2. How many hours a day does that mean that you're at home and awake? _____

3. Which activities do you spend time on? How much time do you spend on each one?

_____   _____hours

_____   _____hours

_____   _____hours

_____   _____hours

4. Do you feel bored when you're at home? _____

5. Can you think of any activities you don't do at home that would make you less bored? _____ Which ones?

_____

_____

_____

6. What activities outside of home (recreational programs, etc.) would be of interest to you?

_____

_____

_____

7. Are there any kids in your immediate neighborhood whom you could invite over more often? _____ Who?

_____

_____

_____

8. Are there board games and guessing games such as "Charades" and "Twenty Questions" which you can do in your home with friends and family?

_____

_____

_____

9. Have there been any books you have ever read that you have enjoyed?

_____

What kind of subjects did they deal with?

_____

Would you be interested in finding similar books?

_____

Can your caseworker go with you to a bookstore and buy a book such as that for you?

_____

Would you be willing to obtain a library card, so that you have access to free books?

_____

10. Do you enjoy drawing? _____ If so, would you like our program to help you buy art supplies?

_____

Accepting Responsibility for One's Behavior

When a youngster enters our program, one of the first goals going forward is to induce them to accept responsibility for their behavior. If our teenage clients are to learn how to stay out of trouble in the future, they must acknowledge what specific negative behaviors of the past they are seeking to change.

Taking responsibility for negative behavior does not always come easily. It is often easier to blame other persons or factors. A favorite line uttered by youngsters in our program is "Trouble has a way of finding me." Taking responsibility for one's behavior is closely tied to one's capacity to make a sincere apology. Youngsters are often so caught up with trying to present a perfect facade to others that apologies appear to represent a form of weakness. We at SCAN-Harbor attempt to reverse this way of thinking by inducing them to see that no one is perfect and that apologies are actually an act of strength.

A central assumption our program has made is that future behavioral change is possible only when a youngster has taken responsibility for past deeds. This is easier said than done. A true acceptance of responsibility usually means that our teenage clients are comfortable making an apology and know how to make it sound sincere. One of the requirements of our program is that each participant write an Apology Letter directed at a person they have done wrong to in some way.

Asking Teenagers to Write an Apology Letter

Every person who reaches adolescence has committed some sort of transgression that they wish they could take back. It might involve lying or stealing from a family member. In extreme situations, a youngster may have shoplifted or even assaulted someone.

Almost every misdeed has a victim who is affected. Developing a youngster's capacity to make a sincere apology is a key requirement of our program. Teenagers need to perceive apologies as a sign of strength, not weakness. In order to accomplish this we insist that our clients write an apology letter to somebody who has been impacted by their misdeeds—a parent, a peer, or a store owner, etc.

Key to making a sincere apology is being specific about the actions one is apologizing for. Only then can one be in a position to make a fresh start.

Taking responsibility for one's actions is always a major requirement for delinquent teenagers, in order for them to move on with their lives. Written apologies are one of the most graphic means of the acceptance of one's actions.

The "Apology Letter" is usually one of the last requirements for graduation from our program. There are two aspects to the apology process—each of which has its own importance.

Teenagers often vehemently resist apologizing for misdeeds which they feel were provoked by others. In these instances, caseworkers may wish to assume a fallback position by helping the youngster sort out his/her role from the roles of others.

What follows is the process we use to assist adolescents in developing their ability to make a sincere apology.

They are able to compose a sincere, fact-based, and remorseful apology verbally or on paper (see Appendix 9D). What follows is a series of questions we use individually or in groups to drive home the importance of youngsters accepting responsibility for their behavior:

<u>HAVE YOU ACCEPTED RESPONSIBILITY FOR YOUR BEHAVIOR?</u>

1. Was there a particular incident you were involved in that led to your coming to our program?

_____

_____

2. What behavior on your part, connected to the incident, do you accept responsibility for?

_____

_____

3. What, if any, behavior on your part connected to this incident do you <u>not</u> accept responsibility for?

_____

_____

4. What could you have done to prevent the incident from happening or for being as bad as it was?

_____

_____

5. Why is it often difficult to accept responsibility for your actions?

_____

_____

6. Why is it important and helpful to accept responsibility for all of your actions?

_____

_____

7. What has been the impact of your getting into trouble on others in your family?

_____

_____

8. Have you ever apologized for how your actions have affected your parents and/or siblings? _____

9. Is apologizing difficult for you? _____

10. Why is apologizing difficult or not difficult for you?

_____

_____

11. Is apologizing a sign of strength or weakness? _____Why?

_____

_____

12. Why is being able to <u>make</u> a sincere apology important?

_____

_____

13. What must an apology contain in order to sound sincere?

_____

_____

14. Why is it important to be able to describe the other person's position in an argument and how he/she appears to feel?

_____

_____

15. Why is it important not to use the word "but" when apologizing?

_____

_____

16. Why is being able to <u>accept</u> an apology important?

_____

_____

17. PRACTICE IN MAKING AN APOLOGY:

A father and son are arguing because the Dad believes the son has lied to him about where he has been. The father has evidence that his son lied. Pretending you're the son, what would you say in an apology?

_____

_____

Appendix 9E

My Apology to the Victim of My Behavior

The following "Apology Letter" is a requirement for a youngster to graduate from our program.

Write a letter of apology to your victim (most recent victim if there is more than one). This letter should include:

1. An admission to your offense (taking full responsibility for it, including verification that the victim did not cause the offense).
2. A description of how you planned the incident and manipulated the victim.
3. A statement showing full awareness of the harm you did to the victim.

4. A statement showing that you understand the emotional impact the incident had on the victim.
5. A sincere apology for committing the offense.
6. An explanation of why you believe that you committed the offense.
7. A description of why you are sure you will never commit a similar offense again. (Use extra paper if you do not have enough space here.)

Dear_____ (your victim's first name)

_____

_____

_____

_____

_____

What follows is the process we use to assist adolescents in developing their ability to make a sincere apology:

But What If a Teenager is Stuck in Denial?

In reality many youngsters, even when confronted with evidence, cannot admit to any misdeeds. Our program has focused on ways of breaking down this wall of denial.

The basic approach needed to confront denial tendencies can often most effectively take the form of the following type of "back-door" approach:

1. What do you think of someone who would steal another person's wallet?
2. Could you ever see yourself stealing someone's wallet?
3. You saw someone else stealing a wallet?
4. If there was video evidence, how do you feel about someone who still denies the act?

5. If you were in that situation, would you deny stealing the wallet?

What is important about the above format is the attempt to induce the youngster to focus on the behavior or comment in general before applying it to him/herself. Hopefully, this strategy undercuts the tendency of denial-driven youngsters to react defensively when confronted with their misbehavior.

Helping Youngsters Take a Personal Inventory

Anyone seeking to assist adolescents with making behavioral change needs first to have them focus on their current personality traits and behavior. For a youngster to end up at Point B, they must have a clear vision of Point A, where they are starting from.

In order to accomplish this, we invite our teenage clients to identify those of their current behaviors which are most likely to get them into trouble. To do so we use the following process:

Appendix 9F has proved helpful to our caseworkers as they try to prioritize those behavioral issues which need to be focused on if a particular teenage client is indeed to stay out of trouble.

Though the basic mission of our program is to reduce the susceptibility of our teenage clients to violent and criminal behavior, there is another related, critical goal. That is to keep our youngsters out of jail.

Preventing incarceration may seem to be an obvious objective, but accomplishing this can be more complex than we might at first have imagined. Furthermore, there is no sadder moment than when it becomes apparent that—despite our caseworkers' best efforts—one of our clients will lose his or her freedom.

Appendix 9F

This exercise is designed to identify which behaviors present the greatest risk of getting into legal trouble.

BEHAVIORS THAT COULD GET YOU IN TROUBLE

Of the behaviors listed below, **check off five which you could see yourself doing**:

___ Lying

___ Stealing from your family (Mother's purse, etc.)

___ Uncontrollable temper

___ Knowing about a crime in advance, or being with someone who

  commits a crime

___ Frequent fighting

___ Ignoring curfew

___ Hitting family member

___ Drug dealing or usage of drugs/alcohol

___ Jumping a subway turnstile to avoid paying the fare

___ Not attending school

___ Disrespect of authority figures (teachers, etc.)

___ Not taking "no" from member of opposite sex

___ Shoplifting

___ Gang activity

___ Stealing a car or riding in a stolen car

___ Carrying a weapon

___ Vandalizing property

____ Accepting an illegal "dare"

____ Other _____

Questions:

- Why are the behaviors you checked off tempting for you?
- What can you do to resist temptation?

In order to help teenagers understand the importance of considering consequences before acting impulsively, we ask them the following questions:

"If I'm Gonna Get Locked Up Anyway..."

Our caseworkers have seen and heard too many times among our teenage clients a particularly dangerous pattern of behavior. A youngster who is prone to delinquent behavior may rationalize future behavior based on the assertion that "If I'm gonna get locked up anyway, what the hell..."

Usually, one of two sets of circumstances will lead teenagers to this desperate statement:

- They may be unwilling or unable to shed delinquent behaviors, and so they will become resigned to the "inevitable," or
- They may feel that past behaviors of any type will cause them to be locked up, so they might as well "let the good times roll," regardless of the consequences.

Of course, caseworkers may regard all this as a self-fulfilling prophecy. They may also look at the youngster's situation and focus on the low self-esteem that the teenager seems to be displaying. After all, this attitude seems to indicate that the youngster is placing a very low value on his/her life and freedom.

A caseworker may want to ask: "Does this mean that the value you place on your future is so low that you don't care whether you have your freedom or not?" Clearly, it is necessary to work on the youngster's self-image, so that in the future, he/she will do what is necessary to preserve his/her freedom.

Helping Teenagers Develop Consequential Thinking

It is often said that teenagers carry around feelings of invincibility, and therefore don't believe that their actions will have any significant negative consequences. Of course, this line of thinking is conducive to delinquent behavior.

Most behaviors have both short-term and long-term consequences. Let's cite the following example:

If a youngster seeks revenge in the form of physical retaliation, the short-term consequences of snuffing an adversary may be a sense of relief and even exuberance. These feelings may last only ten seconds, until an authority figure may arrive on the scene. A witness may have viewed an assault with their eyes, and then...

The long-term consequences set in...interrogation...possible arrest... maybe even incarceration.

Caseworkers have the challenging role of helping probationers anticipate both short-term and long-term consequences. Sometimes, what works best is if the youngster is taught to visualize a symbol of negative long-term consequences—a police badge, handcuffs, a jail cell, etc.

To see how we get our teenage participants sort out the dynamics of consequences, please see Appendix 9G below:

CONSIDERING CONSEQUENCES

1. What was an action that you took during the past month that had negative long-term consequences?

_____

_____

2. What were the long-term consequences?

_____

_____

3. How did you make your choice?

_____

_____

4. Were you influenced by a short-term consequence?_____

5. If so, what was it?

_____

_____

6. What tough, important decision do you have to make now?

_____

_____

7. What will you think about in making your decision?

_____

_____

Encouraging Positive Alternatives to Getting Into Trouble

Our program has developed a Directory of Violence Prevention Resources for our catchment area. Among those resources are cultural, recreational, and paramilitary programs. The resources are coded for their proximity to our clients' neighborhoods.

- Every time one of our caseworkers opens a case, we attempt to reduce the number of after-school and weekend hours our teen clients have to float around unsupervised. In order to accomplish this, we have done the following:
- We have developed an inventory of the youngster's interests.
- We have created a program for the adolescent that reflects those interests, addresses character and behavioral issues, and provides tight supervision.
- We monitor attendance at and outcomes due to such programs.

Some of the out-of-school positive opportunities we have felt it useful to track are the following:

- Boxing
- Ceramics
- Chess
- Computer Instruction
- Dance
- Gymnastics
- Martial Arts.
- Photography
- SAT Preparation
- Squash
- Swimming
- Team Sports
- Tennis
- Tutoring
- Woodwork

Taking an Inventory of a Youngster's Bad Habits

One of the books that has most influenced our staff has been "Don't Give Me That Attitude," which was written by Dr. Michele Borba. The book provides a roadmap for identifying, clarifying and addressing the bad habits that influence teenage (and generally all human) behavior. Dr. Borba has listed 25 negative attitudes and habits, which, if not reversed, can lead to violent and criminal behavior.

Below I have selected a few and linked them to a behavior they may lead to:

Bad Attitude	Potential Criminal Behavior
Bad-Tempered	Assault
Jealous	Robbery
Lazy	Chronic Truancy
Impatient	Assault
Manipulative	Larceny

Since teenagers spend more time with their parent(s) than with their caseworker, it is their parent(s) who is (are) more likely to be impacted by negative behavior. The caseworker's role is to help prioritize which negative habits should be given the greatest priority. The caseworker should then work with the parent(s) on each bad habit, in a sequence following steps similar to those below:

- Uncover the source of the bad habit.
- Help the child understand why the habit is unacceptable.
- Help the youngster understand that the bad habit will not be tolerated.
- Outline alternative behaviors.
- Help the parent assume the position of becoming a role model of desired behavior.
- Monitor the child's progress and track it on paper weekly.
- Discuss the progress of the youngster in the presence of his/her parent(s).

We human beings all have some bad habits—some way more than others. But if we are truly committed to shedding them, we can only focus on a few at a time. For this reason, our caseworkers put parent(s) and child through a process designed to prioritize which of the teenagers' bad habits is seen by his/her parent(s) as the most difficult to put up with.

In order to focus on the bad habits which could stand improvement, we have created the following "Bad Habit Survey". It is best conducted with at least one parent providing the input in the presence of the teenager. (Please see Appendix 9H below):

This survey is best conducted with at least one parent providing the input in the presence of the teenager. Other persons who know the youngster well can provide additional input.

BAD HABIT SURVEY
(Feelings create habits leading to behaviors.)

Client _____**Date** _____

Parent _____

Place "1" before the client's most disturbing habit.
Place "2" before the second most disturbing habit.
Place "3" before the third most disturbing habit.

Then, at the end of this survey, give examples of these three.

____ Arrogant	(know-it-all, brags, shows off)
____ Bad-Mannered	(rude, interrupts, swears, disrespectful)
____ Bad-Tempered	(angry outbursts, physically aggressive)
____ Cruel	(mean to animals, humiliates others, bullies, no empathy)
____ Demanding	(wants it right now, unreasonable expectations)
____ Dishonest	(lies, cheats, never takes responsibility, blames others)
____ Disobedient	(defiant, rebellious, strips parents of authority)
____ Domineering	(bossy, wants to be in charge, won't negotiate)
____ Greedy	(materialistic, never satisfied, wants things for self)
____ Impatient	(wants it right now, can't wait, unreasonable expectations)
____ Insensitive	(doesn't think of others' feelings, self-centered)
____ Irresponsible	(avoids tasks, loses things, forgets responsibilities, misses appointments)
____ Jealous	(never satisfied with what one has, wants what others have)
____ Lazy	(poor work ethic, wastes time, takes easy way out)
____ Manipulative	(twists words, blames others, plays people off against each other, schemes, displays false charm)
____ Poor Sportsmanship	(not team player, blames others, cheats, quits)
____ Prejudiced	(opinionated, negative, intolerant, hateful, bigoted)
____ Quitter	(gives up, doesn't pursue goals, nothing matters)
____ Selfish	(doesn't share, puts self above all, doesn't take turns)
____ Unconnected to Family	(not team player, poor on chores, unsupportive)
____ Ungrateful	(unappreciative, never satisfied, feels entitled)

Example of most disturbing habit:

_____

Example of second most disturbing habit:

_____

Example of third most disturbing habit:

_____

After examining the results of the Bad Habit survey, we work with the adolescent at replacing the identified bad habits with the alternative positive behaviors listed below:

Bad Habit	Intended Replacement Behaviors
Arrogant	Modesty
Bad-Mannered	Politeness
Bad-Tempered	Self-Control
Cruel	Kindness
Demanding	Consideration
Dishonest	Honesty
Disobedient	Obedience
Domineering	Cooperation
Greedy	Generosity
Impatient	Patience
Insensitive	Empathy
Irresponsible	Reliability
Jealous	Gratefulness
Lazy	Positive Work Ethic
Manipulative	Truthfulness
Poor Sportsmanship	Good Sportsmanship
Prejudiced	Tolerance
Quitter	Perseverance
Selfish	Altruism
Unconnected to Family	Team Player
Ungrateful	Appreciation

Questions to Ask:

We have created a series of questions which help parents understand possible reasons why their children have developed bad habits, so that the parents can help the youngsters reduce the impact of the habits. Though the questions for each habit differed somewhat, the basic structure is similar for each:

- Uncover the source of the habit.

- Identify the warning signs of how this habit is displayed at home.
- Have the parents explain what their expectations are.
- Teach the children alternative ways of dealing with situations when the bad habits are on display.
- Show the parents how to reinforce positive behavior when the youngster does not display the negative habit.
- Use consequences when the negative habit is displayed.
- Make notes on how the child is doing. Report back to their caseworker at the next meeting.

The validity of the above process is based on the reality that parents should (and usually do) see their children one-on-one more than anyone else. For this reason, they are in a better position than even teachers or counselors to influence the prevalence or non-prevalence of negative habits. But the key steps are noticing the behaviors and underlying bad habits, reacting to them positively or negatively, and staying with the process over time. It is very helpful when parents, while disciplining, show consistency in tone of voice, types of demands, and gestures.

The Parent as a Role Model of Good Habits

As important as it is for parents to try to attack their children's bad habits, they have an equally vital role as exemplars of good habits.

That being said, parents of teenagers would do well to ask themselves how well they do in measuring up in the following areas, among others:

- "Do I expect others to do things my way?"
- "Do I just want to get by or do I demand much of myself?"
- "Do I allow myself some bad behavior now and then?"
- "Do I have time to spend on what's on my kids' mind?"
- "Do I have to bribe my kids with treats in order for them to behave well?"

If parents are willing to discuss their own attempts to exhibit good habits in their lives, they will have more credibility with their children.

They will then have a greater chance of influencing their children toward positive behaviors. I hope that is now clear to readers of this chapter and that this realization will embolden them to deal effectively with their teenagers' misbehavior.

* * *

<u>Positive Parental Pearls</u>

- "Do you understand the importance of hard work in acquiring possessions which are necessary and important to you?"
- "Can we work together so that you can develop talents, interests, and skills which can lead you to becoming an income producer?"

Chapter 10

The Over-riding Importance of Parents

Skills: Parental Self-Evaluation, Positive Reinforcement, Family Meetings,

There are all sorts of moms. In this chapter, you'll meet some of the more unusual ones—Jack's, Sally's, Belinda's, and Nathan's.

Try explaining that to Jack's mom.

Despite the importance of involving parents in the effort to curb teenage antisocial behavior, some parents are highly resistant, and in some cases, even hostile. The reality is that some parents believe, or want to believe, that the improved behavior of their youngsters can be accomplished without their involvement. Our caseworkers have over the years met some underwhelming parents. I was quite upset when Jack's mom greeted me with the following warm words: "You white, so you right? Eat sh_t, white boy! Bye, Mr. Trump!" (Given the context of those times, I don't think that the use of the Trump name was meant as a compliment.)

Thinking that this so-called mother and I had some racially tinged personality problem, I decided to see how my co-worker, Ms. Segura, would fare with her. Before even having met her, Jack's mom texted the following love-note: "Lady ... you're really reaching ... Don't come at me crazy ... I don't owe you anything ... stop texting me ... I really don't like you... you need counseling yourself." So the lesson here is that those in the delinquency prevention profession need a thick skin. Don't take all of those forms of rejection personally. They are often more about the parents than about the caseworkers.

Responsible parents view their jobs as preventers of problems rather than after-the-fact reactors to problems. Such parents remain consistently in their children's lives. They make a point of monitoring who their children spend time with. They try to get to know the parents of their children's friends and understand their rules and styles of supervision.

PARENTS SHOULD BE ON THE SAME PAGE

Few things are more confusing to youngsters than having two parents whose disciplinary styles are very different. If the attitudes towards discipline of parents of a particular child diverge, they have the responsibility to sort out their differences.

In order to do so, the parents need to deal with the following issues:

What do the parents agree on?

- Are the parenting strategies you and your partner believe in similar?
- Are these approaches consistently applied by both parents?
- Do both parents have reasonable expectations of their children?

Where did your different parenting styles come from?

- What parenting styles were exhibited in the families where each parent grew up?
- Were there aspects of the parenting styles of their parents that the mother or father vowed to apply with their children?
- Were there aspects of the parenting styles of their parents that the mother or father vowed NOT to apply with their children?

- Were there other sources of parenting styles which influenced the mother or father?

How will the parents sort out the differences in their parenting styles?

- Which different disciplinary techniques of the mother and father can be allowed to remain somewhat differently applied?
- On what techniques must one or both parents compromise in order to avoid sending confusing mixed messages to their children?
- If major areas of divergent parenting styles remain unaddressed, a parenting program should be considered.

Examining the Father's Role or Lack Thereof

Research has shown that youth living in single-mother homes are involved in a greater amount of delinquent behavior than in dual-parent households. (Demuth. S. and Brown, S.L., "Family Structure," Journal of Research in Crime and Delinquency, 41 (1), 58-81.)

But just having a father in the house doesn't contribute to positive behavior on the part of the child. A 2009 study by Hoeve et.al. found that poor paternal support was a stronger predictor of delinquency than poor maternal support. (Hoeve, M., et.al., " The Relationship Between Parenting and Delinquency, Journal of Abnormal Child Psychology, 37 (6), 749-775.) In fact, fathers who exhibit a harsh and/or hostile disciplinary style have been found to pose a greater risk to their children than absent fathers. Based on this information, it is important not only to re-engage absent fathers, but also to provide them with training in positive parenting skills.

Loss of Control the by Parent

The power equilibrium between parent and child can shift toward the child shortly after birth. It only becomes obvious when the kid gets into trouble. Loss of power and control by parents is a process which is difficult to reverse. One cause is usually dysfunctional parenting. The first step in reversing the trend is to understand other factors/disorders which are contributing to the situation. A frustration often voiced by parents is, "My kid won't listen to me." In doing something about this problem, the first step is to notice the symptoms:

Some Signs and Symptoms:

- Escalating arguments
- Increased animosity
- Deteriorating emotional well-being
- Family disharmony

Interventions/Solutions:

- Identify the reason for non-compliance.
- Be a role model for good listening.

How Parents Can Best Respond to an Angry Child

- They should lower their voice and speak slowly.
- They should present a relaxed exterior appearance.
- They should avoid arguing—instead show that you are listening.
- They should not lash out in ways that put their kids down.
- They should offer their child a cooling-off period.
- If the parent is seeking compliance from their child, they should restate their expectations at a time when calmness prevails.

Beyond the Child, Other Factors Contributing to Parental Challenges

As stated earlier, life stressors, such as poverty, unemployment, overcrowding and ill health, are known to have an adverse effect on parenting. The presence of major life stressors in the lives of families has been found to create parenting challenges several times greater than in other families.

In addition to external stresses, there are individual psychological factors —including depression—which make parenting more difficult. Other factors include substance abuse and antisocial or criminal behavior.

The following are a couple of examples from our program's cases describing the impact of poor parenting skills:

How To Identify "BREAKTHROUGH" Behaviors Of Youth

Sometimes it is easy for parents to identify their children's good behavior and to compliment them for it. At other times, it may be somewhat of a challenge to identify improved "breakthrough" behaviors and to provide appropriate positive feedback. Breakthrough behaviors can be defined as behaviors that are not only positive ones but represent a significant departure from how the youngsters have responded to similar situations in the past. The following exercise helps the parent distinguish significant breakthrough behaviors from the usual "routine" behavioral responses:

How Doug's Mother's Behavior Affected Her Entire Family

Alice Simmons, the mother of Doug, one of our clients, is another example of how parents' behavior can have a huge impact on their children. Doug and his two siblings have witnessed domestic violence continuously. Alice has treated her family in an aggressive fashion, whether through verbal, mental, emotional, or physical abuse. An extreme version of "tough love" has taken the place of any sign of affection. The children have learned to behave in a similar fashion—disrespectful, unapologetic, and aggressive toward persons inside and outside of the family. They have little empathy for others' pain, nor do they show remorse for even their most violent actions.

And another example...

How Her Mom's Behavior Affected Sally

Sally appears to have learned abusive behaviors from her mother's relationships with men, as well as her physical abuse of Sally herself. Jennifer and her daughter have developed a difficult love-hate relationship. They will curse each other out and fight, with Sally often being thrown out of the house. As a result, Sally would run away and, after a while, return home, with things gradually returning to "normal." Though Jennifer and Sally's relationship is still dysfunctional, our program's intervention has at least curbed the violence between the two.

Many of Jennifer's behaviors have been passed on to Sally. The daughter has learned to be aggressive, unconnected to her feelings, sexually active at an early age, in multiple relationships, and abusive to partners. She has, in fact, chosen partners who embody similar characteristics to those of her mother's partners—gang-associated, demanding, and abusive. In Jennifer's words, Sally is defiant toward her, disrespectful, controlling, and bad-tempered. Sally will "throw tantrums until she gets her way."

Sally's caseworker in an effort to break the cycle of poor parenting, has essentially become a substitute mother, at times. Our program has provided opportunities for mother and daughter to vent and to communicate in other ways. Violence between Jennifer and Sally has been substantially avoided by having both parties feel welcome to call their caseworker when their feelings of anger reach dangerous levels.

In extreme situations, our program must sometimes focus on the problems of the parents before our client—their adolescent child.

A case in point is Belinda, who came to SCAN at 12 years of age, after being arrested for pulling a knife on her brother.

As our program delved below the surface of Belinda's family, it soon became apparent that Belinda's problems lay more with her mother ("Sandra") than with her brother. Sandra was diagnosed as schizophrenic. She has been unable to connect with her feelings. She heard voices which induced her to withdraw into her own world.

Growing up, Sandra was often hit and screamed at by her parents. She frequently was left with strangers. She often experienced feelings of paranoia.

As an adult, Sandra has been in and out of abusive relationships, all of which have been witnessed by her children. Invariably, she chooses partners who are controlling, drug-using, and non-working. Yet she puts her relationships with them ahead of her relationships with her children. Sandra has also used drugs, but had never been treated for this habit or for schizophrenia.

And then, there are times when inaction by a parent has the effect of making a bad situation worse for their children.

Nathan's Untimely Assault

Nathan's case provides a suitable example of parental malfeasance.

Nathan, 15 years old, came to our program for sexually attacking a 12-year-old female schoolmate in the school's recreational yard. Nathan had a generally angry personality, but clearly his behavior toward females was a key presenting problem. As usual, during the first home visit, I asked Nathan's mother to be on the lookout for any time when Nathan had an angry encounter with a female that had a gender-based or sexual-based origin. Nathan's mother, being preoccupied with six children and her job, allowed Nathan's behavior with a 17-year-old live-in female cousin to escape her attention, so she did not alert me—as requested.

Nathan's mother would tell me after the fact that he had developed a pattern of making comments to a cousin ("Britney"). Furthermore, he would begin to touch her in inappropriate ways in the presence of other family members and generally engage with her in arguments.

One afternoon, after school, Nathan and Britney got into an argument in the apartment, which eventually took the form of them throwing ice cream at each other. Britney ran downstairs, followed by Nathan. The conflict culminated in punches. Before long, Nathan landed a blow on Britney's face, which caused her blood to color the sidewalk in front of their apartment building. At this very moment, Nathan's mother approached the building and saw the gory sight. Being concerned for the welfare of her niece—as well as her son—her immediate reflexive reaction was to call the police. The result was that Nathan was arrested on the very evening before he was to make a periodic appearance before the Family Court judge who was processing his case. With this latest chapter added to Nathan's record, the judge had no choice but to send Nathan to a residential juvenile detention center.

In this case, our program was unable to play a crisis intervention role, because Nathan's mother never informed us of the warning signs. For this reason, what happened to Nathan may well have been avoidable if he had a more diligent and aware mother, and if our program had been able, at an earlier stage, to make a crisis intervention response.

As the above examples indicate, by the time our program becomes involved in a case, parent(s) and child(ren) may already be in a divorce mode. Frustrated parents may be exhibiting parenting skills that are inconsistently and erratically applied and less likely to monitor their children's behavior. I hope that some of the strategies advocated in this book can save the day for other families.

So, How Can We Tell If a Parent is Doing Their Job?

The Avoidance of Extreme Parenting Styles

Generally, there are three parenting styles—authoritarian, permissive, and authoritative, which is somewhat a mixture of the previous two.

Authoritarian Parenting is characterized by considerable usage of punitive measures.

Permissive Parenting is the product of parents who put few demands and place few limits or restrictions on their children.

Authoritative Parenting is characterized by clear expectations for their children's behavior and a volume of expectations that is not overwhelming. The authoritative parent generally provides their children with positive feedback quite often and tries to ignore negative behavior.

The most effective parents are often the ones who avoid being overly authoritarian or permissive and who try to provide a flexible mixture of the two extreme styles.

The Ability of Parents to Focus on Their Child's Needs

Some parents are frustrated by what seems like constant conflict with their teenagers. Those parents may be focusing on their own needs and may have difficulty seeing the arguments as a natural by-product of adolescence.

It may be helpful for such parents to focus on some of the following relevant aspects of the situation:

- Recall what you (the parent) was like as a teenager.
- Try to remember what psychological needs you had in order to deal with problems you were experiencing at that age.
- Consider if your son or daughter has those same types of needs.
- Consider how you can best provide the type of support which would help your child address those needs.
- Youngsters need to be appreciated for who they are, how they behave rather than their affiliations (entry into an Ivy League College, etc.) This is bragging about fulfilling the parent's needs more than the child's.

Determining How Involved Parents Are

Here are some questions which parents should ask of themselves:

- How much time are they willing to spend with their child(ren)?
- Have enjoyable family traditions and rituals been developed?
- How much time are they willing to spend on their parental responsibilities?
- How involved are they willing to be with their child(ren)'s school and homework?

- Are their disciplinary practices and monitoring of their children consistently applied?
- Are they willing to be good listeners when their child(ren) are expressing their concerns?
- Are they willing to hold their child(ren) accountable for their family-related responsibilities?
- How consistent are parents able to be with regard to their parental style?
- How open emotionally are they willing to be when interacting with their child(ren)?

Teenagers and their parents, whether they always realize it or not, need an interdependent relationship that includes the following bonding behaviors:

- Emotional intimacy
- Feeling by child of being protected
- Need by child to be soothed at times

An essential aspect of any interdependent relationship between parent and teenager will be their relative contribution to the family. It is clear that a parent has the responsibility to provide housing, food, an educational setting, attention to health concerns, etc.

In exchange, the child is normally expected to do household chores. But it is here the battles often begin. The parent wants the garbage taken out **when** they ask; the youngster wants to finish his video game first. Teens are only too happy to leave uneaten snacks in their rooms and then cover them over with last week's clothes, thus providing an invitation to bugs and rodents.

Too often, today's kids have a sense of entitlement to the benefits of being in a family, without any give-backs. They must be able to visualize what it's like to be in the parents' role and be able to understand what it's like to have to work, shop, cook and **then** have to constantly remind their children about their usually modest duties. Youngsters must be able to have a regard for fairness and a respect for those who gave them their **very life**. Re-enacting such daily confrontations and their methods of resolution are essential to creating the respect, sense of commitment, and feeling of moral responsibility which are the building blocks of a functioning family.

Unconditional Love: The Greatest Support of All

Probably Rule #1 of Parenting is that no matter how deplorable a child's behavior might be, it is vital for him or her to feel loved. Of course, nobody can express sincere feelings of unconditional love better than their parents. So often, when parents and children are together, the conversation focuses on the child's (frequently negative) behavior. So it becomes incumbent on the parent to carve out interactions when the expression of unconditional love ("I love you") is TOPIC NUMBER ONE.

As an example, let me cite Cedric. A 15-year-old client of our program. Cedric usually put on a tough exterior. He was set on demanding the respect of others—never wanting to be pitied or to be seen as vulnerable. For this reason, I was surprised when, during a family counseling session at home, Cedric suddenly bolted from the room in tears.

After a few minutes, I knocked on the door of Cedric's bedroom and entered. I asked him what had just happened. Referring to his mother, he said, "Not once has she told me that she loves me. She only criticizes me." Realizing how important the expression of unconditional love is for Cedric and how challenging it is for his mother, I have encouraged her at least twice a week to tell her son, "I love you." I then check periodically to see whether this has happened. Since his mother has begun to express unconditional love, Cedric's behavior has improved remarkably.

Encouraging Empathy in Our Children

One way parents can reduce the likelihood of having their children engage in cruel, violent, and criminal acts is by modeling the following sorts of behaviors:

- When people or entertainment characters are suffering, demonstrate a concern for what they must be going through.
- Emphasize the importance of preventing the suffering of others or helping them in their time of distress.
- When someone appears to be upset, try to find out why they are in order to try to assist them.
- Demonstrate that you listen keenly to others and try to understand what their feelings and predicament might be.

As important as modeling the above behaviors is, ambitious parents must also discuss the reasons for them and allow their children to react.

What Teens Need to Hear from Their Parents

As a parent of an adolescent or a service provider are you constantly searching for the most helpful types of positive reinforcement to use with them? Here are some guidelines:

1. Assure them that you are listening to them when they are trying to tell you something that is important to them.
2. Let them know that you understand how they are feeling. Teens' feelings should not be dismissed lest they think that their parents don't care how they feel. It is unfortunate if the youngster—whose feelings are not validated—decides not to share them in the future.
3. Teens need to feel that their parents believe in them as persons and in their potential success in life.
4. Youngsters need to feel that their parents are available for them whenever needed. They should be encouraged at all times to reach out to their parents for guidance and support.

Some Relationship-Building Parental Behaviors

When puberty kicks in, many parents experience the feeling that their teens all of a sudden want to exclude from their lives. The reasons behind this phenomenon are complex and parents need to be patient before the relationship can again be re-established. Parents can also use some of the following tactics if they wish a rapprochement to happen sooner rather than later:

- Listen to your adolescent far more than talking to them.
- Let them know that you understand how they feel—if indeed you do.
- Make reasonable efforts to get to know their friends.
- Let them know that you are available to assist with problems which may arise.
- If asked to, participate in their favorite activities—even if it's a video game you have no interest in.
- Search for activities which you and they may have a common interest in – dog walking, working out, watching movies or TV shows together.
- Find excuses to spend time in cars together where they may be a captive audience.
- Stay in touch electronically by forwarding messages, memes, and articles which they might find interesting and/or amusing.

POSITIVE REINFORCEMENT
Rewards for Adolescents Who Have Behaved Well or Achieved Something Special

Participating in activities with friends (e.g., going to a mall, the movies, or a concert)

Having one or more friends over for an afternoon or a sleepover

Taking dance or music lessons

Receiving accessories for grooming or for sports

Hanging a special poster in bedroom

Redecorating own bedroom

Skating or bowling with friends

Talking additional time on the telephone

Having dating privileges

Receiving a gift certificate

Downloading songs onto one's computer

Getting to use an iPod or other MP3 player

Computer time

Getting to sleep in late on the weekend

Going shopping

Getting to stay out late

Staying up late

Staying overnight with friends

Having a date during the week

Getting a chance to earn money

Getting a special haircut or hairstyle

Going to an amusement park

Inviting a friend to eat out

Receiving a magazine subscription

Buying a DVD or CD

Having one's own telephone

Selecting something special for dinner

Buying a book of one's choice on an outing with a parent

Beyond Praise, Rewards as a Positive Reinforcement Tool

The following are some specific options available to parents:

- Everyday Activities — more opportunities to play video games, sports, have music or singing lessons, watch TV, etc.
- Special Activities — going to the movies, a concert, or another event.
- Foods and Beverages — Favorite digestibles at mealtime — extra snacks should not be offered.

- Financial Rewards — money or tokens that can be eventually turned in for money.

Parent Training as an Essential Activity

Earlier in this chapter, comments were presented from the mother of Jack, a teenage probationer who had been referred to our program. Jack's mother at one point asked "What does this program have to do with me?" This woman seemed surprised that we couldn't improve Jack's behavior if the parent to whom he was accountable for his behavior was not involved. In almost all of our cases, we involve the parent in various types of training activities. Parent training can be conducted individually, with other family members, or in a group setting with other parents. In all cases, the primary focus of our parent training activities is on the teaching of disciplinary skills that can be applied in particular situations.

The persons best suited for conducting parent-training sessions have the following characteristics:

- Commitment to the intervention's objectives
- Experience with family interventions
- First-hand knowledge about the community (they either live or work there)
- Good interpersonal communication skills
- Knowledge of group dynamics
- Ability to manage resistance from participants

In any case, parent training should occur almost every time the case-worker and parent meet. Groups, however, are usually more cost-effective, and help the parents realize that their child-rearing problems are not unique, nor should they be immune from discussion.

The key units of a parent training group include the following:

- Understanding What Discipline Is and Isn't
- Communication Skills (active listening, I-messages, etc.)

- Problem-Solving Skills
- Setting Limits with Children
- Disciplinary Tools (timeouts, logical consequences, positive reinforcement, etc.)

One extremely helpful parent training resource has been a "Parent Manual" available from the New York City-based program "Family Dynamics"—of which I happen to have founded.

Any effort to train or retrain parents of teenagers must start by making sure that the parents understand what the developmental needs of adolescents are. Some of these needs are:

<u>Physical</u>:

- Importance of having breakfast
- Why sleeping arrangements, if at all possible, should be private

<u>Social</u>:

- Knowing what type of youngsters the children befriend
- Gradually giving the children more independence if they show signs that they are ready for it.

<u>Emotional</u>:

- Giving the children as much attention as is humanly possible
- Demonstrating that the parents show extreme concern about the well-being of the children.

<u>Educational</u>:

- •Understanding the importance of regularly checking on the children's progress on their homework
- Keeping in close contact with the children's school and teachers

Crisis Parenting:

Sometimes, a family situation has become so acute that a focus on parenting skills to be used in crisis situations may be needed more than "Parenting 101." For that reason, our program has put together a Crisis Parenting Package. The combination of skills in this package is designed to defuse current behavioral problems as a more comprehensive parenting approach is put in place. The package can be taught in individual or group settings.

Family Meetings as a Problem-Solving Tool

Youngsters who are in constant trouble usually are members of dysfunctional families. Negative behavior can seldom be compartmentalized; it has a way of infecting the entire family unit. Generally, it starts with inadequate parenting skills.

It is often difficult to isolate a brother-sister problem from a mother-daughter or mother-son problem. If negative behavior spreads within the family unit, fostering positive behaviors also is a project normally involving the immediate family. As stated elsewhere in this book, one of the advantages of home visits is that the caseworker is more likely to meet family members who can be part of the client's problem and/or part of the solution. It is often beneficial to invite involved outside parties, especially neighbors.

Though the casework can be abetted by pulling in family members on an "as needed" basis, it is the "family meeting" that provides the greatest opportunity for total family involvement in a problem-solving mode. Though every member of the household may have a "bone to pick" with other members of the family, it is important to keep the discussion on a positive note. It is important that the caseworker/mediator, through astute questioning, avoids eliciting accusations and name-calling. It is productive for each attendee to go beyond rehashing past issues in order to focus on what is expected from others in the future. The most effective family meetings are those that avoid getting stuck in the messy events of the past.

In order for the above to occur and for the sessions to be productive, the following format for a series of family meetings is suggested:

Invitations to Family Meetings

Announce that you want to schedule the meeting around family members' schedules. Specify that the aim is to solve a problem that everyone can relate to. Mention that all electronics are to be left in a different room from where the meeting is held.

Scheduling

Clearly, the sessions should be scheduled at a time when as many relevant players as possible can attend. Ninety minutes is an appropriate session length in most situations.

Team-Building Warm-up

Though it is a conflict that has brought the family members together for the family meetings, it is important that the relatives be committed to improving both the behavior of particular members and the atmosphere of the family in general. One way to encourage this to happen is to start the first session on a positive note, such as with the following type of question: "Ms. Roberts, what do you most appreciate about Frank?" (Each member of the family can then be asked a similar question regarding another relative.)

Some Rules:

1. Do listen to others.
2. Don't lecture.
3. Don't be repetitious
4. Don't judge others.
5. Everyone should be prepared to change some of their behaviors.

6. Explore the difficulties family members will have in changing behaviors.
7. Ask questions in a tone of genuine curiosity—with no hint of sarcasm.

Emphasize Needs–Not Just Problems

The central first question is often: "What problems have you had with Mom, Dad, brother, sister, etc.?"

Obviously, family meetings should dwell on what those in attendance need from each other going forward rather than merely rehashing past confrontations. This is most likely to happen by asking questions most likely to elicit such information, such as: "Mary, what do you most need from your dad?" Responses to such questions will inevitably include anecdotes from the past, but if the above procedure is adhered to, hopefully, the answers will be constructive and non-inflammatory. ("I need to be treated with respect by you.") This question should eventually be posed to all attending relatives regarding each other participating family members. The caseworker/mediator should help clarify the needs that are expressed and should record them.

Summarize the Needs Expressed During the Session

Have the list of needs typed up before the next family meeting.

A Review of the Needs List Should be Made at the Start of Subsequent Sessions

It is important to see how much progress each attendee has made in having their needs met. ("Since last week, Mom, has John done a better job of listening to you?") As the family meetings continue, it should become clearer what exact behaviors are needed in order to meet the needs of the attendees.

Invite the Expression of New Sets of Needs

Ask questions such as "Since the last family meeting, has anyone discovered additional needs they have from other family members?"

Number of Sessions Needed?

There is no magic number. It depends on how much progress is being made and whether the amount of conflict has been reduced. If progress is indeed being made, the interval between sessions may be lengthened.

Family Meetings Should be Held Without the Caseworker/Mediator

Hopefully, the value of family meetings has been established so that they will become a family tradition. The suggested process should be typed and given to each family member. Participants could eventually take turns in scheduling and leading sessions without the presence of the caseworker. For this to happen, family members must show commitment, leadership, and respect for the needs of others.

A common agenda item at family meetings is trying to resolve sibling rivalry issues. Some of the aspects of this common problem and guidelines for resolution are as follows:

Signs and Symptoms:

- Escalating arguments
- Increased animosity
- Deteriorating emotional well-being
- Family disharmony

Early Intervention:

- Discover the reason
- Identify the trigger
- Reduce sibling rivalry

Response:

- Stay neutral
- Find time to be alone with each child
- Let each child tell his/her side of the story

Contracts Can Be a Means of Improving Teens' Behavior

An effective way to change the behavior of aggressive teenagers is to use contracts. Basically, contracts are agreements between a caregiver and a youth that clearly spell out what the youth will earn from the parent when he or she behaves in certain ways. With contracts, privileges are contingent on specific behaviors you want to see from the teenager. For example, you can say, "When you finish cleaning your room, you can go out and play ball." If you were to write down this proposal, you would have a contract. Contracts motivate youngsters to try new strategies. Without feeling motivated, behavioral change can be hard to come by.

Contracts have three main features:

- Specify the behavior the youth needs to change.
- Specify what positive consequences and privileges can be earned.
- Specify how long the agreement is in effect.

Contracts can be used in a variety of situations, including the following:

When you want to focus on a particular aggressive behavior. A teenager may frequently lose self-control, take things he or she wants from others, or yell and curse when asked to do something.

When a teenager has a goal in mind. A youngster may want to work toward earning money for a new bicycle, having a later bedtime, or being allowed to go out with friends.

When you have a particular goal you'd like the youngster to achieve. You may want a youngster to stop bullying younger children, decrease the number of times he or she loses self-control, decrease the severity of aggressive behaviors, or increase the number of positive comments the youth makes about others.

Contracts are a great way to help teenagers see the successes they achieve. They also open lines of communication, so caregivers and youngsters can work toward goals together. Identifying goals and planning requires a conversation between the caregiver and the youngster. For both to be winners, negotiation is necessary. The time spent setting up contracts shows teenagers that you care and are interested in helping them succeed.

Before teenagers get to do what they want, they have to keep their end of the bargain. Contracts are simple, straightforward, and geared toward helping caregivers and youngsters make improvements and get things accomplished.

Guidelines for Successful Contracts

State the goal in positive terms: Say, "When you finish your homework, you can watch television," instead of "If you don't finish your homework, you won't get to watch TV." Both of these statements can be true, but it's easier to reach a goal if you're working toward something positive.

Follow through on the agreement: Be sure to review your youngster's progress each day and provide encouragement to keep going. When a youngster reaches the goal, provide the promised reward.

Make the goals measurable: A goal of "completing homework each night" is easier to measure than a goal of "doing better in school." Being specific and clear helps you to know when your youngster has reached the goal.

Make goals that are reasonable: Setting attainable goals is especially important when you are first introducing the idea of a contract.

Sample Contract Format

I, (name of youngster), agree to: _____

_____

_____

Parent or Guardian (name) agree to: _____

_____

_____

This contract begins: (date _____)

This contract will end on   (date _____)

Agreed to by (Youngster's signature _____)

             (Parent or guardian's signature _____)

Date this contract is being signed: _____

As an Example, Virginia's Contract Reads as Follows

I, Virginia, agree not to tease or bully other kids. That means I will not yell, verbally threaten, curse, hit or punch others. I have to do this for two weeks in a row before I earn a later bedtime on the weekends. If I bully and tease other kids during this time, I will have to go to bed a half hour earlier the following two weekends.

We (caregivers) agree to permit Virginia to stay up until 11:30 PM on Friday and Saturday evenings when she doesn't bully or tease other kids for two weeks in a row. We will mark the calendar each day that Virginia does not bully or tease other kids. This will continue for two weeks or until the contract is renegotiated.

_____   _____
(Virginia's signature)   (Date)

_____
(Caregiver's signature)

When a Parent Tries "Everything" — and It's Still Not Enough

What if a parent of an at-risk teenager has received parent training and tried to implement the content, has held family meetings, tried contracts —and still is left with a disobedient child?

Even a well-meaning parent who wants to repair their relationship with their child may find that it doesn't always work out as intended. A cruel lesson about parenting is to do your best and then hope for the best, knowing that the results are never guaranteed.

The reality is that some adolescents may not respond to their parents— so it then becomes incumbent on the parent to help their child find other human resources who may make a difference. Who might the teenager have access to—another relative, a coach, a minister, a teacher, a counselor, or an online resource?

What such youngsters probably need is someone available to them on a fairly consistent basis who can provide the following contributions:

- Someone who serves as a role model
- Someone to whom they are comfortable expressing their feelings
- Someone who will keep sensitive conversations private
- Someone who can help them see nagging problems in a different way
- Someone who can help them uplift their spirits during what might seem like the worst of times

The above ambitious parental behaviors may seem like a stretch, but hopefully this chapter will at least inspire parents to do the best they can within their individual limitations.

Chapter 11

Crafting a Crisis-Oriented Delinquency Prevention Program
Skills: Trust-Building

In this chapter, you will be introduced to our teenage client Lawrence, his family, and their housing challenges.

How Our Program Was There for Lawrence's Family in Their Time of Need

Programs must be flexible and ready to shift gears when necessary. Our Delinquency Prevention Program is usually quite predictable—home and school visits, groups, the occasional field trip, etc.—but frequently a special need of the client family develops. It is probably some sort of emergency resulting in a crisis intervention visit.

Sometimes, the response required is more out of the box. What may be needed is a creative, time-consuming, and perhaps costly method of solving the client's problem.

One situation engraved in my memory is when the family of Lawrence (a client of ours) found three of its members assaulted by his mom's current husband. One of the victims was Lawrence's mom herself, and the other two were his brothers.

The domestic violence incident had occurred only a day after Lawrence's four siblings, his mom, and his stepfather had moved from Harlem to an ex-urban town in Maryland. As soon as the boys unpacked, punches flew.

This unexpected development would cause anger, despondency, and chaos in most families. In the case of Lawrence's family, the event seemed to bring their six family members together. There were, however, certain practicalities in dealing with the situation. The family had already given up its Harlem apartment in favor of the "greener pastures of Maryland," which the stepfather promised. Upon fleeing the violent scene, not only did they not have time to collect their clothes, but they had nowhere to live upon their return to New York.

After a few days of staying with an aunt, Lawrence's family had to move into a shelter in the Bronx. But then there was the matter of pressing charges against the stepfather and collecting the clothes. For these necessities, a trip back to Maryland was required—a trip that the family could ill afford. This is where our program was able to step in to fill the void.

At 7:30 AM on a sunny September morning, a van rented by our organization picked up Lawrence's family near the shelter. As driver for the three-hour trip, I expected that I would be in for a stressful experience featuring five poorly-behaved youths. What occurred was just the opposite. Everyone was courteous and, above all, extremely appreciative that our program was able to help them with the tasks at hand.

Being able to assist Lawrence's family in their time of dire need gladdened my heart. Charges were pressed at a local county courthouse. The family's belongings were salvaged from the house. Before departing again for New York, Lawrence's mother asked him to write a note to be left for the stepfather. It read: "When you get help—and only then—you will be permitted to come back to our family." It was certainly a more-than-gracious note under the circumstances.

This long and emotionally satisfying day reaffirmed for me that social service agencies and programs must stretch their normal routines and budgets on behalf of families in order to be there for them in special times of need.

I'll remember the day Lawrence asked me if I would "adopt" him. This suggestion was personally flattering to me but not the relationship I was striving for. The proper role of a delinquency prevention worker is a facilitator of behavioral change, a counselor for and advocate of the children, and a trainer of and role model for the parents. The trickiest element of our role is how close we come to assuming the duties of a parent. A case will have a greater likelihood of success if it is understood that the goal is to build up the authority and the skills of the parent(s) in order for the child to feel accountable to them. Delinquency Prevention caseworkers must be careful to ensure that the following circumstances are understood:

- The parent is not allowed to abdicate his or her role to the caseworker on more than an exceptional basis.
- The child is clear that his/her primary accountability is to the parent.

Procedures Conducive to Successful Delinquency Prevention Outcomes

Our staff has found that two of the most important foundations of successful violence prevention casework are consistency and clear expectations. So many of our teenage clients have had parents who have died prematurely, have been incarcerated, or have otherwise disappeared that consistency in being there for the youngster goes a long way. Also important is that the parent be asked to sign an agreement regarding what the expectations of them in the delinquency prevention process should be. (See Appendix 4B.)

The Importance of Trust

In order for a child to develop normally, it is helpful for at least the primary caretaker to engender trust. This is most readily accomplished by parents with nurturing personalities.

But, by the time they become teenagers, our young clients have had adult family members, friends, and authority figures disappear on them many times before—through abandonment, incarceration, or premature death. These events have led to an erosion of trust in people who claim to be there for them. For that reason, a social worker must be prepared to spend a great deal of time being able to display trust in order to earn the youngster's trust. To obtain trust, the professional must be empathetic to the experiences and emotions the teenager is going through. Only by doing so can the relationship build sufficiently for the caseworker to be influential in the life of the youngster. Our program has outlined some questions which are pertinent to this process.

The teenagers have also likely been let down during their lives by peers who may have pretended to be friends but who showed in the final analysis not to have the best interests of our clients at heart. Many times, our clients have evoked a variation on one of the following themes: "I don't need friends" or "I don't trust anybody—even if they're my age." If peer influence is meant to play a part, then the same considerations around trust issues must be addressed with regard to both adults and peers.

Trust-building between the client and caseworker is especially crucial to the success of counseling. It is an ongoing process. Without mutual trust, parents and/or children may deny violence within or outside the family. In the interests of avoiding their children being placed in an institution, they may also deny violations of the conditions of probation. Parents may also doctor their family's reality so as not to be seen as ineffective in their child-rearing role.

The caseworker can facilitate the development of that trust in several ways, including serving as the sort of role model who invites trust and, if necessary, conducting trust-building exercises.

It is also important for caseworkers to point out behaviors on the part of teenage clients which lead others to mistrust them. One example would be when youngsters refuse to make eye contact with others. This important mannerism can be practiced. It is also important to clarify what the underlying causes for not making eye contact are. For example, looking away from a caseworker might be a means of resisting the counseling process.

Our caseworkers use the questions in Appendix 11A below with our teenage clients in order to help them clarify some of the issues regarding trust.

Appendix 11A

These questions can be posed to a youngster individually or in group.

WHOM SHOULD YOU TRUST?

1. Who among your friends in the last two years have you been willing to share important secrets with?

_____

_____

_____

2. Are you glad that you trusted those friends?

_____

_____

_____

3. Did your relationship with those friends change after you opened yourself up to them?

_____

_____

_____

4. How did your relationship change?

_____

\
---

5. Would you still continue to trust these friends?

\
---

6. Who in your family have you been willing to share your secrets with?

\
---

7. Are you glad that you trusted these family members?

\
---

8. What were the benefits of trusting these family members?

\
---

9. What disappointments occurred from trusting these family members?

\
---

10. Do you have anybody now whom you can trust to discuss your private feelings and problems?

_____

_____

_____

11. What are the sort of topics about which you would never share?

_____

_____

_____

12. Do you see your caseworker as somebody whom you can trust?

_____

_____

_____

13. Why or why not?

_____

_____

_____

14.   What are the benefits of sharing more with your caseworker?

_____

_____

_____

15. What are the sorts of topics you wish to discuss with your case-worker in the future?

_____

_____

_____

The Need to Respond to Crises

Too often today, social workers meet with their clients—even during periods of greatest stress and violence—at the social worker's most convenient time and place. Clearly, the practitioner can be most useful by meeting where and when the most critical situations emerge.

Since every worker's caseload at any particular time has at least one crisis situation, if not several, it is necessary to assess on a daily basis which case has the greatest degree of urgency. For that reason, it is often most program- and time-efficient to schedule appointments within a period of two days before. This avoids continual cancellations and keeps the focus of resources where the need is greatest. As stated elsewhere in this book, crises are best dealt with where the threat exists (at home, school, other programs, etc.).

In Crisis Intervention: "You Gotta Do What You Gotta Do"

Often, crisis intervention responses by our caseworkers are made when there is a disturbing pattern of behavior, a physical altercation, or a threat of violence. At other times, crisis intervention is planned because it becomes obvious that without a bold move, the youngster or parent will commit an act that puts him/herself and/or others in danger. Parents must be aware of not only how their actions contribute to domestic violence but also when their inability to defuse a situation makes matters worse. Though the parents' greater experience may put them in a better position to defuse such a situation, they may allow themselves to become so angry that they are unable to do so. They must recognize their responsibility to be a true adult.

As an example of Planned Crisis Intervention, the case of Stuart will be cited. Before our staff had become involved, Stuart had perpetrated a number of violent acts. He'd trashed the lobby and windows of his mother's apartment building and had bloody fights with his brother, sister, and godmother.

Stuart, however, despite needing psychiatric help, had never been charged with a crime, nor would he voluntarily go for help. As a result, one of our caseworkers and his mother planned a crisis intervention, in order to get him into a secure facility where he could be evaluated. On a Wednesday morning, while Stuart was still sleeping, our case worker had arranged for an ambulance and police backup to transport him to the local residential adolescent mental health diagnostic center. Obviously, Stuart was enraged over this scheme, but in crisis intervention, you gotta do what you gotta do.

Out-of-the-Box Thinking — How Token Gifts Can Help

When our caseworkers try to encourage certain types of behavior, making pertinent token gifts to youngsters can be helpful. Here are a few examples:

1. When teenagers avoid reading: the reason may be that they do not feel connected to the topics of books they are required to read in school. It may be helpful to buy them a paperback on a subject of interest to them. Reading is certainly one positive activity our program wishes to foster in our teenage clients.
2. When youngsters are absent from an appointment "because of the rainy weather": buy them an "el cheapo" umbrella. That should end at least one excuse.
3. When one of our clients seems to be so lacking in hygiene that he projects an odor that is offensive to his neighbors, buy him deodorant. He will get the message and hopefully be on the road to adopting socially acceptable habits.

Mentors — A Potentially Important, But Complicated Resource

A mentor is a trusted adult who has a consistent relationship with a child over time which involves shared activities and emotional support.

Our Mentoring Program grew out of the realization that our caseworkers were too occupied with crisis-oriented services to provide mentoring activities themselves.

Our Mentoring Program has the following **objectives:**

- To develop adult-teen relationships that will help compensate for such common parenting deficits as a lack of positive reinforcement and unconditional emotional support;
- To expose the youths to activities and events in our geographical area which help broaden their horizons beyond their frequently poverty-ridden, crime and drug-infested neighborhoods;
- To assist our teen-clients in developing academic, cultural, and athletic skills, which will keep them out of trouble, improve their self-image, and help them build a productive, violence-free future.

Effective mentoring does not come cheap; it requires substantial costs to cover the recruitment, screening, training, and monitoring of the mentors. For that reason, a mentoring program of modest size might seek assistance from an agency specializing in mentoring to provide those responsibilities.

Regardless of how a mentoring program is organized, special attention must be focused on dealing with the following questions:

- How can mentors and mentees be matched in terms of the mentor's gender, personality profile, skills inventory, interests, and other factors?
- How can the mentors be trained so as to reduce the significance of cultural, educational, and other gaps?
- How can the mentoring program be coordinated most effectively with the overall delinquency prevention effort?

Relating to the Cultural and Demographic Features of the Participating Youngsters

In most cases, mentors' backgrounds will be significantly different from those of participants in terms of age, lifestyle, ethnicity, and class. Mentoring efforts must take those differences into account and develop activities and techniques for bridging gaps. These interventions must also recognize the power of other influences in the lives of disadvantaged youths, such as poverty, exposure to violence, and lack of parental supervision.

Big Brothers/Big Sisters (BB/BS), founded in 1904, is the oldest and best-known community-based mentoring organization in the United States. It has also been studied more than any other. Its mission is to provide young people with one-on-one relationships that help them develop according to their full potential and become confident, competent, and caring adults. There are more than 500 local BB/BS agencies in all 50 states, serving more than 100,000 youths. Mentor-mentee pairs meet one-on-one for three to five hours each week for at least one year. There are no prescribed activities–they may include taking a walk, watching TV, going to the library, or just sharing thoughts.

Site-Based Mentoring

Site-based interventions have one particular location where all sessions take place. Most site-based efforts are implemented in schools, but they can also occur in workplaces, churches, community centers, detention centers, and public housing neighborhoods. Group mentoring interventions with targeted activities such as academic projects and career- or skill-building exercises are more likely to be site-based.

School-Based Mentoring

In school-based mentoring interventions, volunteers meet with children for an hour or two once or twice a week on school grounds. In these sessions, mentors focus primarily on activities that build academic and social skills, but they also involve the children in fun activities.

Screening and Selecting Mentors

Selecting mentors requires a great deal of forethought; being too lenient in your selection process can have very serious consequences. Develop written eligibility criteria to guide staff in making wise, objective selections. Above all else, you want to make sure there is nothing in an individual's past or about his or her character that would make that person unsuitable for mentoring. Red flags behaviors include the following:

- Substance abuse problems
- History of child abuse, neglect, or molestation
- Previous criminal conviction
- History of acting out or emotional instability
- Evasion of child support
- Interference with policies or procedures

Some Practical Considerations Regarding Mentoring

- Proximity to the mentee or the intervention site. If a mentor lives far away, travel time may become an obstacle to regular meetings.
- Age and other demographic characteristics. Whether these factors are important will depend on your intervention activities and on your mentees' preferences.
- Ability to meet regularly and make a long-term commitment. It would be unwise, for instance, to accept a volunteer who travels frequently or is thinking about moving in a few months.
- Compassion and tolerance. Mentors must be caring and accepting of views and attitudes that differ from their own.
- Desire to spend time with children. Mentors should enjoy interacting with children and feel comfortable with youths who may be "cold" toward them at first.

Mentor Training

Mentors should receive comprehensive training before being matched with mentees. Some general areas to address are the roles mentors are expected to play and the overall values, philosophy, and goals of the intervention. Specific areas to cover in training include the following:

Trust. An effective mentoring relationship is built on trust.

Keys to gaining the trust of mentees include showing up to meetings and keeping promises.

Patience and perseverance. Youths are likely to feel uncomfortable sharing intimate information. Some youths may be reluctant to talk about anything in the beginning. Mentors must be patient and realize that the relationship may be one-sided initially.

Communication skills. Mentors must be able to share ideas with youths and suggest alternative behaviors and attitudes without sounding like they are passing judgment. And they must listen intently to mentees while watching their body language and picking up on other cues that might indicate hidden feelings. Good communication skills will help develop the relationship and set a good example for mentees on how to interact with others.

Problem-solving skills. Mentees often face difficult social and academic problems. Mentors should be trained in how to help their young people come up with solutions.

Self-esteem building. One of a mentor's roles is to help the mentee build self-esteem. Teach mentors how to guide their youths in setting initial goals that are attainable quickly and with relative ease. Early accomplishments will help mentees recognize their capabilities and develop pride in their achievements. As the relationship progresses, goals should become increasingly more challenging.

Developmental stages. Mentors need to know about the developmental stages that children and adolescents go through. This will help them better understand mentees' behaviors and create age-appropriate activities.

Cultural and economic issues. Mentors should be informed about their mentees' cultural and economic backgrounds so that they can tailor activities to address the challenges mentees face in their families, neighborhoods, and schools. Because no two young people have identical backgrounds, some of this information should be provided to the mentors individually when a match is made rather than in group training sessions.

Sustaining the Mentor-Mentee Relationship

The drop-out rate for mentoring interventions is fairly high. Some researchers have estimated that half of the relationships fail. Mentors must work to keep participants interested in the mentoring relationship. The following guidance for mentors can increase the likelihood that young people will stick with the program.

- Listen to the youths and respect their viewpoints.
- Involve mentees in deciding how to spend time together.
- Respect mentees' need for privacy; do not push them to share intimate information.
- Be available to talk at any time.
- Change strategies and goals as mentees get older; if necessary, change mentors to meet mentees' developing needs.

Planning Appealing Activities for Mentees

Keep the following guidelines in mind when planning your activities:

- Make activities fun as well as educational.
- Focus on activities that promote mutual exchange, rather than on instruction for the mentee.
- Plan activities that offer challenges.
- Provide support and encouragement, but do not solve problems for the mentee.

A particularly effective model can be one emphasizing corporate involvement. It is a multifaceted school-to-work initiative that targets disadvantaged high school juniors and seniors who have average academic and attendance records and demonstrate commitment and motivation. Mentors support students in exploring college and career options through educational workshops, career-specific training, and quality summer work experiences.

Examples of Mentoring Activities

Social

Talking about life experiences
Having lunch together
Visiting the mentor's home

Academic

Working on homework
Working on the computer

Job- or career-related

Visiting the mentor's workplace
Developing a resume
Talking about career options
Practicing interviews skills

Event-related (field trips)

Camping or hiking
Attending a concert or an art exhibit
Attending a sporting event

Recreational

Playing games or sports
Doing arts and crafts
Walking in the park
Going to the mall
Visiting the library
Reading together

Civic

Helping in a community clean-up effort
Working at a soup kitchen

Life Skills-related

Developing a fitness or nutrition plan
Attending a cooking class
Discussing proper etiquette
Participating in a public-speaking class

Social Work Interns as a Mentoring Resource

An effective addition to professional delinquency prevention workers can be interns from institutions of higher education, which specialize in social work.

Being relatively close in age to the teenage clients, student interns can be perceived by the clients to understand their situation better than a professional who is decades older. This can be even more the case if the intern's socio-economic background mirrors that of the client.

Interns can be helpful during individual and family counseling sessions as well as during group sessions. To be most effective, it is important for the interns to be briefed clearly as to what is expected of them. They need to operate within the philosophy of the program to which they are assigned. Their added value normally comes in the form of helping clarify clients' statements and helping brainstorm approaches to problems.

In order for our teenage clients to clarify the amount of interest they have in seeking a mentor, we ask them the questions in Appendix 11B below:

Appendix 11B

These questions are best posed to a teenager when seen individually.

ASSISTING YOUNGSTERS WITH BUYING INTO THE IDEA OF HAVING A MENTOR

Our program asks prospective mentees the following questions:

Who is someone you know who you look up to?

_____

Why do you look up to that person?

_____

If that person has helped you in the past, how has he/she helped you?

_____

_____

Are there any areas of your life you would now like help with?

_____

_____

What are the qualities you would like your mentor to have?

_____

_____

My intent is that readers of this chapter will understand the human resources necessary to prevent juvenile delinquency. Also, I hope they realize that the development of mentors has great potential benefits for youngsters but requires substantial time and quality control for that to happen.

Chapter 12

Preventing Delinquent Behavior in our Schools

Skills: Dealing with Behavioral Problems and Bullying, Educational Motivation

In this chapter, you will be introduced to our teenage client Patricia as she attempts to deal with threats at school. And then there's Carl, who saw the importance of having strong relationships with school personnel.

The Evolution of Aggressive Behavior in Schools

As a parent or an educator, do you find yourself wishing that schools are consistently part of the solution to misbehavior rather than part of the cause? In this chapter, a timely issue is dealt with. The extent of the role of schools is much debated across the U.S. these days. There was a time when aggressive behavior in schools was considered to be throwing a spitball or leaving one's seat without permission. Conflicts between students usually were conducted with words and fists.

Around the 1970s, studies indicated how a dramatic turning point occurred. Over a three-year period in American schools, homicides increased by 19%, rapes and attempted rapes increased by 40% and robberies by 37%, assaults on teachers by 78%, and on students by a whopping 85%.

These statistics have remained fairly consistent since the 1970s. Research has shown that despite the fact that teenagers spend only 25% of their time in school, 41% of robberies and 37% of assaults committed by adolescents occur in school.

I am aware of all sorts of school-based delinquency prevention programs. The most effective ones seem to emphasize creating student trust and teaching conflict management and peer leadership skills. Below, Patricia recounts her school experience.

Our Teenage Client Patricia Recounts Her Experience

As a young child, I never got into fights. That was until I moved up to New York and started my first year of high school. It seemed as though a lot of my schoolmates wanted to start fights with me. I was a country girl from South Carolina. My classmates sometimes made fun of my accent. The boys loved my accent; they thought it was different.

After about three months into the new school year, I started to become familiar with my classmates and started making friends. I would go to Saturday school for extra credits (I tried my best to maintain an 85 and above average). One Saturday morning as I sat in the gymnasium, my classmate Jasmine and I were talking. She asked about my transition to New York. She asked about my opinion of the school and my classes. Then she asked about how I got along with others. I told her I was still figuring people out—and that there was one girl, in particular, I thought hated my guts. Every time I saw this girl, she would give me dirty looks, roll her eyes, and make smart remarks. But I never understood why she did not like me. I learned that this girl was on the cheerleading team. So she was very popular. Her name was Mary, a very petite and pretty sophomore. Jasmine told me not to worry about that and not to take her actions personally. I decided to take Jasmine's advice and let it go.

One Monday morning, the bell rang, and I was heading to my next class. As I'm walking through the staircase with a friend of mine, I bumped into Jasmine and her friends—and, of course, Mary was there.

I assumed Jasmine thought it was the right time to bring up the conversation that we had during Saturday School. It actually was the perfect time. Jasmine turned to Mary and asked what her problem was with me. If I could only repeat why this girl said she didn't like me, anyone listening would have a good laugh. She didn't like me because of how I looked, the way I carried myself, and that "you think you're a big shot." I didn't know this girl from a hole in the wall. I had only seen her walking the halls and didn't even know her name until the past Saturday.

During the entire confrontation, I asked one question of this crazy cheerleader Mary, "You don't like me because of how I look?" I was confused, but still, she went on screaming. At this point, the staircase was full of people. Mary started taking off her big gold hooped earrings and walked toward me, indicating that she wanted to fight. I handed my book bag over to a friend, walked up to Mary, and punched her right in the face. From that point, IT WAS ON. I threw her onto the floor and kept hitting her. Although I blacked out, I was still able to hear all that went on around me. I heard people yelling, telling me to get off of her. I felt someone pull me, and I turned around and hit a school safety security guard. I was so angry. I wondered how in the world this girl could say that she didn't like me.

After the fight was finally broken up, I was taken to the principal's office. My principal, Mrs. Hooper, questioned me as to why I chose to fight. She asked if Mary and I already had any kind of conflict or if we were fighting over a boy. I told her my side of the story, and Mrs. Hooper laughed. She knew that I wasn't a troublemaker. I told her that I felt threatened by Mary because she started to take off her jewelry and proceeded to walk toward me, so I hit her. Mrs. Hooper asked if I would sit down with Mary, and I agreed. I knew there was something more to the story as to why this girl didn't like me. When Mary walked into the office, her face was bruised and swollen. She sat down and started crying. Once again, I was confused. Why was this girl crying? Shouldn't I be the one crying hysterically? Mrs. Hooper questioned both of us. It was clear that my story was the same as Mary's. Mary turned to me and asked me why I hit her. I explained to Mary that when I'm having an exchange of negative words with another person and the other person starts taking off their jewelry, that tells me that they want to fight. I told her that was the vibe I caught from her.

Mary put on a show that day in the office, apologizing and saying she would never judge another person as she judged me. Thankfully, due to the fact that we settled everything in the office, we were not suspended. We actually became friends.

We were sent back to class, and when I walked into class, my classmates started chanting my name, PATRICIA, PATRICIA, PATRICIA! They were all shocked because I was a quiet pre-teen and had never created any drama. I knew that my classmates and friends would have never thought I was going to be in an altercation—let alone with a cheer-leader. Before my class even ended, the word got around the school that I had been in a fight. Lunch period rolled around, and I couldn't believe that people were talking about it. Of course, my friend Jasmine, who witnessed the entire fight, was right there telling EVERYBODY how it happened. I personally didn't want to talk about the incident. I kind of felt bad for Mary. I was quite sure she was embarrassed. After all, she had started it with her crazy yelling.

By the end of the day, my classmates and other students whom I didn't even know were referring to me as "little Miss Mayweather." But I was tired. The fight drained me. My head was pounding, and I just wanted to crawl into bed. Honestly, I was happy the day was over.

The moral of the story: No matter who you are, people will judge you for some random reason—and they may not have a clue as to who you really are. Try to avoid all confrontations as much as you can. It doesn't really help to be violent unless you want to get hurt or end up incar-cerated.

Specific Provocative In-School Behaviors

A child with a perfect attendance record would spend some 1,500 hours a year in school. Apart from anything academic that is learned, the school represents a stage where the battle against one's own temper is played out. Many parents are notoriously out-of-touch with details of their children's life at school. For that reason, it is often beneficial for caseworkers to visit the school at the same time as the parents so that both of them have the same information. This may also instill in the parent a pattern of visiting the school.

An Anger Management program focusing on fights within schools must zero in on the specific behaviors common to youngsters, which often precipitate fights. Examples of such behaviors are the following:

Play Fighting:

Play fighting (make-believe fights which lead to actual fights): Play fighting should be discouraged because what may be a play fight to one person is a real fight to another. Play fighting clearly threatens the necessary orderly atmosphere required for the educational process to take place. The best defense against a play fighter is just to walk away.

In order to try to have youngsters stop play fighting in school, we often ask them the questions which can be found in Appendix 12A below:

Appendix 12A

The following questions can be posed individually or in groups.

1. What do you find enjoyable about playfighting?

---

2. What risks do you think there might be in playfighting?

---

3. How do you know if playfighting has gone too far?

_____

4. Have you lost friends due to playfighting?_____

5. When are the rules of playfighting broken?

_____

6. With this in mind, do you plan to continue to playfight?

_____

_____

7. If so, how would you determine who is safe to playfight with?

_____

_____

8. Where should playfighting not be done?

_____

_____

Sniping

Sniping (when young "snipers" joke about peers to their face in an insulting manner, though there may be some truth to what is said). Again, this is a behavior that provokes fights. Especially sensitive are comments made about one's ethnicity, family, or pertaining to physical characteristics (obesity, etc.).

Snipers, who usually have aggressive personalities, may have a need to lash out at others, but they may have concluded that verbal aggression keeps them safer than physical attacks. Again, we have a series of questions designed to discourage sniping. They can be found in Appendix 12B below.

_____

Appendix 12B

SNIPING

The following question can be posed individually or in groups.

1. What do you find enjoyable about sniping?

_____

2. What risks do you think there might be in sniping?

_____

3. How do you know if your sniping has gone too far?

_____

4. What type of person should you never snipe with?

_____

5. Have you lost friends due to sniping?

_____

6. What type of subjects should be avoided by snipers?

_____

7. Where should sniping not be done?

_____

Some strategies to put a stop to sniping:

- Encourage students to look at themselves in positive ways. Hopefully, they will feel less of a need to put others down in order to feel better about themselves.
- Help students focus on accomplishments rather than failures.
- Some strategies to defend against snipers:
- Teach students to use "comebacks" when they are "put down."
- Teach the victims of snipers to reach out for allies who might be peers or adults.

Bringing snipers and snipees together:

- Explore how their relationship could be improved.
- Draw up a plan to either ignore each other or mend the fences.
- Hold a class meeting in order to discuss the issue of sniping.

Serving as a Protector

Students who establish themselves as willing to come to the aid of others who are threatened or who seek protectors are threatening the peace within schools. This protective syndrome also sets the foundation for gang-type behavior.

When students volunteer to be someone else's protector, they are offering one of the "services" that are part of the recruitment process. Of course, there are "strings" attached—and they can come at a high price. Would-be protectors are usually troublemakers who are trying to line up someone who will come to their aid when they are involved in a confrontational incident that will likely spark retaliation. Teenagers normally are preoccupied with their own perceived enemies without having to worry about other people.

When discussing the subject of protectors with teenagers, our case-workers often focus on the following sorts of questions which can be found in Appendix 12C as follows:

Appendix 12C

<u>PROTECTORS</u>

The following questions can be posed individually or in groups.

1. What would lead you to seek "protectors" (someone who will back you up in case of a fight)?

_____

2. When you have had understandings with other kids to protect each other, what has been the result?

_____

3. How can seeking and serving as a "protector" actually be risky?

_____

4. Why might today's protectors become tomorrow's gang members?

_____

5. With this in mind, will you seek and serve as a "protector" in the future?

_____

Quasi-Sexual Behavior

Quasi-Sexual Behavior: Kissing and prolonged hugging in the school are becoming more common, particularly as a means of showing off. The problem is that such demonstrations of affection can create feelings of jealousy and can lead to fights. They have no place in school. Youngsters must set and observe boundaries for themselves.

Our caseworkers try to assist our adolescent clients in setting personal boundaries for themselves. We have found the following exercise to be helpful in doing so. It can be found in Appendix 12D as follows:

_____

QUASI-SEXUAL BEHAVIOR

The following exercise can be administered individually or in groups:

Place a check next to those behaviors which you consider inappropriate for you to engage in within your school:

_____ Telling jokes with sexual content about someone in school

_____ Using dirty language with sexual content (SMD, etc.)

_____ Suggesting to another kid that you'd like to hook-up with him/her

_____ Telling a girl that you like her looks

_____ "Lap-dancing"

_____ A boy wearing pants so low that his underpants are extremely visible

_____ Kissing a girl or boy on the cheek

_____ Staring repeatedly or for an extended period at someone's body part

_____ Hugging in the hallway

_____ Discussing the body parts of someone in school with your friends

_____ Having a secret affair with a teacher out of school at the teacher's request

_____ Showing nude or sexually graphic pictures or images

_____ Touching someone's boobs, butt, or crotch

Bullying

A large percentage of bullying takes place in and around schools. Studies have shown that 25% of kids acknowledged being the victim of bullying, and 17% admitted to being bullies. Bullies tend to identify their victims based on having a power advantage over their targeted victims. Bullies tend to seek out kids with disabilities or different sexual orientations—characteristics that are seen as different or indicating weakness.

Some Warning Signs that a Child Is Being Bullied:

- Increased social isolation
- More frequent displays of worrying and anxiety
- Declining school and class attendance
- Reduced participation in activities where there is supervision (recess, lunchroom, non-academic activities, etc.)
- Increased moodiness and agitation
- Bruises, scratches, skin cuts, or torn clothing

In order to help parents, educators, and other students identify bullying situations, we have created "Signs a Youngster Has Been Bullied," which can be found in Appendix 12E as follows:

SIGNS A YOUNGSTER HAS BEEN BULLIED

This exercise can be presented to parents, educators, and youngsters individually or in groups.

Have you noticed a child or teenager who is ...

_____ Appearing distressed, depressed, or tearful?

_____ Experiencing a sudden or gradual deterioration in schoolwork?

_____ Afraid or reluctant to go to school?

_____ Getting teased in nasty ways?

_____ Staying close to teachers or adults rather than peers?

_____ Coming home with unexplained bruises or scratches?

_____ Having torn clothing or damaged books?

_____.Choosing odd routes to go to and from school?

_____ Spending a significant amount of time alone?

_____ Needing extra money for no apparent reason?

In order to have tweens and teenagers understand the dynamics of bullying, we have developed "Bullying Experiences," which can be found as follows:

_____

Appendix 12F

BULLYING EXPERIENCES
(This exercise is best presented to groups of tweens or teenagers.)

1. There are physical bullies and emotional bullies. What is the difference?

_____

_____

_____

2. What feeling does a kid hope to get from both physical and emotional bullying?

_____

_____

3. In addition, one who physically bullies may seek to gain what types of material things?

_____

_____

_____

4. What factors motivate emotional bullies?

_____

_____

_____

5. Have you ever been bullied? _____

If so, what did it feel like?

_____

_____

If not, what would you imagine it would feel like?

_____

_____

6. What might the long-term effect of being bullied be?

_____

_____

7. Have you ever physically bullied anyone? _____

If so, why do you think you did so?

_____

_____

8. Have you ever emotionally bullied anyone? _____

If so, why do you think you did so?

_____

_____

9. Are you likely to bully anyone in the future? _____

Why or why not?

_____

_____

When teased or bullied verbally, youngsters should be advised to respond in one of several ways. They can accept the comments gracefully or make a joke of them or simply ignore them. They should avoid retaliatory responses which foster aggression.

Schools are increasingly creating anti-bullying initiatives. The most effective ones avoided being overly punitive. They focus on getting the bullies to understand why they have chosen this form of behavior.

When bullies realize that they have a particular type of problem, they may well decide that they wish to cease bullying and focus on addressing their problem.

Schools and parents need to be on the lookout for indications that a particular child is a bully. Among the warning signs are the following:

- Obsession with winning
- Over-inflated ego
- Frequent angry outbursts
- Poor grades
- A need to impress their peers with displays of their "power"
- A lack of empathy for others who are suffering

What Parents Can Do to Discourage their Children from Bullying

- Teach the importance of having their children respect individual differences.
- Emphasize the importance of anger management.
- Let your children know that you are checking with their school regularly to see whether they have recently committed a bullying act.

In order to help parents and youngsters understand what options are available to them in reacting to bullies and how parents can coach them toward doing so, we have created "How Kids Can Deal with Bullies," which can be found in Appendix 12G as follows:

HOW KIDS CAN DEAL WITH BULLIES
AND
HOW THEIR PARENTS CAN HELP

(These responses can be discussed with individual children or parents or with groups of them.)

Here's what <u>not</u> to do and why:

1. Don't cry if you can avoid it. Bullies love having power over people. When you cry, you give them what they want,

2. Don't try to get even. Bullies hate this. It makes them madder and meaner.

3. Don't fight back physically. Bullies usually pick on people who are smaller and weaker than they are. You could get hurt.

4. Don't make threats. Bullies respond to threats with more bullying.

5. Don't ignore the bullying. Bullies want a reaction from the people they're picking on. If you ignore them, they'll try harder.

6. Don't stay home from school. Bullies who can scare people away from school feel really powerful. In addition, skipping school keeps you from learning.

Here's what you <u>can</u> do:

1. Tell a friend—someone who will listen to you, support you, and stick to you. **Tell your parents, too.** Clearly explain what kind of help you need.

2. Tell a teacher, especially if the bullying happens at school. Bullies are sneaky—they do most of their bullying where adults can't see or hear it.

So your teacher might not know about the bullying unless you tell him/her.

3. When someone bullies you, stand up straight, look the bully in the eye, and say in a firm, confident voice, **"Leave me alone!"** or "Stop it! I don't like that!" Bullies don't expect their victims to stick up for themselves. This might be enough to make them stop.

4. Stay calm and walk away. **Walk toward a crowded place or a group of your friends.** Bullies usually don't pick on people in groups. They don't like being outnumbered.

5. **Plan alternate routes.** Decide when and where the bullying most often occurs, and then find safer routes. If it's on the bus, find other transportation. If it's in the park, stay away.

6. **Develop a sense of humor.** Laughing at yourself or cracking jokes about your own shortcomings can help defuse situations.

7. Go out of your way to **give sincere compliments** to those who might bully you. This makes it harder for them to be mean.

8. **Become interested** in what potential bullies (and other kids) are doing and talking about.

9. **Develop more peer friendships.** Learn how to initiate conversations, etc.

10. **Learn martial arts.** Some kids find that learning martial arts, boxing, or weight-lifting improves their self-confidence. Might this be you?

Cyberbullying

This can be defined as bullying that occurs using electronic technology (texts, voice messages, etc.) or social media (Facebook, Instagram, Twitter, X, Snapchat, etc.). The purpose of cyberbullying is usually to threaten, embarrass, or exclude a youngster from a particular group. Cyberbullying messages can spread to large numbers of other people in a short amount of time. Another advantage of this form of bullying is that it can be done anonymously by creating fake accounts. Anonymous bullying can create increased anxiety in victims as they worry about "who is out to get them."

The Human Toll of Cyberbullying
(www.security.org/cyberbullying)

Before the pandemic-related lockdowns were implemented in 2020, a majority of youngsters were already spending many hours a day on social media. When COVID-19 hit, it is estimated that the number of hours increased by another 20%. YouTube, TikTok, Snapchat, and Facebook are the social networks of choice for cyberbullies. Victims of cyberbullying report a range of emotions after being cyberbullied—including anger and fear. It is reported that two-thirds of the victims of cyberbullying felt worse about themselves after an incident took place.

In order to assist tweens and teenagers in refraining from cyberbullying, we have created "Cyberbullying," which can be found in Appendix 12H as follows:

Appendix 12H

<u>CYBERBULLYING</u>
**(exhibiting bullying behavior through internet messages,
which create public embarrassment)**
(This exercise can be presented to individual youngsters or in groups.)

1. Have you ever been the victim of cyber-bullying? _____

If so, explain:

_____

_____

_____

2. Have you ever done cyberbullying? _____

If so, explain:

_____

_____

_____

3. What do you imagine the effect was on the "victim"?

_____

_____

_____

4. Were the victim's rights violated? _____

Explain:

_____

_____

_____

5. What feelings would cause somebody to become a cyber-bully?

_____

_____

_____

6. When one has these feelings, what is the responsible way to express them?

_____

_____

_____

In order to assist actual bullies or possible future bullies in refraining from this destructive behavior, we have developed " Helping a Child Stop Bullying Other Kids," which can be found in Appendix 12I as follows:

What Parents Can Do to Discourage Cyberbullying

- Tell your children not to post anything online that they wouldn't say to a peer in person.
- Realize that all online communications except Snapchat should be considered permanent and likely to be passed on to others.
- Tell your children not to share their passwords with anyone but you.
- Get your children to agree to report cyberbullying to school authorities.

Parents and school administrators who wish to maintain a violence-free atmosphere in their schools clearly must attack the above dangerous but all-too-frequent behaviors in an aggressive manner.

_____

HELPING A CHILD STOP BULLYING OTHER KIDS

1. Bullies have a **need for domination** and/or control. Help them question that need.
2. Bullies often intimidate victims in order to **obtain something of value** (cash, clothes, CDs, etc.). Help them see what the consequences of such behavior might be.
3. Bullies often intimidate because of the following reasons:

- They don't like someone;
- They want revenge on someone who'd gotten them in trouble; or
- They are jealous of the attention that a girlfriend or boyfriend has given to someone of the opposite sex.

Help youngsters understand why they are bullying and **help them seek other ways of dealing with their feelings and needs.**

4. When bullies intimidate because **someone is different,** have them make positive statements about the uniqueness of others.
5. To show bullies what it means to treat others as they would like to be treated, use a **reverse role-play exercise** Have bullies play the part of their victims. Put bullies in the position of being verbally teased or physically intimidated because they are too short or too thin.
6. Help a bully make a **sincere apology to victims.** To do this, he/she should:

- Look at the person.
- Using a sincere tone of voice, tell the person you would like to apologize.
- Begin by saying, "I want to apologize for..."
- Clearly state what you did.
- Take responsibility for everything you did wrong. Do not make excuses for what you did or why.

- Say that you will try to avoid making the same mistake again. If you took or damaged something, offer to replace or repair it.
- Follow through with your offer.

Gun Violence in Schools

When a Potential Shooter is Identified:

It is not always easy to identify potential school shooters before the fact. They do not normally have a long history of disciplinary problems. They do, however, often find themselves socially marginalized as a result of being rejected by peer groups. As a consequence, they may suffer from depression.

Some students may bring themselves to the attention of authorities by engaging in communications that cause concern:

- A student submits a story for an English assignment about a character who shoots other students in his school.
- A ninth grader, who is known to be feared by his classmates, cocks a finger at another boy on the playground and says, "You're gonna die."

Other students of concern come to the attention of authorities through second or third parties:

- A school bus driver tells the principal of a school that a group of students has been overheard whispering about bringing a gun to school.
- A neighbor of a student calls the school to report suspicions that the student is experimenting with bomb-making materials.

If the above sorts of events create a significant level of concern, school officials should initiate a threat assessment inquiry immediately.

The following information should be sought in a threat assessment inquiry:

- Facts that drew attention to the student, the situation, and possibly the targets
- Information about the student
- Information about "attack-related" behaviors
- Motives

Students and adults familiar with the student who is the subject of the threat assessment inquiry should share communications and behaviors that may indicate their observations that a violent act might be contemplated.

The parents or guardians of the student of concern should usually be interviewed.

Interviews with a student of concern often are critical in a threat assessment inquiry.

Individuals who have been identified as potential targets of the student of concern should also be interviewed.

Information obtained from the above sources should be organized and analyzed as follows:

- What are the student's motive(s) and goals?
- Have there been any communications suggesting ideas or intent to attack?
- Has the subject shown inappropriate interest in school attacks or attackers, weapons, or incidents of mass violence?
- Has the student previously engaged in attack-related behaviors?
- Does the student have the capacity to carry out an act of targeted violence?
- Is the student experiencing hopelessness, desperation, and/or despair?
- Does the student have a trusting relationship with at least one responsible adult?
- Does the student see violence as an acceptable—or desirable—or the only way to solve problems?

- What circumstances might affect the likelihood of an attack?

Creating a Safe School Climate

- Emphasize the importance of looking and listening for danger signs in schools.
- Take a strong but caring stance against the code of silence.
- Work actively to change the perception that talking to an adult about a student contemplating violence is considered "snitching."
- Find ways to stop bullying.
- Empower students by involving them in planning, creating, and sustaining a school culture of safety and respect.

School Visits Targeted At Particular Underachieving Students

Of course, there are many more reasons to collect data from schools besides school shootings. Typically our teenage clients are not performing well academically or socially in their schools. School visits provide important data that helps our caseworkers deliver appropriate service for our young clients. We have been able to verify whether the child's learning problems are known to the school and are being dealt with appropriately. (In a large school, serious diagnostic and programmatic mistakes are often made.) Therefore, the school visit provides an opportunity to share pertinent background information of which the school may be unaware.

A youngster's respect, or lack thereof, for authority is an indicator of behavior. For that reason, finding out from teachers and administrators how the child responds to them can provide a roadmap for what sort of delinquency prevention counseling is needed. Most important of all is noting pertinent incidents. If a security guard requests one of our clients to take his hat off in school—and he responds defiantly—this provides something live to work on.

It is also valuable to hear first-hand the litany of fights that the youngster may have been involved in and their origins, as an aid to developing an appropriate anger management curriculum.

We have been able to develop contracts between our client and school representatives regarding behavior going forward.

The results produced by school visits can only be maximized if a methodical effort is made to collect information pertinent to the student's behavior and the learning process. The child's academic and behavioral record at school can best be understood if information is sought regarding the following circumstances:

- The educational program developed for the student;
- Classroom environment including the size of classes;
- Teaching styles to which the student is exposed and apparent effects;
- Academic performance;
- Perception of student by school staff;
- Disciplinary approaches and apparent effects;
- Testing history; and
- Parental involvement.

Students with a Conduct Disorder

A bi-directional relationship exists between academic performance and conduct disorder. Frequently, children with conduct disorder exhibit low intellectual functioning and low academic achievement from the outset of their school years. In particular, reading disabilities have been associated with this disorder, with one study finding that children with conduct disorder were at a reading level 28 months behind normal peers (Rutter, Tizard, "Language Dysfunction and Childhood Behavior Disorder," 1976).

In addition, delinquency rates and academic performance have been shown to be related to characteristics of the school setting itself. Such factors as physical attributes of the school, teacher availability, teacher use of praise, the amount of emphasis placed on individual responsibility, emphasis on academic work, and the student-teacher ratio have been found to be factors. (Carolyn Webster-Stratton, "The Incredible Years," 2021).

Triangular Casework

Teenagers and even younger children are very adept at playing authority figures (mothers, fathers, teachers, counselors, probation officers) against each other. For that reason, it becomes extremely important for youngsters to hear the same message from more than one authority figure at the same time. Triangular casework consists of sessions with two non-familial authority figures (including one of our caseworkers). Other key authority figures might include therapists and school personnel.

When a student has had behavioral problems in school, it is important to establish communication with the appropriate Dean or guidance counselor early in the school year—with the youngster present. Expectations for the child's behavior must be clearly set. By doing so, it will be made perfectly clear to the youngster what is known about his/her behavior and what will be expected in the future. The child must feel encircled to the extent that lying is not an option because one person or another within the triangle will find out and share the information. This dynamic creates important leverage in the process of attempted behavioral change.

The Relationship Between Carl and Ms. J.

One of the benefits of triangular casework can occur when there is a strong relationship between the youngster and an adult staff member at his/her school. As an example, this occurred when we visited Carl's school.

Carl had difficulty developing positive relationships and had virtually none at school. He had alienated almost all of the students with his standoffish manner and annoyed the adults by constantly breaking school rules. And yet, somehow, Carl had forged a positive relationship with "Ms. J.," the school psychologist. Our caseworker scheduled an appointment with Ms. J. and Carl.

As we discussed the evolution of Carl's relationship with Ms. J., it became apparent that it was no accident that they had become close. Carl had treated Ms. J. in a polite manner, which was distinct from how he approached others. As we tried to run back to how the relationship had developed, Carl came to understand how his behavior and words had put Ms. J. at ease and made her interested in becoming an ally of his. This school visit provided an example of how triangular casework can help identify available resources.

Remediation Measures

School visits should not be viewed as a one-time event. They should set the stage for remediation measures that have the input of parents and educational/social service providers. The information gleaned from a school visit can be supplemented by additional data from "Conduct Reports," which can be required to be signed by teachers every day and brought home for parents to see.

Based on all of this information, it is expected that a Plan of Possible Remediation Measures will be established. Such a plan may include a consideration of the following action steps:

- Change in seating arrangements
- Additional monitoring of student
- Additional expectation of parental involvement
- Positive reinforcement of strategies
- Tangible rewards at home for positive changes at school
- Detention, suspension, or removal from the school

Clarifying What Teens See as the Meaning of School

One of the depressing learnings often gleaned from a school visit is that many teenagers don't want to be in school—nor do they see any important relationship between what is learned in school and how satisfying their later life will be.

Conversations with clients and their teachers can provide a clue as to how a caseworker can best attempt to instill a long-term sense of meaning in the teen's life. Some of the options include the following:

<u>Focusing on Role Models</u>:
Try to find out who they admire—especially non-athletes. Discover with them how these persons worked for the success they achieved.
Key Question:
Ask them, "What would you like to be doing in ten years?" The answer may provide some clues as to the right approach for a particular child.

<u>Prioritizing Life Goals</u>:
Have the children select which goals are most important for them (accomplishment, excitement, social recognition, etc.). This will help them understand what's important to them and what they need to do in the next day or week to head toward their goals.

Helping Youngsters Buy Into Long-Term Goals

Teenagers can have feelings of invincibility and can act impulsively. They can live for the moment without considering how their behavior relates to the sort of life they want for themselves down the road.

It is important for parents and caseworkers to induce youngsters to ask themselves the following sorts of questions:

• What type of life do you want?

• What type of life would you have if:

→ you have a good education

or

→ you don't have a good education

and with regard to

• job satisfaction;

• the type of neighborhood you can afford to live in;

• the level of opportunity you will be able to provide for any children you may have;

• how much variety your life will have?

For inner-city youngsters, the idea of long-term goals may seem to be a total abstraction. So it becomes the role of parents and caseworkers, first of all, to help teenagers realize:

• Having and working toward long-term goals can lead to a happier life.

• Seeing that their daily behaviors—even as teenagers—either advance long-term goals or make their achievement less possible.

The first step in the process of our program is to help the youngsters understand what they wish their long-term goals to be. We ask our teenage clients to rank ten possible goals in order of importance. Several of the goals deal with the relationship between educational achievement and decent jobs, and long-term goals. Examples of such goals are included in Appendix 12J as follows:

LONG-TERM GOALS
This exercise can be administered individually or in groups.

Directions: Rank from 1 (most important) to 10 (least important) goals for your life. To what degree you have accomplished a goal so far should not count. Each blank space should have a different number.

____ Inner Harmony (freedom from inner conflict)

____ Freedom (independence, free choice)

____ Self-Respect (self-esteem)

____ An Exciting Life (stimulation, adventure)

____ Comfort (enough money)

____ Love (sexual and spiritual intimacy)

____ Salvation (deliverance from sin, eternal life)

____ Accomplishment (making a lasting contribution)

____ Family Relationships (taking care of loved ones)

____ Respect by Others (positive feedback)

How do you see education as helping you attain each of the above life goals?

Long-term goals can only be achieved if short-term steps toward those goals (daily, weekly) are attended to. In Appendix 12K below are some of the steps we ask our teenage clients to focus on in order to plan their daily routines:

_____

STEPS TOWARD ACHIEVING YOUR LONG-TERM GOALS

(This exercise is normally conducted with individual youngsters in order to help them plan their daily routine.)

When you have time on your hands which can be used for the following activities, which are you most likely to choose?

Rank from 1 (most likely) to 9 (least likely):

_____ Log into a social media site

_____ Do an extra credit project for school

_____ Work on improving your artistic or musical skills

_____ Play a video game

_____ Work at an after-school job or look for a job

_____ Read a book which you are not required to read

_____ Work on improving your athletic skills

_____ Help a family member who needs your help

_____ Hang out with friends

What do your responses tell you about your priorities?

_____

_____

Do you need to change your priorities? _____

If so, how?

_____

_____

THE IMPORTANCE OF EDUCATION

What can be found in Appendix 12L below are questions our caseworkers have asked our teenage clients in order to help them clarify the importance they consider education to have:

1. Do "Long-Term Goals" Exercise (See Appendix 12K on previous page)

2. Have an adult co-leader share his/her goals and discuss how education has played a role in his/her achieving happiness in life.

3. Asked of Co-Leader:

   Did you always see the relevance of school to achieving happiness?

4. Asked of Co-Leader:

   What sacrifices did you need to make in order to do okay in school?

5. Asked of Co-Leader:

   How did you get yourself to make those sacrifices?

6. Is there anyone in the group who has difficulty seeing the relevance of school to achieving happiness in life?

_____

_____

7. Who has discovered that connection?

_____

_____

8. Have you made sacrifices in your present life in order to have a brighter future?

_____

9. How do you get yourself to make those sacrifices?

10. What sacrifices are others in the group willing to make?

At times, in cases where struggling students need additional motivation, our program has offered to reward students with financial stipends for academic improvement. For instance, if a student improves grades in particular subjects or in their overall grade point average, payments can be made in installments. Such financial enticements can then be extended into new timeframes with new goals—if this seems to make sense. The format for such an agreement can be found in Appendix 12M as follows:

AGREEMENT TO PAY EDUCATION-RELATED STIPENDS

Our organization agrees to pay three installments of $100 each to
_____ on the following dates:_____,
_____, and_____.

The payments will be made if_____ attains the following grades in
the designated subjects for the marking period ending on: _____.

The latter two payments will be made if the student is still maintaining positive work habits
as of those dates.

<u>Subject</u>	<u>Grade</u>
1.	
2.	
3.	

Signed:

_____   _____
(Sponsoring Organization)   (Student)

                                                         _____
                                                         (Parent)

Assisting Youngsters With Executive Functioning

Teenagers who are intent on staying out of trouble need to actively
manage their lives and schoolwork as opposed to allowing themselves to
become victims of events swirling around them. The process by which
youngsters take control of their lives and their educational responsibilities has come to be known as Executive Functioning.

The major aspects of Executive Functioning include:

Becoming More Organized

> Understanding the consequences of disorganization, and
> Applying the consequences to one's own life and education.

Time Utilization

> Understanding the difference between "time using" activities
> and "time wasting" activities and
> Making choices between alternative activities.

Examining One's Lifestyle
Amount of sleep, homework time, exercise, eating habits, substance
usage?
Fun activities, creative expression, time with friends?

Issues Pertaining to Emotional Safety

> Rejection, failure, abandonment, emotional hurts?

Boosting One's Confidence Level

> Helping youngsters get in touch with their positive features; and
> if they were honored, what nice things would be said?

The Problem of Procrastination

> Understanding the reasons why a youngster avoids particular
> tasks; and the problems caused by procrastination.

In short, schools would be well advised to focus not only on the academic subject areas but also on the organizational skills which enable students to succeed educationally. Beyond that, as has been discussed in this chapter, schools have a huge role in identifying and responding appropriately to a substantial variety of behavioral problems.

Chapter 13

Leveraging Positive Peer Pressure to Prevent Delinquency

Skills: Developing Leadership Skills, Choosing Friends Wisely, Dealing with Gangs

In this chapter, you'll meet Joel, who though meaning no harm, made some bad decisions that caused him to spend many years in prison. Fortunately, Rex fared better. But not Barton.

The Impact of Positive and Negative Peer Pressure

Do you, as parents or service providers to adolescents, feel that you are doing your job but are unable to counteract the effects of peer pressure?

When caught doing something illegal, teenagers often blame their actions on others or on peer pressure in general. A peer can be considered to be a youngster of approximately the same age.

Young people themselves can be considered to be one of the important resources that can be targeted to prevent juvenile delinquency. They can effectively contribute to developing and engaging in significant and meaningful ways.

Young people are the ones who are most often directly affected by youth violence. Therefore, it can be helpful for them and their peers to enhance their communication skills, avoid risky situations, and select positive relationships as well as activities to succeed in reducing violence. Below are approaches we have used to accomplish these aims:

Before responding to situations with a potential for conflict, youths need to seek help from trusted adults, respond non-violently, or seek a safe place to move to. These options are significant because when young people control their feelings and try to resolve conflicts in a nonviolent way, they automatically reduce the odds of hurting anyone or getting hurt themselves.

Shortly after entering our program, we ask our teenage clients to develop responses to situations that could escalate into physical conflict. See Appendix 7G on page 108.

In order to avoid violent and criminal behavior, teenagers must seek out those who are at low risk in terms of such behavior. Youngsters must choose friends who are not consumers of alcohol and/or drugs. The youths must try to differentiate those friends who intend to perform well academically from those who have a history of delinquent behavior. It is helpful to become involved in varied activities, including clubs, volunteer work, and sports, so that they will avoid the boredom that is often produced by long periods at home and directionless "hanging out." Anti-social behavior is often a reaction to feelings of boredom.

Teenagers Influencing Other Teens

Youths can significantly influence others directly and can help prevent delinquent behavior by helping others understand that such behavior is not acceptable. Some steps that can be executed to prevent anti-social behavior include the following:

Support others to become law abiding alongside helping those who are the victims of illegal acts. Youths must be encouraged not to just wait and view the occurring violence. If they see any of their friends getting upset and possibly on the road to criminal misconduct, youths must assist them in calming down and using peaceful approaches to conflict.

They can also let others understand that bullying or any other violent acts are not permissible. On the other hand, if they feel that it is not safe

262 Youth in Jeopardy

for them to resolve the problem on their own, they must seek help from trusted adults. Besides, youths must support those people who are the victims of such violent acts so that they may not be bullied or victimized again and possibly retaliate violently themselves.

Youths must also encourage others to remain safe. They must show other peers how to increase their safety by avoiding violent acts, drugs, and alcohol. They can further encourage others by making healthy and safe choices. When minors try to resolve conflicts in nonviolent ways without the use of weapons, they tend to help their families, peers, friends, neighbors, and themselves remain safe.

The Highest and Best Use of Peer Leaders

What peer leaders most have to offer our other teenage clients is the benefit of their past experiences. By definition, a peer leader has discarded many of the attitudes and behaviors which might have gotten him/her in trouble and has developed new approaches to life.

One of the ways our caseworkers first utilize our peer leaders' past experiences is to match a client with a peer leader whose forms of misbehavior, to a large degree, mirror each other's. In other words, a peer leader with a past history of gang membership would be a good resource for a current gang member. Similarly, a peer leader who has abused drugs in the past can be helpful to a youngster still struggling with that problem.

Once these matches have been made, we bring together the peer leader and teenage client in an informal setting. Usually, the client's caseworker is present in order to help make relevant connections ("Felix, how did you manage to get out of the gang you were in?") The resultant dialogue, which may take place over many months, may provide the client with the belief that seemingly unattainable objectives are actually achievable.

Some of the ways in which peer leaders have been especially helpful to other youngsters have included the following:

- Welcoming new members to the group and making them feel comfortable;
- Providing support and encouragement to other youngsters who are struggling with decisions and new behaviors;
- Co-leading teen group sessions with a violence prevention counselor;
- Being trained in anger management techniques, so as to help resolve conflict;
- Developing a level of comfort in taking unpopular stands without fear of a negative reaction.

Job Description for SCAN-Harbor's Peer Leaders

- Go through training in preparation for his/her role;
- Co-lead support groups;
- Meet with co-leaders before and after groups for planning and evaluation;
- Contact support group members who have stopped attending the group or who have special needs;
- Accompany caseworkers on home visits when needed;
- Model healthy, mutually respectful relationships with your co-leader;
- Help orient new members of the Violence Prevention Group;
- Help mediate conflict in the group.

Peer leaders serving our program receive stipends for their work. As much as peer leaders have contributed to the success of our program, we also wish to see them benefit in ways in addition to financial rewards. A major goal has been to enhance the knowledge level of the peer leaders and perhaps even generate some careers in the helping professions. In order to make this possible, the peer leaders are asked to complete summaries at the conclusion of each counseling session that they attend. It is hoped that these summary sheets will generate significant learnings for both present casework and future skills development.

One thing I have learned from experience is that peer leaders should not let their role go to their head. They must retain a vulnerable side so as to be seen as accessible by the other youngsters. When their behavior is less than perfect, it is important for them to listen to feedback from others and to apply the feedback in future situations.

"Trouble Finds Me" – The Classic Cop Out

Several conversations between our caseworkers and their teenage clients have gone something like this:

> Caseworker to Teen Client: "It seems like you've been in a lot of trouble lately."

> Client to Caseworker: "That's because **trouble finds me.**" The implication is that a youngster is somehow entrapped by an unspecified form of peer pressure.

Of course, this is a classic example of a youngster playing the "victim card." Despite the attempt to characterize "trouble" as having human qualities, this line of reasoning is a naked attempt to deny and shift responsibility for one's misdeeds. The bottom line is it is the teenagers' responsibility to avoid negative relationships, and it is the parents' responsibility to monitor their associations.

Youngsters Who Want To Act Older Than Their Age

One dynamic of peer pressure is the 13-year-old (for example) who wants to act as the peer of a 16-year-old. Unfortunately, the younger teenager may be focusing mostly on, and trying to emulate, the more negative behaviors of the older teenager – perhaps the consumption of drugs or alcohol, sex (of a nature for which he/she may not be emotionally prepared), or all-night escapades.

Studies have shown that the most stable and law-abiding adults are those who progress in an age-appropriate fashion through their teenage years. In other words, a youngster who fully lives life as a 13-year-old, then a 14-year-old, etc., will likely feel more fulfilled later on and less susceptible to negative peer pressure in later years.

So how do we instill within a younger teenager a feeling of contentment with their current age? One approach is to help the youngster understand what is behind his/her seeming need to hang out with older kids. Another approach is to help the youngster realize that whereas 13-year-olds may have fewer privileges than 16-year-olds, they also have fewer responsibilities. (16-year-olds, after all, probably have more courses and homework in school and may need a job in order to buy the clothing they desire.) It is, therefore, important to help the younger teenager see the relationship between an increase in responsibilities and an increase in privileges. What's more, parents need to make the latter dependent on the former.

Appendix 13A

<u>THE PRESSURE TO ACT OLDER THAN YOUR AGE</u>

(These questions can be posed with individual youngsters or in groups.)

1. How old are you? _____

2. What are the benefits of being your age?

_____

_____

3. How old are the kids you hang around with? _____

4. What additional responsibilities do older teenagers have that you don't have?

_____

_____

5. What would you like the freedom to do at your age that you currently don't have?

_____

_____

6. Are the freedoms that older teenagers have worth the responsibilities that go along with them? _____

7. What do you do in your free time?

a. _____   d. _____

b. _____   e. _____

c. _____   f. _____

8. Could any of those activities (Insert the letters above which apply):

_____ get you in trouble?

_____ make you uncomfortable?

_____ be dangerous for you?

_____ be more appropriate when you are older?

9. Of those activities mentioned in #7, why do you feel the need to do them?

a._____

b._____

c._____

d._____

e._____

f._____

10. Which of the items do you do because of peer pressure?

_____

_____

11. Concerning those items in #10, could you tell your friends that you would rather not be involved in those activities at this point in your life?

_____

12. In order for you to tell your friends that, what would need to happen?

_____

_____

Next, we present an exercise designed to help adolescents and their families determine whether they are leaders or followers. This, of course, helps the family understand how susceptible the teenager is to peer pressure. This exercise can be found in Appendix 13D as follows:

_____

<u>ARE YOU A LEADER OR A FOLLOWER?</u>
(this exercise can be presented individually or in groups)

Enter "Y" for "yes" or "N" for "no" in the spaces at the left

Do you....

_____ 1. Feel okay expressing an unpopular opinion when a group of your peers is around?

_____ 2. Let your partner know if you sense there is something wrong with your relationship?

_____ 3. Do what the majority does since the majority "must be right?"

_____ 4. Walk the streets with someone you've just met who asks you to?

_____ 5. Follow your conscience when you're not sure how to act in a situation?

_____ 6. Criticize peers who make offensive or prejudiced statements?

_____ 7. Consider loyalty to friends important—even if this presents a risk of getting into trouble?

_____ 8. Criticize a disruptive person in class who is making it difficult to hear the teacher?

_____ 9. Think you'd intervene if your friend is being bullied right in front of you?

_____ 10. Suggest solutions when the group you're in has a problem?

_____ 11. Find your partner usually decides what you'll do on dates?

_____ 12. Like to play a role in solving conflicts within a group?

_____ 13. Take drugs or alcohol because that's what everyone else is doing at a party?

_____ 14. Wait for others to choose you as a friend?

_____ 15. Tell someone in your family that you love them, before they say that?

_____ 16. Apologize after both persons behave badly during an argument before the other person does?

_____ 17. Break off a relationship with someone you've been in trouble with before they do?

Scoring Appendix 13B

Indicating Leadership Qualities: Questions 1-Yes; 2-Yes; 3-No; 4-No; 5-Yes; 6-Yes; 7-No; 8-Yes; 9-Yes; 10-Yes; 11-No; 12-Yes; 13-No; 14-No; 15-Yes; 16-Yes; 17-Yes

Indicating a Follower Role: Questions 1-No; 2-No; 3-Yes; 4-Yes; 5-No; 6-No; 7-Yes; 8-No; 9-No; 10-No; 11-Yes; 12-No; 13-Yes; 14-Yes; 15-No; 16-No; 17-No

Ten or more "leader responses" indicate the youngster is more of a leader. Seven or more "follower responses" indicate the child is more of a follower.

When Negative Peer Pressure Intrudes on Friendships:

The type of friends people need changes as they go on through life. The qualities one needs at 5 and 9 and 13 years of age may greatly differ as tastes and favored activities evolve. We may move in different directions than even our longest-standing friends.

Certainly, when two friends get into serious trouble that presents a warning signal that a risky chemistry exists between them. Walking down the streets together could lead to trouble. In most cases, indoor activities pose less risk.

Youngsters should at least take a close look at the pros and cons of their peer relationships. If there are more negatives, thought should be given to breaking off. But there may be logistical challenges when moving on. What is the other person's reaction likely to be?

Hands-on parents make an earnest effort to get to know their children's friends. In the final analysis, children have the right to choose who they wish to surround themselves with. But a parent is in a position to identify the personal qualities of other youngsters (e.g. dishonesty, insensitivity, disloyalty, etc.) which their own children may hardly notice. Wise parents provide their kids feedback on what they have noticed about their friends and suggestions for their consideration.

We encourage our teenage clients at some point to discuss with certain friends problems connected to getting in trouble together. If one's friend doesn't seem to care about this issue, they may be leading you toward a lawless life. It may then be time to discontinue the relationship. Youngsters need their own welfare as the number one priority. The enticements of others should be placed on a lower rung.

Encouraging Youngsters to Choose Friends and Associates Wisely

For the purpose of this book, it is helpful to distinguish friends from associates. As most teenagers see it, a friend is someone you go out of your way to spend time with—whereas an associate is somebody you bump into now and then but only have a sporadic and superficial relationship.

It is vital that an adolescent—particularly an Inner City resident—take care in choosing both their friends and associates. Let's start with an incident where a decision to hang out with an associate had consequences for Ronald, one of our teenage clients.

The Wrong Associate

Ronald was sitting at home one evening at his home in the Bronx when Paul, a teenager whose family had only recently moved into the building, knocked on Ronald's family's door and asked Ronald whether he would like to take a walk through the neighborhood. Not knowing much about Paul, Ronald made a huge mistake by agreeing to the idea.

Ronald and Paul walked through the streets and when 15-year-old Edwin Hammond refused to hand over his cell phone to Paul, he was stabbed to death by Paul (see the tragic article below from *New York Daily News*, February 16, 2008.

2 Boys Fingered in Slay Over Phone

TWO 13-YEAR-OLDS have been fingered as the thugs who stabbed a Bronx teen to death while trying to steal his cell phone, cops said yesterday. A police source said Paul Smith and another boy tried to snatch the phone from Edwin Hammond, 15, just before 7 p.m. Saturday. When Edwin refused to hand over the phone, Paul Smith stabbed him to death, police said. "Over a cell phone?" asked neighbor, Rhonde Jenkins, 49, who saw the bloodied teen right after the stabbing. "That means life has no value to them." Smith, who has prior assault and burglary arrests, is to appear in Family Court today on a second-degree murder charge. A police source said he's already in custody on an unrelated charge. Edwin, a 10th-grader at All Hallows High School, was born in New York but lived for a time in Liberia. He moved back to the Bronx four months ago. He was described as a popular student and a computer whiz who stayed out of trouble. But Edwin's run-in with the younger boys ended with him collapsing in front of his mother, Patricia Hammond-Church. Neighbors said Edwin was walking toward his home on Andrews Ave., talking on his cell phone Saturday, when he was attacked. Edwin staggered home while the suspects ran, one tossing a knife. Police said yesterday that Smith would be charged as an adult. But a spokesman with the Manhattan district attorney's office said that determination hadn't been made.

So what mistakes did Ronald make which caused him to be charged with Edwin's senseless murder? After all, Ronald didn't try to grab Edwin's phone, nor did he stab him. Ronald erred by agreeing to walk the streets of the Bronx with someone whom he hardly knew—much less knew what misdeeds he was capable of. Ronald's next mistake was that when it became apparent what Paul was up to, he didn't move away from the scene as fast as possible. So Ronald was charged as an accomplice and was sentenced to 15 years in prison. He threw away a good portion of his life because he did a poor job of selecting an associate. (For a group discussion of this incident, please see" "Could you find yourself in Ronald's shoes?" in Appendix 13C.)

Appendix 13C

COULD YOU FIND YOURSELF IN RONALD'S SHOES?
(This exercise can be conducted individually or in groups)

1. What was your first reaction when you heard about this murder?

_____

_____

2. Do you look at the crime any differently because the victim seemed to be a "good kid?"

_____

_____

3. What was your reaction to the victim's collapsing in front of his mother?

_____

_____

4. What mistakes did Ronald appear to make during the minutes leading up to the crime?

_____

_____

5. Were you surprised that Joel could be charged with such a crime?

_____

Why or why not?

_____

_____

6. What personality traits made Joel a candidate for such a crime?

_____

_____

7. Are there parts of Ronald's personality which you see in yourself?
_____

Which ones?

_____

_____

8. What do you have to do to make sure that you don't ever find yourself in Ronald's shoes?

_____

_____

Almost as important as who teenagers choose to "hang out with" is where they will go with them. In terms of the amount of risk posed, it is one thing for a youngster to spend time with a negative peer indoors, where relatively little damage can be done. It is quite another thing for a teenager to walk the streets with a peer who little is known about or who has a history of being charged with committing assaults and starting fights.

Helping Adolescents Form and Maintain Positive Friendships

Many teenagers believe that selecting friends just happens organically or maybe they "just keep those friends they've always had." Our caseworkers try to get our young clients to see that they will be best served by selecting the friends they need at a particular time consciously. The behaviors of kids go up and down as they get older—so a youngster who has the right friendship at 11 years of age may become a "nightmare" at 14.

What are the sort of friends a child might be on the lookout for? The most basic criterion might be to have positive rather than negative friends. Positive friends will intervene in situations when their buddy is about to get into trouble. They're looking out for each other. Negative friends don't particularly care what happens to each other.

So it is smart to select your friends rather than be selected. By selecting your friends, you will most likely be surrounded by the sort of youngsters you need. If you waive that prerogative, you may be subject to flatterers who gravitate toward you for the wrong reasons.

Of course, when children select their friends, it is important that they know what they are looking for in friends. Are they seeking someone with similar interests (basketball, Playstation, etc?) Are they drawn toward someone with a sense of humor? Do they need someone who is there to compliment them and support them?

On the flip side are "red flag" behaviors which might make a youngster want to stay away from someone who is trying to become their "new best friend." The process our program provides to identify "red flag" behaviors can be found in Appendix 13D as follows:

_____

IDENTIFYING "RED FLAG" BEHAVIORS
(This exercise can be conducted with individual youngsters or in groups)

Which of the following behaviors should make you consider not getting too friendly with someone? Check those behaviors:

____ Cutting classes

____ Sudden aggressive behavior

____ Ignoring curfew steadily

____ Trying to make every decision rather than allow others to have

   their say

____ Showing frequent disrespect of others

____ Constantly lying

____ Getting into fights often

____ Seeming to be jealous of you

____ Having been arrested

____ Ignoring or dismissing your feelings

____ Not listening when you talk

Evaluating Current Relationships

Our caseworkers encourage our teenage clients to focus on their closest friends. Some of the questions we ask them to consider are:

- Is he/she good or bad for you?
- What does he/she contribute to your life?
- Is he/she there for you when you have a need?
- Does he/she watch your back?

- Have you ever gotten into trouble with him/her?
- Are there any behaviors you wish he/she could change?

Assuming that nobody's perfect, an adolescent at some point will likely have to say "no" to a friend who's suggesting to do something that could get both youngsters in trouble. It is important to be able to take a stand with a firm voice, then possibly walk away from the situation.

GANGS

A National and Local Problem

As a parent, are you trying to provide a positive family environment for your teenagers, while gangs are trying to lure them into their "family?" The rapid increase in the number of street gangs is a major problem on the national and local levels. It is estimated that the total number of gang members in the United States runs in the millions. Gangs are organized groups involved in criminal activities, drug use and sale, and violence. They frequently wear certain colors, use symbols on their clothing or bodies, and enforce strict codes of behavior for their members.

How Gangs Recruit

Recruitment of gang members often takes place around schools. Gangs are most successful in recruiting young people with weak family attachments who are looking for a sense of identity and belonging and frequently view the gang as a substitute for a family.

However, gangs do not provide their members with a caring and safe environment. Gangs require their members to steal, sell drugs, fight, and even murder. As a gang member, you run the risk of being arrested and spending much of your life in prison. You also run the risk of being hurt, maimed, or killed either by members of your own gang or by rival gang members.

What is Expected of Gang Members

Young people who want to join a gang are required to participate in a rite of passage called an "initiation." The initiation rites may involve being beaten up by other gang members, assaulting others, or providing sex to gang members. In order to gain prominence in a gang, you must continually prove your loyalty. Often, you prove your loyalty by committing crimes which, over time, escalate in degree of seriousness.

It is nearly impossible to leave a gang because as a member you have knowledge of illegal activities committed by others in the gang. Other members fear that you will "snitch." The penalty for "snitching" is often death.

Current Gang Trends

During the 21st century in New York and other major American cities, the structures and communication patterns of gangs were noticeably shifting in the following ways:

- Instead of gangs being closely tied to national and regional organizations such as the Bloods and the Crips, they were becoming extremely local, being defined by blocks and housing projects. Often, they were identified by three letters (OYG, FDZ, 2MF, etc.)
- In another return to past form, conflict between gangs has become centered once more on turf. ("I better not catch you anywhere near the Washington Houses.")

A youngster growing up in a housing project doesn't need to apply to be a member of a crew. Merely living in such an environment can make one feel that he/she needs such protection for mere self-preservation. The NYC police report that project-affiliated crews account for about 40% of the city's shootings. Most of the violence, in fact, stems from the slightest of disses on the street or in social media.

Within a school, the approach is similar, in that school safety administrators are unlikely to be effective in protecting a youngster. They may,
however, be able to identify student peer mediators who can get the job
done by cooling off gang members. Investigations should also be
conducted with the assistance and input of young people.

In addressing gang members, it is important that mediators understand
how gang members view themselves. Many of the older members are
trying to change the violent image of gangs, and they may consider
themselves agents of social change and community empowerment.
Those roles should be acknowledged, rather than their criminal activities being referred to.

Guidelines For a Teenager who Wishes to Resist or End Gang Membership

- Use the above suggestions in order to get to the local gang
  representatives.
- Appeal to the gang member's need for respect. Refer to his/her
  positive goals—not to gangs.
- Don't threaten to go to the police or engage in other forms of
  snitching.
- Gang members will be most persuaded when a youngster refers
  to his/her pressure from home to quit. This is because gang
  members' families have a weak structure, causing them to long
  for and respect family attachments.

There must be a collaborative effort by school staff, an agency with
expertise working with gangs, and another agency specializing in medi-
tations. Before these parties embark on a gang mediation, they must
agree on goals and have all parties be considered equal in terms of their
influencing the outcomes. There must also be rules governing the
process—no personal remarks, interruptions, or acts of intimidation,
etc.

If a gang member sees through the following promises and WANTS
OUT, extreme care must be taken with regard to how the situation is

handled. Any discussions should be held in a neutral location such as McDonald's, so that the possibility of physical retaliation is minimized. Fortunately, in cities such as New York, there are resources available to intervene between would-be exiting gang members and gang leaders.

These resources consist of former gang members who know some current members of a gang in a particular geographical area. These "gang intervention specialists" have on many occasions helped our teenage clients ease their way out of gangs without retaliation.

Helping Families Limit Their Children's Contact with Gangs

Parents may wonder, "What do gangs have to do with our neighborhood? We don't have any gangs around here." In terms of how inner city street gangs operate, there may be some truth to that. But there also can be gang-like behaviors in the most unexpected communities. Youngsters act like gang members when they form cliques which exert concentrated peer pressure to carry out anti-social acts. Such acts might include bullying, cyber-bullying and shaking down fellow students for money or property.

With this in mind, I'd like to portray the sorts of gangs which our program interfaces with in Harlem and the Bronx. Some gangs form along ethnic lines—African-Americans, Dominicans, Puerto Ricans, Mexican-Americans, etc. Others have ethnically mixed populations. Virtually all engage in criminal behavior, though some will try to hide core activities, such as drug trafficking and larceny, behind "community service" activities. Our goals have been two-fold: to reduce gang membership among our clients and to reduce violence-related incidents in which they are involved.

In recent years, gangs have become less hierarchical and regimented. They are also less racially segregated. The so-called "sets"—subgroups of national gangs —often owe their loyalty to housing projects. Today's gang life is often characterized by class and in-fighting. As older leaders are locked up, brawls erupt over who will be successors.

But amidst all the craziness, gangs still appeal to those who long for what they believe are the feelings of family attachment. One of our clients, James, for instance, always wanted a brother. But in one Blood-related set, he proudly exclaimed, "I've found dozens of brothers." On top of that, gang membership provides some of life's petty luxuries—a dinner out with a girlfriend or a pair of sneakers which are widely admired.

The New Faces of Gangs and Crews

Tragically, some of our teenage clients view jail-time as a somewhat anticipated milestone on the way to adulthood—not unlike summer at a sleep-away camp. It is a place where they will hobnob with many of their homies from the hood. They know at least that they'll have their own bed.

A 2014 report from the New York City Police Department showed how the evolving profile of street gangs and crews are often feeding into a sense of inevitability of incarceration. "Corporate" gangs such as the Bloods and Crips have been replaced by local teenage "crews" with names such as Very Crispy Gangsters, True Money Gang, and Cash Bama Bullies.

Some Hints for Kids Who Might Be Harassed by Gangs

How should someone being stalked by gangs address gang members?

> Gang members have a high need for respect. Many of the older members are trying to change the violent image of gangs, and they may consider themselves agents of social change and community empowerment. Those roles should be acknowl-edged, rather than the criminal behavior status being exclusively referred to.

How can the local police precinct be used to help a youngster who is threatened by a gang?

Most youngsters would rather not go to the precinct themselves to report gang harassment, for fear of retaliation by the person being reported. It is advisable to have a family member file the report. When making a report, it is best not to mention specific gangs, but refer to the incident as being "between kids."

Should a youngster being threatened by gangs relocate?

If a student is so frightened that his/her capacity to attend school and/or learn is genuinely affected, a school safety transfer should be requested. Ideally, the transfer should be made to the furthest school which is accessible to the student. Obviously, the new school should not have the same gang represented as the old school. For instance, Bloods and Crips speak to Bloods and Crips across community lines.

If a youngster's residence and family are being threatened, a relocation to a home in a different community may be necessary.

What procedures should a youngster observe when walking around the city?

Areas where gang members are known to congregate should be avoided.

A youngster being threatened should try to walk with someone without a gang reputation.

If a youngster sees danger approaching, he/she should enter a building or move toward third parties on the street.

What should a teenager being harassed carry for self-defense?

As a last resort, pepper spray, which can be bought at some stores specializing in security equipment. Youngsters should be trained in its usage.

What training is helpful for youngsters who are being threatened by gangs?

>Self-defense
>Karate
>Boxing
>Anger Management
>Communications skills

Fortunately, Our Teenage Client Rex Escaped

At age 13, Rex had been arrested twice for activities he committed as part of the "6-Wild Gang." When I became Rex's caseworker, I was able to convince him to leave the gang. The reaction from a 6-Wild leader was somewhat predictable: "If you leave the gang, we'll kill you." At the same time, Rex was also being stalked by the YGs, a rival gang who "had beef" with 6-Wild. He had hit the sister of a YG member with a stick.

Rex was terrified to go anywhere without a weapon. At school, security guards removed a knife and a box-cutter from his book bag. His violent threats at school had caused him to be expelled from a total of 11 schools. Once Rex had gone so far as to beat up his principal in the course of stealing her pocketbook.

Various gang members were camped out near the entrance to Rex's apartment building. He became so frustrated at not being able to leave his home that he agreed to pursue a possible solution to his problem. In New York, there is a coalition of former gang members known as "Save Our Streets" (SOS).

The SOS employees maintain their relationships with current gang leaders to the extent that they are often able to have them agree to intervene on behalf of teenagers who wish to break their ties with gangs. I was able to find just such a person named Lorenzo, who was able to convince the leaders of 6-Wild and the YGs to keep their hands off of Rex.

The Sad Tale of Barton

Unfortunately, we are not always able to achieve such a successful conclusion in cases where adolescents are being harassed and stalked by angry gang members. In the case of our 14-year-old client Barton, his older brother William had been assaulted by a member of the Rocksolid Gang—and Barton "snitched" about the incident to the police. In the world of gangs, this is a "sin" which can be punishable by death.

From that moment on, Barton couldn't go anywhere without looking over his shoulder. He had to leave school at a time when somebody would be unlikely to be waiting for him. He took a circular route home in order to avoid stalkers. He couldn't even take the subway. I enrolled him in a boxing class and at first wondered how he could afford to always take a taxi to the gym. I came to realize that his safety had become the number one financial priority of his impoverished family.

But no amount of money could guarantee Barton's safety. One morning, he stepped out of his building with his younger brother and was mortally gunned down by a Rock Solid gang member. In our line of work, we become emotionally attached to our clients. It was hard for me to get over Barton's passing.

* * *

I hope that readers of this chapter will recognize how terribly important it is for adolescents to develop safeguards against surrendering consistently to negative peer pressure.

Based on the results of the Leader/Follower exercise (see Appendix 7C), our caseworker hopes that the participating youngsters will modify their behavior in order to resist becoming vulnerable to peer pressure.

HOW DETERMINED ARE YOU TO BECOME A LEADER?

As a result of the previous exercise, will you make an effort in the future to do the following?

Check off either "unlikely," "perhaps" or "definitely"

		Unlikely	Perhaps	Definitely
1.	Express unpopular opinions?	___	___	___
2.	Let your partner know if you sense there is something wrong with your relationship?	___	___	___
3.	Refuse to do what the majority wants to do, if you have doubts?	___	___	___
4.	Refuse to walk the streets with someone you don't know?	___	___	___
5.	Listen to your conscience when you're about to do something dishonest?	___	___	___
6.	Criticize peers who make offensive or prejudiced statements?	___	___	___
7.	Consider staying out of trouble more important than loyalty to friends who act in ways that can get you in trouble?	___	___	___
8.	Criticize a disruptive person in class who is making it difficult to hear the teacher?	___	___	___
9.	Criticize someone who you see bullying a friend of yours?	___	___	___
10.	Suggest solutions when the group you're in, is in trouble?	___	___	___
11.	Share in decisions about what to do on dates?	___	___	___

		Unlikely	**Perhaps**	**Definitely**
12.	Play a role in solving conflicts within a group?	_____	_____	_____
13.	Turn down offers of drugs or alcohol at a party, even if everyone else is consuming them?	_____	_____	_____
14.	Choose your friends, rather than wait to be chosen?	_____	_____	_____
15.	Be the first to tell a family member that you love them?	_____	_____	_____
16.	Be the first to apologize after you've had an argument?	_____	_____	_____
17.	Break off a relationship with someone you've been in trouble with, before they do?	_____	_____	_____

Chapter 14

Additional Delinquency Prevention Initiatives

Skills: Teen Groups, Self-Defense Programming, Challenge and Prison Trips

Pro-Social Activities

So far, this book has presented anti-delinquency strategies in chapters 4, 5, and 7 through 13. It is especially important that our program offers our teenage clients opportunities to share experiences with other participants. This provides our staff with the opportunity to view how each youngster interacts with their peers. Because of this, we are better able to provide services that are on target. What follows are examples of prosocial activities.

<u>TEEN GROUPS</u>

Weekly teenage groups have been an essential part of our Delinquency Prevention Program. Normally we have had a mix of more positive and more negative types in terms of their attitudes and past behaviors. A major goal of the groups is for the more positive types to have a healthy influence on their less positive colleagues.

The agenda of the group sessions is taken from "Violence Prevention Curriculum" categories which can be found in Chapter 4. In reality, a good percentage of the time is usually spent on Anger Management, Relationships, and Media Usage. The Teen Group is described below.

Teen Groups only work if there is agreement by the participants to abide by certain rules. These rules are summarized in the "Teen Contract" which can be drawn up as shown in (Appendix 14A).

The Teen Group:

- Our weekly 1½ hour delinquency prevention group sessions have several purposes, including the following:
- Creating opportunities for positive peer pressure to occur;
- Discussing the participants' personal problems, so that the youngsters can feel a communality of experience with their peers.
- Assisting the participants in developing skills useful in problem solving—including I-messages, Active Listening, cooperation and conflict resolution skills.
- Anger management is the core curriculum of the group, but many other problem areas are addressed.

Among the key learnings from the group sessions have been the following:

- Groups should reinforce the problems which run through individual counseling sessions. For this reason, the agenda should be designed to encompass the problem areas most frequently surfacing during individual sessions.
- Some teenagers are so emotionally disturbed and undisciplined that they can only have a disruptive effect on such a group—and should therefore be excluded.
- Pairing resistant or quiet group members with peer leaders or other strong members in dyads can generate discussions which can help the quieter members share their experiences and problems with the group.

- It must be communicated that non-participation in the group is not an acceptable option, although some flexibility should be allowed during the first session someone attends. (A non-participant from the second session onward should be marked "absent.")

Teen Groups are effective only if there is an agreement by the participants to abide by certain rules. These rules are summarized in the "Teen Contract" which can be drawn up as follows (Appendix 14A):

TEEN GROUP CONTRACT
(The contract should be presented to new group members when they are starting in the group)

The following are rules designed to keep Teen Groups both productive and civilized:

General Rules:

1. Participants must conduct themselves in a respectful/responsible manner at all times when on our organization's premises.

2. When a group participant breaks a rule, he/she will be given a "pull-up," which is a final warning. A second pull-up will result in an "absence" and a report will be made to the referred source.

3. Participants must be on time to group. Two latenesses equals one absence.

4. When attending leadership skills groups, participants will dress appropriately. No gang colors, beads, hats, durags, headbands, cell phones, I-pods, etc.

5. Seating placement will be at the discretion of our program staff.

Participation:

6. Participants are expected to share their experiences after the first session, and to respond to questions directed to them.

7. If, in the opinion of the group leaders, a member does not participate, the whole group may be kept over at the end of the session. Also, a non-participant shall be marked absent on the attendance sheet.

Unacceptable Behaviors:

8. Refusal to carry out instructions of the program staff

9. Using abusive or profane (cursing) language

10. Stealing, fighting, gambling or destroying someone else's property

When in Group:

11. No "put-downs." Affirm other's good points.

12. Do not interrupt staff or each other. No side discussions.

13. Volunteer yourself only.

14. Maintain confidentiality.

15. Help group leaders enforce group rules.

Agreed to: _____
Date: _____

Appendix 14B

It is helpful to start the sessions by having participants share what is happening in their lives, with reactions and support from the others in attendance. The Sentence Completion exercise below which helps bring current problems into the open are often helpful:

SOME ANGER MANAGEMENT SENTENCE COMPLETIONS AS OPENERS FOR GROUPS

1. The last time I felt like hitting someone was ...
2. The hardest person for me to deal with at school is ...
3. Kids often get in trouble during the summer because ...
4. The last time a kid disrespected me, I ...
5. In school, I feel most disrespected when ...
6. The most frequent reason I get into arguments is....
7. The quickest way to get me angry is ...
8. The last instigator I had to deal with was ...
9. A time recently when I needed help from an adult was ...
10. The biggest beef I have with my parents is ...

* * *

Considerations Regarding the Composition of Groups

If group leaders decide to include both delinquent and non-delinquent youngsters, caution is suggested when designing intervention activities. While negative teenagers may be impacted for the better by more positive participants, aggressive adolescents need special attention. A treatment plan intended for a general population may not succeed. And if the proportion of delinquent to non-delinquent teenagers is too high, the non-delinquent ones could be negatively affected. Some examples of how groups can go wrong follow:

When a Violence Prevention Group Itself Turned Violent

When arriving late for a group session one day, one of our teenage clients, Stephen, was searching for a seat. One chair was empty, except for the presence of Giselle's bag, so Stephen, with no advance warning, took it upon himself to remove the offending accessory. Giselle reacted by directing one of the most disrespectful-looking grills at Stephen.

In the world of teenagers, the wrong sort of glance can be all it takes for all hell to break loose. On this occasion, Stephen bounded from his seat and charged Giselle—dragging her out of the building by her hair with one hand and punching her with the other. Fortunately, our staff intervened to prevent the worst from happening. Certainly, this episode provided a reality-based backdrop for the following session's discussion of Anger Management techniques.

Long Memory — Short Fuse

When they were 14, two members of a group had been involved in an incident on the streets of the Harlem, with familiar details. One of Frank's crew had jumped Danny. Frank had boasted about the incident on YouTube. Now, some 18 months later, here was Frank entering the same group as the one Danny was in. The memory of the incident had lengthened Danny's memory and increased his sense of embarrassment. So upon the sight of Frank, Danny leapt out of his chair and, seeking revenge against Frank, chased him. Fortunately, other group members intervened so as to prevent serious injury. But the incident demonstrated how the Internet has expanded the statute of limitations on revenge situations. It has a way of keeping angry feelings from being extinguished.

The Self-Defense Program:

Especially in inner-city communities, teenagers are regularly harassed, sometimes even assaulted, as they walk the streets. Some youngsters even feel the need to carry weapons for self-protection. Unfortunately, the presence of weapons during a stressful event can lead to tragic outcomes for all involved.

Our Self-Defense Program was created in order to eliminate the need for youngsters to carry weapons. This goal is accomplished by teaching 12 defensive skills which are designed to make our teenage clients feel safe without the use of weapons.

Goals of Our Self-Defense Program

1. To reject any need to carry weapons
2. To increase self-esteem, self-respect, and respect for others
3. To become more aware of one's surroundings
4. To become more disciplined when experiencing anger
5. To use techniques designed to avoid bodily harm to oneself
6. To learn how to use exercise as a tool and to apply it to self-defense
7. To increase appreciation for health and fitness
8. To have the necessary confidence to exhibit before an audience what has been learned

Our program has tried to simulate in our groups the types of situations that they may encounter while walking around town. One such situation is when they are accused of being "in someone's face." What follows are some of the issues we discuss:

Self-Defense Techniques When "You're in My Face"

In view of the high rate of teenage violence in inner-city communities, it is critical that:

Youngsters learn how to defend themselves from assaults in the most effective but least violent manner possible.

They also must be clear on the boundaries between legal and illegal self-defense tactics. (The key provision of the law is that if one is assaulted, the response cannot be more violent than the original action. In other words, if you are pushed, you are not permitted to retaliate with a closed-fist punch. If you are punched, you may not take out a weapon, etc.)

Often, youngsters will consider a provocative act to be merely when "he (or she) is in my face." Obviously, a key issue is how "being in my face" is defined. Our program addresses this topic by exploring the following:

How close is the aggressor to you?
What sort of threatening gestures or language is being used?
Has this pattern of behavior been building up?

Should a youngster feel physically threatened, we attempt to provide him/her with both verbal and physical methods of reacting to the situation:

Verbal:
"I don't want problems."
"I'm feeling uncomfortable."

Physical:
Put one's hands up and decide what the necessary next least violent step should be.

In our Self-Defense Program, we teach the following defensive skills for use in situations where they feel threatened:

Skills Required for Graduation:

1.	Kata Moves	7.	Defense Against Punches
2.	Roundhouse Kicks	8.	Horse Stance
3.	Break Piece of Wood	9.	Falls and Rolls
4.	100 Jumping Jacks	10.	Wrist Grab
5.	50 Push-ups	11.	Sparring Drills
6.	50 Sit-ups	12.	Side Head Lock

Equipment Needed for our Self-Defense Program:

- Music
- Jumping Ropes
- Punch Mitts
- Resistance Bands
- Breakable Boards

Expectations of Behavior by Participants

When deciding how to act in the class, participants should forget about what they may have seen in martial arts movies. (Here, the emphasis is more about discipline, self-defense, and self-control than about combat.)

Regular attendance and being on time are necessary for the program to be successful.

Participants must listen to and follow directions.

There will be no contact below the waist or hitting in the face. It is critical that participants in no way see martial arts training as instruction in how to fight.

"Slap-Boxing" is not allowed.

It is important that the participants view the self-defense classes as more than entertainment. In order to gauge how true this is, our program regularly asks the participants to respond to a series of questions which can be found in Appendix 14B:

<u>REVIEW OF IMPACT OF SELF-DEFENSE ON PARTICIPANTS</u>

This review is conducted periodically with the group of self-defense participants.

1. On a scale of 1 to 10, how do you feel about the Self-Defense Class? _____ (1 = hate it; 10 = totally excited about it)

2. What about the class makes you feel that way?

_____

_____

_____

3. What was the most useful thing you learned in this class in the past month?

_____

_____

_____

4. How might you use this learning in your life?

_____

_____

_____

5. How would you describe the instructor's style of discipline?

_____

_____

_____

6. Does his style of discipline cause you to act differently than usual? __

If so, how so?

_____

_____

_____

7. Do you feel you have more control over your emotions? _____

How so?

_____

_____

_____

8. How might this greater control be a result of the Self-Defense Program?

_____

_____

_____

9. Does it make you feel differently about yourself? _____

If so, how so?

_____

_____

_____

10. Any suggestions you wish to make to the instructor?

_____

_____

_____

Some Lessons Gleaned from Our Self-Defense Program

- Our focus has been on what is usable in the streets—proper reactions to specific situations (blocks, defensive strikes, trapping, etc.)
- In order to deliver a firmer response and quicker reactions to aggression, we have included in the sessions conditioning routines including pushups, abs training, leg exercises, etc.
- We have found meditation and relaxation techniques to be helpful as well. These activities are aimed at the minds of the participants and enable them to focus on the particular task at hand.
- At times, youngsters in our Self-Defense Program have been injured—thus raising the question as to whether they should participate on a particular day. The injured and disabled, however, are seen as prey in the streets. For this reason, we have encouraged our teenage clients to participate with those assets they have working on a particular day.

Pro-Social Activities: Field Trips

Field trips provide a body of time and an unstructured atmosphere where a level of bonding occurs between the teens. This is beyond what the regular weekly groups can produce. But the learnings from and the benefits of the field trips cannot be left to chance. Immediate discussion and analysis of the experience are vital to creating a significant learning and motivational experience.

The Need to Behave in Public Places

When our participants go on field trips—needless to say—their behavior is not always appropriate. Some types of misbehavior that have occurred over the years have included the following:

- Loud and profane behavior which intruded on other's right to privacy
- Physically aggressive behavior on the subway or buses
- Graffiti
- Scare tactics used on random people in the streets
- The use of insulting language in front of or in reference to strangers.

Clearly, before embarking on a field trip, a caseworker should be clear as to what the expectations for the youngsters' behavior are.

In addition, should inappropriate behavior occur, the caseworker should analyze the incident with the youngsters including the following aspects:

- What behavior was inappropriate?
- What attitude led to such behavior?
- What was the effect on persons unrelated to the organization taking the field trip?
- What rights do people frequenting public space have?
- Did the behavior reflect poorly on the organization you are affiliated with?
- What are the responsibilities of young clients to avoid behavior that reflects poorly on their sponsoring organization?
- How will the behavior on the recent trip affect a program's ability to hold future trips?
- In Appendix 14C below is the format our program uses to elicit the above sort of information from our adolescent clients.

Appendix 14C

BEHAVING IN PUBLIC PLACES

This exercise can be conducted either before or after field trips with the group

1. What rights do you have when you're out in public among strangers?

_____

_____

_____

2. Do other people have the same rights as you _____

3. Is it acceptable behavior to curse out strangers or use sexually graphic language? _____

4. What would cause you to do that?

_____

_____

_____

5. Is it acceptable to label someone you just met as gay? _____

6. What would cause you to do that?

_____

_____

_____

7. Is it acceptable to throw ice on a stranger?_____

8. What would cause you to do that?

_____

_____

_____

9. What behaviors on the subway violate the rights of other passengers?

_____

_____

_____

10. Is using subway handlebars to do gymnastic exercises acceptable
behavior?_____

11. What could the consequences be?

_____

_____

_____

12. What do we mean by violating others' space?

_____

_____

_____

13. Do you ever do it?_____ Why?

_____

_____

Visits to Prisons

One of the requirements for youngsters to graduate from our program
is that they must visit a local prison to catch a close-up view of where we
hope they will never reside.

Most of our prison visits have been to Sing Sing Correctional Facility, a
maximum security institution located in Ossining, NY. Sing-Sing
provides a program for visiting teenagers which is staffed by adult
inmates, who, in most cases, are serving long-term or even life sentences
for violent crimes.

On prison visits, there are usually two main components:

A walk-through of the facilities where the lack of privacy and space is readily apparent (including living quarters, bathrooms, dining room, etc.).

Having well-prepared inmates share the poor decisions they made in their teenage years—and how those decisions destroyed their lives. We have found that our teens have been quick to see how their initially "minor" misdeeds gradually got them into trouble with the law. This sharing should occur not only in a group setting, but is particularly effective in one-on-one dyads, if the prison staff permits.

When we arrive, we undergo a lengthy security check. Photo IDs are required, as well as thorough body searches. Usually, during the initial stages of the visit, a prison guard accompanying our group will identify even minor transgressions of rules by one or more of our youngsters. This serves to provoke the teenagers and force them to understand and adjust to the higher degree of authority and control which prisons demand.

A preliminary tour of the premises features a visit to the solitary confinement "shoebox," where rule breakers are sent. At Sing Sing, tours of the cells are permitted, thus affording visitors a view of the conditions and the desperation of the average inmate. A phrase our clients often apply to the living conditions is that "they're living like caged rats." Our kids then enter a large room where they meet seven or eight inmates. Each of them makes a presentation, discussing how he landed in jail and the pain it has caused them.

A highlight is their discussion of how their progression of misdeeds at age 13 or 14 escalated gradually in terms of violence and hostility toward authority. The youngsters in our program are usually able to visualize the similarities between their current behavior patterns and the past patterns of the prisoners. Our participants usually see how their own "minor" misdeeds can gradually get them into deeper trouble with the law.

The emotional peak of the presentation for many is when the inmates share the voids within their lives, as a result of their incarceration. ("I'll never be able to attend any of my daughter's birthday parties.")

The intimate dialogues can be enhanced when one of our caseworker/chaperones joins in long enough to provide a focus for the interaction. ("I notice that you, the inmate, and Jack, the visiting teenager, both got into trouble by joining gangs.") This intervention can help make the interactions more productive by helping the inmate focus on relevant behaviors rather than "going on a fishing expedition." Planning is important. Our case workers must decide in advance of the visit what aspects of the youngsters' behavior need to be focused on.

Both our adolescents and the inmates have an enormous need for each other at this moment. The teens are eager to learn how somebody could "throw his life away." At the same time, the prisoners find meaning in their own lives by attempting to save those of other young persons.

The obvious message for our youngsters is: clean up your behavior, so that you'll never land at a place like Sing Sing.

Following these interactions, the inmates leave the room without saying goodbye. The leader later explains to us, "We want the kids to remember the message—not the messenger. So it is important that the kids don't feel a personal attachment to them."

Key to the success of a prison visit is scheduling a discussion of the experience with our clients immediately after leaving the prison. Such debriefing sessions clarify important learnings from the experience.

In Appendix 14D are the questions we ask our teenage clients immediately after returning from the prison trip:

Appendix 14D

<u>DEBRIEFING THE PRISON TRIP</u>
These questions are posed in groups.

1. What memory will you carry with you longest from the prison trip?

_____

_____

_____

2. One of the questions asked by an inmate was: "When does a young person really land in prison?" His answer was: "It happens at home and school when one develops a bad _____."

3. When I think of the inmate's situation, I feel _____

because _____

_____

4. What were the most frequent patterns of behavior as kids that eventually landed the prisoners in jail?

a._____

b._____

c._____

5. Which behaviors are most likely to make you a candidate for prison?

a._____

b._____

c._____

6. What do you need to do, starting today, to change those behaviors?

_____

_____

Challenge Trips

As previously stated, a major goal of our Delinquency Prevention Program is to make our teenage clients accountable to their parents or guardians. This challenge is made considerably easier if the family has opportunities to meet common challenges in a fun, non-threatening atmosphere. Other goals of challenge trips are to expand the family members' view of their potential. Exercises can also be developed that provide opportunities for demonstrating cooperation, patience, listening, leadership skills, and the ability to ask for help.

Family camping, or other forms of challenge trips, provide just such an opportunity. Key to the full-day or weekend experience is having skillful trainers who develop a program aimed at having family members form teams which together undertake challenges that may involve climbing, balancing, or other activities. Interspersed with the physical challenges are psychological exercises and group discussions, which are aimed at creating parent-child commitments when the family returns home. At the end of the experience, it is hoped that the family members will have bonded, have understood each other better, and have developed a mutual respect which can lead to positive behavioral change. Follow up is clearly needed.

Obviously, joint planning between caseworkers and trainers is crucial to the success of the experience. Our caseworkers have found it important to communicate the following information to the trainers:

- What are the sorts of issues that need special emphasis during the challenge trip?
- What are issues to be avoided for certain families?
- What are the behavioral problems of attendees, which the trainers should factor into the planning process?
- How and when will the expectations of the attendees be communicated to them?

The Cultural Stretch

Our caseworkers have found that a key element in inducing behavioral change in teens is to provide them with the opportunity to focus on life beyond their respective neighborhoods. Inner-city youngsters often have apprehensiveness about venturing into new areas of the city. We have found it helpful to widen their exposure to institutions representing human achievement and presenting opportunities to establish interests to pursue. To graduate from our program, each youngster must participate in a "cultural stretch."

Not all of our field trips have been to museums, businesses, and governmental institutions. It is important to allow the teen group to play a role in suggesting trips to movies, amusement parks, and other favorite attractions.

Boot Camps and Cadet Programs

"Boot camps" have been widely targeted as the cure-all for unruly teens, so it would probably be helpful to define the term. A juvenile boot camp is "a paramilitary program with a highly regimented schedule of discipline, physical training, work, drill, and ceremony characteristic of military training." Also provided are regular remedial education and counseling about substance abuse and other mental health problems. Responsibilities, regard for authority, physical fitness, and life skills are normally taught.

Boot camps can be sold as an easy solution—just what parents want to hear. Many boot camps have been conducted in a fraudulent manner. Several widespread evaluations of boot camps have shown them to be ineffective or even counter-productive. For this reason, great care should be taken before a boot camp is selected for the prevention of criminal behavior.

"Cadet programs" are likely to be more locally based than boot camps and are often less harsh and confrontational in their style. They may be conducted by local police precincts.

Probably the greatest advantage of such paramilitary programs is that troubled youngsters can grow and become officers—so authority no longer seems an abstract concept to be rebuked.

Delinquency programs are unlikely to be able to include all the pro-social activities mentioned above, but hopefully readers of this chapter will have an assortment to choose from.

* * *

I hope that readers of this chapter will have discovered some components of a Delinquency Prevention Program which can be used in order to achieve the program goals.

Chapter 15

Managing the Usage of Electronic Devices by Teenagers

Combatting Computer Addiction, Reducing Screen Time

As parents of and service providers to adolescents, are you frequently feeling frustrated by the effects of video games and social media? An average youngster will have played about 10,000 hours of video games by age 21. Recently, I asked our teenage clients to find a 24-hour period during which they pledge to stay off all media—social media, TV, movies, electronic games. Some of the reactions to this "nightmare of an experience" include the following: "I began going crazy." "I felt paralyzed". "I went into panic mode." "I felt as if I was being tortured." In recent times, most perpetrators of mass murders in school settings had been major consumers of violent electronic games. Theoretically, these young men may have wanted to have close, in-depth friendships. They may have cared for other people, and wished to share with and give to others.

But at some point, the impact of watching violent movies and television programs and playing violent video games has seemed to anesthetize them to the value of human life. Their frustrations within their lives and the low value they came to place on their own survival contributed to their heinous crimes.

Research has also indicated that when teenagers view R-rated movies the risk of using marijuana increases more than fivefold. There is also a correlation with lower academic performance and behavioral problems.

The negative effects of technology have infiltrated the attitudes and patterns of behavior of both parents and children. For this reason, to be successful, the battle against excessive and harmful screen time must be a full-scale war, and it must be waged by both generations.

Facebook...YouTube...surfing the web...texting—activities which are usually neither educational nor socially meaningful—have come to dominate the lives of many of today's teenagers. Consider a few examples from today's world of portable electronics:

- Maggie sends and receives 27,000 texts a month, as she carries on as many as seven text conversations at a time.
- Lazlo intentionally wakes up at 2:00 AM on school nights, in order to send Facebook status updates. He then sleeps through many of his classes.
- Stefan's social life is almost non-existent in the traditional sense, as he escapes into his far more controllable world of video games.
- Linda spends much of her time as a member of a cyberbullying gang that harasses peers online continuously.

All of the above youngsters lack a social life that is both positive in its orientation and even moderately deep in its relationships with peers. This means that teenagers who do not have in-depth peer relationships often are unable to show empathy with the feelings of others. IPhones and desktops relieve boredom and eliminate the need to develop social skills. They certainly don't lead to relationships built on human caring and mutual respect. It is no accident that violent and criminal behavior thrive where there is little caring and respect for others. Tragically, there is within some teenagers an almost total disregard for human life. For them, killing has become an enjoyable act, barely distinguishable from the slaughters occurring in a video game.

Some Causes of Computer Addiction

Anxiety caused by work or school-related stress, social relationships, or financial problems

Depression

Physical illness

Boredom

Types of Computer Addiction

<u>Internet Addiction</u> – The result of an individual's desire to spend time online performing any one of a number of tasks in excess. Sub-categories include:

> <u>Internet Compulsions</u> – shopping, gaming, gambling, stock trading

> <u>Cybersex</u> – participating in internet sex through chat rooms, adult websites, fantasy role playing, watching pornography

> <u>Social Network Addictions</u> – Spending more time socializing online than socializing with people in real life. Finding online relationships more meaningful than offline relationships.

Tips to Recognize Healthy Use of the Computer:
(versus unhealthy use)

Healthy use of the computer will NOT:

Directly interfere with other members of your family or their well-being;

Interfere with your obligations at home, work or school;

Reduce your interest in other activities (your health, well-being or personal care); nor lead to negative consequences (in your relationships or your finances).

Symptoms in an Individual who is Addicted to Computers:

Isolation

Defensiveness

Distractedness

Lateness

Some Signs that an Adolescent is a Computer Addict

Isolation from other persons

Failure to carry out responsibilities

Feeling a burning desire to go online to play a game, socialize or develop programming codes

Youngsters saying that he/she is doing homework, but whose parents suspect they are actually playing a computer game

Having anxious feelings when you know that your use of the computer will be limited

Mood swings or irritability when you are not permitted to spend as much time on the computer as you would like to, or if your computer time is interrupted

Telling yourself that you will get off the computer at a certain time, and then spending more time than you had committed to

The Dangers of Computer Addiction

In the 21st Century, current technology has produced many benefits, but not without a number of unintended adverse consequences. One stark example is that the accessibility of the Internet—with its games, photos and varied messages—has spawned its own type of addiction.

Someone experiencing computer addiction from excess usage will likely suffer social, financial, physical, and/or emotional consequences. A preoccupation with computers can lead to problems with relationships, productivity, self-care and hygiene.

Some Effects of Computer Addiction

- Inability to interact socially, except when online in chat groups or social networking sites
- Inability to experience pleasure when performing tasks that are not done on the computer
- Overspending on computer hardware and software
- Loss of relationships due to spending too much time doing entertainment-related activities on the computer
- Lack of productivity with regard to schoolwork because of computer-related distractions
- Poor self-esteem because of feeling socially inept
- Poor hygiene, because you are "too busy" on the computer to take time to shower, eat, brush your teeth and otherwise take proper care of yourself.

The Impact of the 2020-21 COVID-19 Quarantine

Most American families found themselves homebound after the start of the pandemic-related quarantine in March 2020.

Parents soon become aware of the huge increase in the amount of time their teenagers' spent on video games and social media. This was time — as much as 40 hours a week — that used to be spent on healthy activities such as basketball or ballet.

But after a month or so, the trend sunk into the parents' minds. When they tried to discuss the problem with their children, the sad response was something like "But my phone is my whole life."

It took a while for these particular consequences of the 2020 quarantine to fully register in the parents' minds. And this was a time when computers, tablets, and phones became the focal point not only of the kids' social life, but also their daily school activities. What seemed like a quarantine of a few weeks duration soon rambled on for a year or longer for many families.

Normally, adolescent minds can adapt to short-term, altered circumstances without having their core identity affected. But as the months dragged on, so did the digitalization of young minds. Looking back on this period, many parents wished that they had turned off Wi-Fi except during school hours. By doing so, their children might have felt less at the mercy of videos and social media. Without such restrictions, the technology platforms increase their profits through the lure of limited edition bonus time.

And so as 2020 unfolded, parents hardly recognized their children, who became increasingly obese and lacking in social skills. In many cases, they escaped onto YouTube. The result often was a decline in academic motivation and performance.

Tips to Help Overcome Computer Addiction:

- Limit your computer use to work or school;
- Place limitations on the location at which you will use the computer;
- Look for social support;

- Keep a computer diary (amount of time spent on computer, activities performed on the computer; and
- Get outside help.

As a parent of or service provider to adolescents, how can I find resources for the treatment of computer addiction? You might wish to start with the following

Computer Addiction Hotline: 800 – 895-1695
addictions.com/computer

Our caseworkers want our teenage clients to see how the amount of time they spend on electronic devices negatively impacts other aspects of their lives. Some questions which can help clarify this can be found in Appendix 15A as follows:

Appendix 15A

DOES THE AMOUNT OF A TEENAGER'S "SCREEN-TIME" IMPACT HIS/HER SOCIAL SKILLS AND CONCERN WITH PEOPLE?
(The following questions can be posed individually or in groups.)

1. Check those traits below which you hope to develop:

____ Someone who has close, in-depth friendships.

____ Someone who genuinely cares about other people, values others for who they are and not what they look like or own, and shows love for family and friends.

____ Someone who demonstrates responsibility and can set and work toward long-term goals.

____ Someone who is willing to share with and give to others.

2. Do you think that spending large amounts of time watching television, playing video games, surfing the net, etc., helps you achieve any of the above? _____

Why or why not?

_____

_____

_____

3. Do you think that being plugged into I-pods, headphones, and hand-held toys helps you achieve any of the traits listed in #1?

_____

_____

_____

Why or why not?

_____

_____

_____

4. What are "people skills?"

_____

_____

_____

Does technology help one develop them? _____

Why or why not?

_____

_____

_____

5. Do you feel that violence in the media and video games cheapens the importance of creating positive relationships? _____

Why or why not?

_____

_____

_____

6. Thinking about the above, do you plan to decrease your screen-time? _____

Why or why not?

_____

_____

_____

7. Do you plan to change the types of electronic entertainment you expose yourself to? _____

Why or why not?

_____

_____

_____

Finding the Proper Parental Response to Electronic Devices

Unfortunately the continuous availability of smart-phones to teenagers has many negative consequences:

- Most youngsters admit that they are "addicted" to smart-phones and therefore allow their usage to play an overwhelming role in their lives.
- When schools allow students to bring smart-phones into educational buildings, their usage and the resultant discussions about their usage undermines the educational process.
- When teenagers text and go on social media late at night when they should be sleeping, they often lack the energy and alertness necessary for educational achievement the following day.
- Social media should be seen for what it is in the lives of most teenagers—entertainment. It seldom is a substitute for meaningful in-person social interaction or the development of in-depth personal relationships.

It should be clear from the above observations that the common over-reliance of teenagers on smart-phones has a frequently negative impact on their education. And who is legally responsible to see that youngsters obtain an education? Their parents, of course.

Our caseworkers feel that it logically follows that a parent is responsible to see that impediments to their children's education are kept to a minimum. This means that—even if a teenager has saved up money to purchase a smart-phone—it does not necessarily follow that he/she should be permitted to own one. It should be a parental decision.

It is suggested here that youngsters should not be permitted to own a smart-phone until they have demonstrated a commitment to learning that is more powerful than the electronic distractions which tempt them at every turn. A hands-on parent should probably set minimum standards of educational effort that must be met over a specified period of time in order for their child to own a phone with access to the internet and to social media.

Parents Need to Understand Their Children's Social Media Usage

Both parents and children must be aware of the particular website policies. Some potentially dangerous sites are Omegle, KK, Tik Tok, Telonym, Snapchat, and Whispers.

> Have youngsters identify sites they have an account on.
> Are any posts too private to be made public?
> Decide if they should be deleted.
> Time restrictions can be placed by parents on children's access.
> Consider that a youngster will survive a day without social media.
> Parents have available social media protection sites such as calculator vault, Hide it Pro, Cover Me, Private Photo Vault, and Secret Folder.
> Internet providers (Verizon, T-mobile, etc.) can provide assistance to parents on accessing controls.

How Parents Can Counter Teenage Computer Addiction

Most adolescents are happiest when they feel connected to friends and family. Yet the invasion of technology-oriented entertainment (TV, video games, surfing the net, on-line chat rooms) undermines the development of interpersonal skills which lead to positive personal relationships.

Parents can help foster these relationships by teaching their children that happiness normally is achieved through warm personal relationships rather than the acquisition of material possessions. Parents can also facilitate such relationships by teaching their children simple social skills, such as how to introduce oneself and carry on a satisfying conversation. But youngsters are unlikely to create intimate relationships unless they are required to adhere to the following sorts of rules:

- The amount of screen time is limited, with electronics not permitted in the bedroom, at the dinner table, and during family activity sessions.
- Computers must be restricted to places where they can easily be checked to see how they are being used.
- It is important for parents to watch any borderline violent videos with their children and to share their concerns about the content, so that any prohibition of watching particular videos will be grounded in a firsthand experience.
- Parents can offer incentives for earning more screen time if they devote a prescribed amount of time to other positive activities. Examples of such activities might include spending a certain amount of time with a younger sibling, achieving greater academic success, or participating in a community service project.
- Children with the collaboration of their parents should keep track of how much time they spend on electronic devices—with the goal of decreasing the number of hours. (A form we use to track screen time is shown in Appendix 15B.)

Surrendering Digital Devices Before Bedtime

It is advisable for parents to insist that their children turn off their digital devices before bedtime. This policy usually leads to an improved quality of sleep and is conducive to better functioning the next day—physically emotionally, and cognitively.

Other Screen-Time Rules for Parents to Consider

- Limit their on-line use (including text messaging) to under 90 minutes a day, aside from special school projects.
- Keep them off of social networks or on-line dating sites.
- Talk to them about not meeting strangers offline.
- Keep computers in a central location in the home.
- Teach them to keep their passwords private since password theft is a serious problem.

- Teach them not to pirate software or motion pictures.
- Have them Google themselves often, including screen names, telephone and cell numbers, address, full names and nicknames.
- Try to limit their use of chat rooms to monitored or themed chat rooms on safe topics.

What if my adolescents show that they have learned to curtail unhealthy media usage?

> Parents are then advised to let their children make their own decisions regarding media consumption. It is still necessary for parents to conduct spot-checks to make sure that a backslide is not occurring.

Ways of Guarding Against Internet Predators Who May Target Younger Teens

- Respect their privacy to the extent possible and talk with them about their online experiences.
- Filter sites that are inappropriate for young teens, instead of blocking all but approved sites. Some bad ones will get through, though. So, talk about this beforehand.
- Give them more leeway on people they can expect contact from. But check and account for everyone on their "buddy list." No "friends of friends."
- Make sure you filter or block image searches, which are often a way around many filters.

In order for youngsters to be able to track the amount of screen time they rack up on a daily and weekly basis, we have created a form which can be found in Appendix 15B as follows:

SCREEN TIME USAGE (No. of Hours Per Day)
Client: _____ (used individually)

Week of

	Mon.	Tues.	Wed.	Thurs.	Fri.	Sat.	Sun.
Snap Chat, etc.							
Games							
Netflix/TV							
Other							

Week of

	Mon.	Tues.	Wed.	Thurs.	Fri.	Sat.	Sun.
Snap Chat, etc.							
Games							
Netflix/TV							
Other							

Week of

	Mon.	Tues.	Wed.	Thurs.	Fri.	Sat.	Sun.
Snap Chat, etc.							
Games							
Netflix/TV							
Other							

Week of

	Mon.	Tues.	Wed.	Thurs.	Fri.	Sat.	Sun.
Snap Chat, etc.							
Games							
Netflix/TV							
Other							

CHOOSING UPLIFTING FORMS OF EXERCISE AS ALTERNATIVES TO SCREEN TIME

Below are types of exercise based on the Ayurvedic principles of medicine. Adapted from the work of chiropractic and naturopathic medicine expert Dr. John Douillard ("Body, Mind and Sport," 2001), these clusters correspond to the three doshas, or body types.

Type 1 Activities for anxious youngsters that are slow and calming.	Type 2 Activities geared toward those who are highly competitive which require stamina, speed and strength	Type 3 Activities for calm youngsters who do well under pressure. These require endurance and mind-body coordination.
Low-impact Aerobics	Basketball (and other team sports)	
Dance	Ice skating	Body-building
		Soccer
		Gymnastics
Ballet		
Baseball		
Swimming	Touch football	
		Inline skating
		Rock climbing
Doubles tennis	Diving	Tennis
Walking		Volleyball

	Noncompetitive racquet sports	
		Lacrosse
Martial arts		Handball
Weight training	Yoga	Cross-country running

SETTING BOUNDARIES FOR THE USE OF TECHNOLOGY IN YOUR LIFE

Using checkmarks, indicate which of the following technological devices you own or have access to. If you have a device not listed, add it to the list. Then, keep track of how much time you spend using each of these devices per day for one week.

Type of Device	Own or Have Access To (√)	Hours per Day Used						
		Mon	Tue	Wed	Thu	Fri	Sat	Sun
Cell Phone								
MP3 player								
Tablet (e.g., Kindle, Galaxy, iPad)								
Desktop computer								
Laptop computer								
Television								

DVD/Blu-ray player								
Radio								
Video game system								
Handheld PDA (e.g., iPod Touch)								

In order for youngsters to determine whether they are screen addicts, we have developed a series of questions which can be found in Appendix 15C as follows:

<hr>

Appendix 15C

<u>**Some Questions for Potential Screen Addicts**</u>

Is anyone in your life concerned about your use of these technological devices? If so, who?

<hr>

<hr>

How might these technological devices interfere with your ability to pay attention to important tasks? (For example, do you text your friends when you should be doing chores or homework)?

<hr>

<hr>

List any ideas you can come up with for limiting your use of these devices.

<hr>

<hr>

Questions and Answers for Parents Regarding Screen Time

1. Q: At what age should a youngster be allowed to have a smart-phone?

A: At no particular age. The timing should be based on his/her behavior, maturity level, and attitude toward their educational responsibilities.

2. Q: If parents want their child to be able to check in with parents and emergency services (but little else), what are the available options?

A: TracFones.

3. Q: What are some of the larger companies providing TracFones?

A: Safelink, Assurance, Access Wireless, True Wireless, Terracom, Life Wireless.

4. Q: How many **minutes per month** are allowed on most of these TracFones?

A: Typically 250 minutes of talk and text a month.

5. Q: Who is eligible for free TracFones?

A: Families who participate in one of the following public assistance programs — Food stamps, Medicaid, SSI, free lunch programs, Section 8 housing. Also, a family whose household income is at or below 135% of the Federal Poverty Guidelines for that state.

6. Q: For how long is a family **eligible** for TracFones?

A: One year — No contract needed. The service can be renewed annually with a quick certification process.

7. Q: Can TracFones be used only during certain hours of the day?

A: Yes. You can block out hours when school is in session or late night hours.

8. Q: What sort of parental controls exist?

A: Typically they are designed for either C7+ (children); T13 (teens) or YA 17+ (young adults).

9. Q: When youngsters do have smartphones, what additional controls are available?

A: All wireless carriers /phones have parental controls which are accessible through settings. The ability to block Internet access is built into I-Phones. As for android phones, they contain a special app to do so. It is called MM Guardian Parent. Parents are then able to customize the settings to limit time spent browsing the digital world, the downloads of apps, filter materials available on the web according to age, block unwanted communications and track their children's location. Once these settings are in place parents would set a password. Children would not be able to change the settings without this password.

10. Q: What are some parental controls that should be considered?

• Resources are listed at www.Screenagersmovie.com

• Avoiding divulging private information such as your child's name or birth date;

• If you have concerns about Snapchat or the addictive Boom Beach, simply block the apps.

• Parents can also use Family Link to see how often a child is using a certain app or game, and choose to have a conversation with the child about using the software responsibly, or blocking the app temporarily.

• Parents can also track the whereabouts of their children by turning on the "locator Switch".

• Parents can also use Family Link to create restrictions on how young-sters browse the web. You can turn on a filter that blocks mature websites. Inside the dashboard, you can create time limits for specific apps or categories of apps - - like social networking or games. When you run out of time with an app, you are locked out.

• Parents also can have control over time usage. For instance, you can give a child two hours of screen time on weekdays. You can also schedule regular bedtime hours that lock down the device at specific times - - between 9PM and 7AM, for instance. No screens - - including TV's and computers should be permanently installed in children's bedrooms.

11. Q: How can parents get teenagers to agree on **additional restrictions**?

A: Youngsters can be required to sign a contract with their parents which could include:

• No nude selfies;

• No meeting of strangers based on Internet introductions;

• No cell phone usage at the dinner table by any member of the family. Parents of course must set the proper example regarding the use of elec-tronics.

• Parents must be given all usernames and passwords. Any changes must be given to parents. If parents try to log on and can't, kids can lose phone privileges for a period of time.

12. Q: What are some resources available to computer addicts?

• Computer Addiction Hotline (800)895-1695

• Addictions.com/Computer

In order to formalize youngsters' commitment to operating within acceptable guidelines for the usage of electronic devices and software, we ask them to read, fill out, and sign a pledge which can be found in Appendix 15D as follows:

Appendix 15D

OUR PROGRAM'S INTERNET AND DIGITAL DEVICE USE PLEDGE

I WILL NEVER RESPOND TO ANY ONLINE COMMUNICATION THAT MAKES ME FEEL HARASSED, UNCOMFORTABLE OR THREATENED – I will tell a trusted adult if I come across anything that makes me feel scared, uncomfortable, or confused. I will never respond to any messages that are rude or offensive in any way. I will show the message to a parent, guardian or caseworker right away. I understand that my caseworkers have my safety at heart and that they will respect my feelings and help me.

I WILL RESPECT OTHER PEOPLE'S RIGHTS WHILE ONLINE AND WHILE USING DIGITAL DEVICES

The Internet is a large community and digital devices have broad capabilities; my behavior on the Internet and my use of digital devices affect others. This includes the avoidance of explicit language or images, sexting, cyberbullying, and other forms of social cruelty perpetrated online against others. I will not use someone else's device without the approval from the device's owner, a teacher or a school administrator.

I WILL KEEP IDENTITIES PRIVATE- I will never share personal information such as names, mailing addresses, telephone numbers, passwords, the name of my school, or any other information that could help someone determine my actual identity. I will also not reveal any personal information about my friends or any person. I will never send or post media (pictures, video, audio etc.) or any personal information, my own or that of others in my community, without first checking with my parents, caseworker, or guardian. I will never meet in person with anyone I have first "met" online without discussing it with my parents or guardian or caseworker.

I WILL TALK WITH MY PARENTS/GUARDIAN AND CASE WORKER ABOUT THEIR EXPECTATIONS AND GROUND RULES FOR GOING ONLINE (parents, please go over guidelines with your children) – I will talk with my parents or guardians at home, and my teachers at school, so that we can set up rules for going online. The rules will include (but are not limited to):

The times of day that I may be online:

_____

The length of time I may be online:

_____

Whom I may communicate with while online:

_____

Appropriate areas for me to visit while online:

_____

I recognize that my parents/guardians have the right to access my accounts:

Client initial: _____ Parent/Guardian Initial: _____
Caseworkers initial: _____

Our program strongly encourages parents and students to work out additional digital device guidelines and contracts for home, especially surrounding non-school devices and services (e.g., texting, or online media and games).

Child's Signature: _____ Date: _____

Name: _____

Parent/Guardian Signature (s) : _____ Date: _____

The challenge parents, caseworkers, and educators face in managing the usage of electronic devices by teenagers will evolve just as technology evolves. Hopefully readers of this chapter will be better equipped to update their responses

Chapter 16

The Special Challenges Of Keeping Girls Out Of Trouble

Skills: Dealing with Emotional Distress, Dating Issues, Provocative Attire

Healthy girls do not ordinarily feel the need to be like a boy. After all, they seem to be operating with advantages as compared to their male contemporaries. Their fine motor skills seem to develop faster than those of boys—as well as their verbal skills. They tend to have extended conversations earlier than boys and develop internal self-control mechanisms. Girls on average get better grades than boys and are more likely to move on to college right after graduating from high school. Girls are also more likely to graduate from college.

But boys may have some advantages over girls. They more often attribute their inevitable instances of failure by attributing them to external factors. This tendency may save them from feeling that the barriers to success are permanent and inevitable. Boys may therefore be quicker than girls to work on eliminating both external and internal obstacles to success.

<u>Some Vulnerabilities Girls May Face</u>

Girls are much more likely than boys to develop symptoms of post-traumatic stress disorder, anxiety, and depression: In a recent year one in three girls seriously considered attempting suicide, according to the center for Disease Control and Prevention. Girls often feel pressured into committing defensive measures in reaction to awful acts committed by adults. They are victims of physical and/or sexual assault five times more often than the rate of boys. They may also have witnessed domestic violence against their mother. In addition, the entertainment industry reinforces the sense of vulnerability girls experience with its streams of violent acts against women shown on TV and in movies.

As a result of these acts and images girls witness, teen girls may go elsewhere for emotional support—gravitating toward people who may not have their best interests in mind. Some girls may come to tolerate abuse and begin to mistakenly feel that such acts are part of what happens when they are in a "loving" relationship. Family rules and traditions also are part of the mix. Some girls are not allowed out of the home to play with their friends and are told to clean the house and do other chores.

Some Causes of Female Violence

Some girls seeking respect are quick to respond aggressively when being "dissed." Even the "wrong look" can be considered disrespectful. Not responding to such instigating incidents may cause a girl to lose the respect of her peers and make her a target for future aggressive acts. Retaliation against the above provocative acts is especially important to girls who have few familial attachments. Girls whose parents should be responsible for their development and protection, too often fail them. They often receive too little supervision at home by uncaring or even rejecting caregivers.

The result of this emotional abandonment is that girls may come to feel little empathy for others. With considerable arrests of hostile persons outside the home, some girls will feel that pre-emptive aggression is necessary. Unfortunately their parents may dismiss their daughters as "bad girls." This characterization provides an excuse for not guiding such daughters toward positive values and appropriate behavior.

Clearly, what's needed are caregivers who are available, consistent and responsive to the emotional needs of their daughters. If parents feel the need to require demanding household and family responsibilities from their daughters, it is best if they do so early. If done later, the responsibilities may be seen by girls as a form of punishment and may create resentment and further cracks in what may be an already fragile parent-daughter relationship.

Some Issues Facing Teen Girls and Their Parents

Developing a Positive Identity

Parents of young daughters might be advised to monitor the source of information which their girls are exposed to and which affect their view of women. Such parents should be on the lookout for degrading comments about women and negative stereotypes. They should seek opportunities to make them aware of places they can go in order to share in the celebration of female achievements.

A proactive parent might ask their daughters what personality traits they are trying to display. Hopefully, included in the list will be such characteristics as intelligence, strength, happiness, and concern for others.

Access to Social Media

Girls tend to turn to digital technology earlier and for somewhat different reasons than boys. They are more likely to use social media to manage uncomfortable feelings such as loneliness. In order to encourage their daughters to deal with distress by confiding in other trusted individuals, parents may want to hold off on providing them with early access to social media. By doing so, parents may be providing their daughters with more time to have conversations about heavy emotional issues with persons who can assist them in meaningful ways.

Dealing with Emotional Distress

Boys often deal with emotional challenges by focusing on another topic such as schoolwork, social media, or sports. Girls, on the other hand, tend to manage emotional distress by seeking out support in order to talk about their feelings with their parents or friends. Parents should encourage this course of action. Should a teen girl find herself wallowing in emotional distress for extended periods of time, parents may be advised to suggest that their daughters focus on alternative activities—as boys often do.

The Pressure for Girls to Start Dating Early

It is normal for girls as young as 10 years of age to have crushes on one or more boys. A girl may even talk about having a boyfriend. In reality, your daughter may just be part of a particular boy's social circle, but may not be ready to spend time alone with him. Parents might want to suggest double dating as a means of postponing the frequent awkwardness of their daughter being alone with a boy for the first time.

Parents should be available to discuss sooner rather than later about what makes for a healthy dating relationship. It is preferable for a girl to learn this from her parents rather than from other girls, social media sites—or, worst of all—pornography sites. If parents see their daughters go on a date with too much cleavage or thigh showing, they should speak up and set guidelines for appropriate attire.

Parents should also be available to discuss their daughter's relationship with their boyfriends. They should be on the lookout for any tolerance of verbal abuse. Too often girls may endure a barrage of rude comments because they "don't want to hurt his feelings." Some boys may manipulate a girl by telling her how nice she looks or express discomfort about her even talking to other boys. Girls may embrace such comments because they would only be directed at a "loveable person."

Effects of Girls' Earlier Physical Maturity

On average, girls experience puberty about two years earlier than boys. For that reason female 7th graders may gravitate towards 9th and 10th grade boys in pursuit of dating relationships. But when a girl dates a boy more than a year older than her, there are often negative consequences.

Studies have shown that sexually transmitted diseases are more likely—as are pregnancies and drug usage.

If a boy starts kissing their daughter or touching her breasts, parents should help her develop a plan. The dangers of unwanted pregnancies and sexually transmitted disease should be stressed. On a more positive note, potential benefits of emotional intimacy with a partner as opposed to mere consensual sex should be pointed out.

Girls should be encouraged to enjoy their romantic life. If your daughter wishes to discuss her dating relationship with you, such an opportunity should be welcome. Potential lectures should be kept to minimal duration. An important parental message might be to avoid having social status be the only incentive for dating a particular boy. The relationship itself should be what's most important—not how outside parties view their relationship. Hopefully, a girl's level of self-esteem will not be based solely on romantic relationships. It is a healthy sign when self-esteem is based on a variety of factors, perhaps including academic success, athletic prowess, same sex friendships, volunteer work, and paying jobs.

Provocative Attire

At an early age, girls will view through social media and advertising campaigns what clothes are most likely to attract the attention of males. They may even wear daring attire exposing more flesh than their parents would prefer. Teen girls may not necessarily see a connection between looking sexy and being sexual. They may not intend to back up their appearance with sexual activity. Proactive parents may seek a compromise between having overly rigid attitudes and totally abdicating their right to express what they consider the parameters of decency to be.

Parents might insist on the right to accompany their daughters on shopping expeditions in order to select the less offensive alternative of two flawed choices. Parents may need to emphasize that a look that is permissible by an adult may not be appropriate for a 13-year-old.

Teen Girls Suffering from Eating Disorders

Those teenage girls who have a bad self-image often blame their weight as a contributing factor. Girls are exposed at an early age to images which celebrate their bodies. The result is often that girls will become dissatisfied with their own bodies. They may be shown gymnasts or ballet performers and feel that any excess weight will be an impairment. Or they may associate super-leanness as something that potential boyfriends would value.

It is vital that parents emphasize the importance of healthy eating habits and body image. Parents should inform their daughters that rigorous diets can compromise growth and health. Parents should also help their daughters understand why they might be so concerned about their body image. Is she afraid of getting fat? Do her peers tease her about her looks? Is she afraid that her body may not be functioning properly? Parents should be prepared to provide feedback on these issues, since their perception may be different than their daughter's fears.

The opposite type of eating disorder is *bulimia*. Girls suffering from this variation will stuff themselves with food, react with feelings of guilt, and disgorge the food by vomiting or using laxatives. In either case, the bottom line is for parents to advise their daughters to eat when they feel hungry and to stop eating when their body signals that they are full.

I hope that readers of this chapter who are entrusted with teenage girls will be better equipped to react appropriately to any uniquely female phenomena which may surface.

Conclusion: Summary of Delinquency Prevention Techniques to Be Found in This Book

My hope is that those of you have persevered up to this stage—whether parents or professionals or both—feel better equipped to manage their relationships with youngsters. But it is my intention that the impact of this book on readers will be more than engendering feelings. The significance of *Youth in Jeopardy* will have been ratified if you readers check off those problems and techniques which are most pertinent to your particular relationship(s) with teenagers and implement at least a few within the next month. Without doing so, today's "easy child" can become tomorrow's at-risk youngster.

Readers of this book hopefully will have a better understanding of the factors which place youngsters in the at-risk category. Readers should understand how the risk factors—whether related to mental health, emotional health, conditions at home or peer relationships—can be addressed with significant success.

Counseling professionals will hopefully feel motivated and better equipped to develop delinquency prevention programs in their schools and communities. It is my intention that professionals will understand how such programs can be organized and staffed and how they can reach out to and inform parents. Finally I have tried to highlight how the ability of parents to manage the electronic devices available to teenagers is a central factor in delinquency prevention.

And so, when you finish reading this book, I urge you, within the next day or two, to plan how you will implement the techniques found therein. After you have checked off those problems and techniques which are most pertinent to your particular relationship(s) with teenagers I suggest that you prioritize them and determine the times and occasions when they most often present themselves. This will help you try on your new parental or programmatic behaviors systematically. Should your new behaviors not be immediately successful, don't throw in the towel. Important changes sometimes require fine-tuning and a few attempts in order to achieve the desired results.

Whatever your results might be, don't hesitate to keep us informed by posting on our website www.youthinjeopardy.com

Acknowledgments

Of course, no social service initiative is worth much until some combination of funders is willing to step up and offer their financial support. One of the advantages of growing up on the Upper East Side and attending independent schools, holding memberships in social clubs, etc. was that I met quite a number of philanthropists. Fortunately, I was seen by many of them as someone who would put their dollars to good use - - someone that for them seemed to represent a vehicle toward the achievement of meaningful outcomes.

Several persons tied to foundations knew me from the days when they helped me launch the organization Family Dynamics. Among those are Bill and Michael Rudin of the Rudin Foundation, the late CEO Margot Gibis of the Leir Foundation, Lloyd Goldman of the Joyce and Irving Goldman Foundation, and Barbara Slifka of the Joseph and Sylvia Slifka Foundation. Despite the volume of requests they receive, these foundation executives have chosen to support our program consistently. They believe in me and I believe that I have provided good reasons for their confidence in me.

In addition, I appreciate the many people who provided me with wise advice about how I might approach "Youth in Jeopardy." These inhabitants of the worlds of publishing, editing, social service, and psychology included Gail Brussel, Alex Merrill, Peter Harper, Bob McGee, Hal Fessenden, Peter Bogardus, Nancy Nereo, Khani Smart, Paul Dinas, Oliver-Crespo, Brunilda Rivera, and my daughter Brooke Monaco.

Of course, nobody plays a more crucial role in launching a book than the publisher. Red Penguin Books has been a consistent and resourceful problem solver dedicated to creating a superior finished product. I must specifically express my appreciation of Head Penguin Stephanie Larkin, Editor Katherine Abraham, and Marketing Specialist Denise Reichert.

A key to the success of authors is the freedom granted by those who live with them. Book-writing is a time-consuming activity. My thanks in this regard to my dear wife Patricia Lowe Schuster and my teenage son Preston. Their patience with me as the reams of paper and computer entries flowed has meant a lot to me. And has made the completion of "Youth in Jeopardy" possible.

Additional Delinquency Prevention Resources Recommended

Alberts, Connie and Farris, Michael. "Parenting Beyond the Rules," NavPress, Colorado Springs, CO, 2019.

Atencio- MacLean, Psy D, "Overcoming Oppositional Defiant Disorder, Althea Press, 2019. Emeryville, CA

Bernstein, Jeffrey, "The Stress Survival Guide for Teens," New Harbinger, Oakland, 2019.

Borba, Michele, "No More Misbehavin", John Wiley + Sons, San Francisco, 2003.

Burkett, Wynn, "The Power of Mindful Parenting," Mindful Parenting Press, Chicago, 2019.

Caselman, Tonia, Ph.D. and Cantwell, Joshua, MSW, Youth Light, Chapin, SC, 2011.

Covey, Sean, "The 7 Habits of Highly Effective Teens" Simon + Schuster, New York City, 2004.

Daley, Daniel Ph.D., "Working with Aggressive Youth", Boys Town Press, Boys Town, NE, 2011.

Damour, Lisa, Ph.D., "Untangled: Guiding Teenage Girls," Ballantine Books, New York, 2017

Fay, Jim and Cline, Foster, "Parenting Teens with Love and Logic," NavPress, Colorado Springs, CO., 2020

Fulks, Bart, "X-Plan Parenting," Howard Books, Brentonwood, TN, 2019.

Graham, Stedman, "Teens Can Make it Happen," Simon + Schuster, New York, 2000.

Geltman, Joani, "A Survival Guide to Parenting Teens, AMACOM, New York City 2014.

Hansen, Sharon, MSE, "Executive Functioning Workbook for Teens," New Harbinger, Oakland 2013.

Johnson, Brian, Ph.D. and Berdahl, Laurie, MD, "Warning Signs," Chicago Review Press, Chicago, 2016.

Josephs, Shelia, Ph.D., "Helping Your Anxious Teen," New Harbinger, Oakland, 2016.

Lee, Nicky and Sila, "The Parenting Teenagers Course Guest Manual," Alpha North America 2012.

Mack, Cassandra, "Young Gifted and Doing It," Authors Choice Press, New York City, 2007.

McCready, Amy, "The MeMe Epidemic," Tarcher Perigee, New York 2016.

McGrady, Kat, Ed.D., "Building Resiliency in Youth," Boys Town Press, Boys Town, NE, 2021.

Miller, Jennifer, "Confident Parents, Confident Kids, Fair Wind Press, Beverly, MA, 2019.

Micco, Jamie, Ph.D., "The Worry Workbook for Teens," New Harbinger, Oakland, 2017.

Nelson, Jane and Lott,Lynn,"Positive Discipline for Teenagers," Harmony, New York, 2012.

Peter, Val and Dowd, Tom, "Boundaries: A Guide for Teens", Boys Town Press Boys Town, NE, 2000.

Phelan, Thomas, "1-2-3 Magic Teen," Sourcebooks, Naperville, IL 2016.

Shapiro, Lawrence, Ph.D., "The ADHD Workbook for Kids," New Harbinger, Oakland, 2010.

Shipp Josh, "The Grown-Up's Guide to Teenage Humans," Harper Wave, New York City 2018.

Skeen. Michelle, PsyD. and Skeen, Kelly, "Just as You Are, " New Harbinger, Oakland 2018.

Thompson, B., "Parenting Teenage Girls," Create Space, Scotts Valley, CA., 2016.

Thompson, Jessica, "How to Help Your Anxious Teen." Harvest House, Eugene, OR, 2019.

Willard, Nancy, "Cyber-Safe Kids, Cyber-Savy Teens," John Wiley + Sons, San Francisco 2007.

Wingate, Molly and Woodward, Marti, "Slow Parenting Teens," Norlightspress.com, 2012.

About the Author

The focus of Derek Schuster's professional life has been on the prevention of family-related social problems. That is to say, he has shown consistent interest in addressing a social problem before it reaches an acute stage.

In the year 2000, Derek started a Violence Prevention Program for the highly regarded organization SCAN-Harbor. Many of the at-risk teenage clients have been arrested. The program has been consistently able to reduce re-arrests by over 70%. And throughout its 20-plus years in existence, Derek has maintained a personal caseload of six to ten youngsters. This means that his experiences in Violence Prevention are first-hand. As the father of six children ranging in age from 19 to adulthood and as a former teacher Derek's life experience has prepared him in multiple ways to be the author of "Youth in Jeopardy." He has not only preached about parenting techniques, but has used them on the home front and in school settings.